shmexperts

how ideology and power politics are disguised as science

marc e. fitch

 WND Books

shmexperts

Unless otherwise indicated, Scripture quotations are from the NEW AMERICAN STANDARD BIBLE*, © The Lockman Foundation 1960, 1962, 1963, 1968, 1971, 1972, 1973, 1975, 1977, 1995. Used by permission.

Published by WND Books, Washington, D.C. WND Books is a registered trademark of WorldNetDaily.com, Inc. ("WND")

Book designed by Mark Karis

WND Books are available at special discounts for bulk purchases. WND Books also publishes books in electronic formats. For more information call (541) 474-1776 or visit www.wndbooks.com.

Hardcover ISBN: 978-1-936488-88-9
eBook ISBN: 978-1-936488-89-6

Library of Congress Cataloging-in-Publication Data
Fitch, Marc E.
Shmexperts : how ideology and power politics are disguised as science /
Marc E. Fitch.
pages cm
Includes bibliographical references and index.
ISBN 978-1-936488-88-9 (hardcover) -- ISBN 978-1-936488-89-6 (e-book)
1. Science in mass media--United States. 2. Science--Political aspects--United States. 3. Expertise--Political aspects--United States.
4. Specialists--United States. I. Title.
P96.S332U64 2015
306.4'5--dc23
                                        2014048410

Printed in the United States of America
14 15 16 17 18 19 MP 9 8 7 6 5 4 3 2 1

For my parents, Ed and Paulette Fitch

contents

acknowledgments   *vi*

introduction: vienna and the gulf   *vii*

1. who are the "experts"?   1

2. experts and media: a call to impotent activism   21

3. culture of crisis   55

4. higher learning and the credentialed age   77

5. quantum confusion: a postmodern science?   105

6. experts, complexity, and chaos   129

7. the culture of death   145

8. media manipulation   165

9. pseudo-reality prevails! now what?   183

notes   *197*

bibliography   *203*

index   *212*

acknowledgments

First and foremost I would like to thank my wife, Erin, for all her love and support through the years. I would also like to thank the Robert Novak Journalism Fellowship and The Fund for American Studies for supporting my work. Special thanks to Zachary Janowski and Mollie Hemmingway for their support and help opening doors for me that might have been previously closed. A big thank you to Geoffrey Stone and WND Books for giving me this opportunity, as well as the copy editors that put the finishing touches on this book. Last, but not least, I would like to thank those who were kind enough to answer some of my questions and offer their opinions for this work.

introduction

vienna and the gulf

A man going quietly about his business all day long expends far more muscular energy than an athlete who lifts a huge weight once a day. This has been proved physiologically, and so the social sum total of everybody's little everyday efforts, especially when added together, doubtless releases far more energy into the world than do rare heroic feats. This total even makes the single heroic feat look positively miniscule, like a grain of sand on a mountaintop with a megalomaniacal sense of its own importance.

—robert musil

[B]ut it's just that a man of culture is bored with the alleged wonders of purely material ingenuity. . . . He simply refuses to get excited about plumbing.

—ayn rand

On the night of April 20, 2010, the *Deepwater Horizon* oil drilling rig suffered an explosion and fire that would leave eleven men dead and begin a massive underwater oil leak in the Gulf of Mexico that would last for the next eighty-seven days. *Deepwater Horizon* was drilling the Macondo underwater well and had reached a depth of 18,360 feet when the crew—a month behind schedule and facing numerous difficulties—decided it was time to end the drill and move the rig to new territory. The well had been sealed and, as far as the experienced crew could tell at the time, everything was fairly normal. However, the concrete seal on the well ruptured, and gas blew up the drill line. The blowout preventer failed to stop the onslaught, and the resultant explosion eventually capsized the rig and left a gusher of oil pouring from the bottom of the Gulf of Mexico.

It was to be one of the worst environmental disasters in U.S. history and one that would, frighteningly, call into question humanity's ability to control its own technology. Could humanity marshal the will, technology, manpower, and knowledge necessary to stop a vast underwater geyser that threatened an ecosystem and an entire region's economy?

Deepwater Horizon was owned by TransOcean but was under lease by BP (British Petroleum), one of the world's largest corporations. Following the initial response to the loss of life, the fire, and the subsequent sinking of the rig, it became apparent that thousands of barrels of oil were flowing to the surface from three separate locations in the Macondo well. By law, BP was on the hook for all cleanup costs and damages. They set up an operations command in Houston, Texas, and a flotilla of ships, skimmers, and support watercraft was dispatched to the Macondo site. The media were slow to catch on to the true extent of the situation, but in the weeks to come, this leak would become the biggest story of the year.

The rest, as they say, is history; there is virtually no end to news articles, scientific papers, and blogs regarding the BP oil leak in the Gulf of Mexico. Joel Achenbach beautifully captured the eighty-seven-day ordeal in his book *A Hole at the Bottom of the Sea*, and for the purposes of this work there is no need to relive those days. We were all there; we watched for nearly an entire summer as a black geyser spewed crude oil into the idyllic Gulf of Mexico. It was a surreal time: fires were burning on the water's surface, the president was talking about kicking someone's ass, BP CEO Tony Hayward was yachting, and we were beset by new technical jargon, like "junk shot," "top kill," "static kill," and "relief well." It was a modern-day suspense novel played out in reality with massive stakes: big multinational corporations, the U.S. government, scientists and engineers, working men and women suffering on the Gulf Coast, and birds and turtles covered in black grime. It spurred intrigue, conspiracy theories, anger, lawsuits, and fear.

But there was something insidious lurking in the coverage of the

Deepwater Horizon blowout, manifesting itself in the undercurrent of society, media, and technology. It was the failure of the "experts" to not only solve the problem but more important, to assess and communicate it to the American public as well. A rift began to emerge in the illusion that the best among us, the most highly educated, the people with the numbers and in the know, can solve the problems that society and the world face. The twenty-four-hour media cycle propagates a delusion that anonymous "experts" can accurately assess a situation or problem and dispense an answer with abilities that would confound the average Joe or Jane. The BP oil leak added a political element. A new president, already facing a number of difficulties, had to win the confidence of an American public that soured on government disaster intervention following Hurricane Katrina. The mix of politics, public outcry, the news media, and technology created an illusion of security meant to comfort the masses. But things were not going well, and the mirage was fading. Achenbach, himself a member of the media elite—a writer for the *Washington Post*—addressed this issue in some knowing asides throughout his work:

> What this political climate meant for the Obama administration was that it would not only have to handle the disaster effectively but also would need to be perceived as handling it effectively. Obama had to get the right people in place, doing all the right things, and he also needed to appear to be fully engaged. Image management isn't a crime, it's sensible politics—and necessary to the extent that it would bolster public confidence in the response.[1]

In other words, to reference Ayn Rand's quote at the opening of the introduction, President Obama—a man of culture—quite suddenly had a major plumbing problem.

As it became increasingly obvious that the efforts to solve the oil leak were not working, the president addressed the public on June 15, 2010, in an effort to bolster confidence:

> Because there has never been a leak of this size at this depth, stopping it has tested the limits of human technology. That is why just after

the rig sank, I assembled a team of our nation's best scientists and engineers to tackle this challenge—a team led by Dr. Steven Chu, a Nobel Prize–winning physicist and our nation's Secretary of Energy. Scientists at our national labs and experts from academia and other oil companies have also provided ideas and advice.[2]

Achenbach dubs this team a kind of scientific X-Men, but there was one problem with this team that had been assembled:

> They were as smart as the day is long, but what did they know about Gulf of Mexico petroleum engineering? Chu's scientific advisers could wallpaper an airplane hangar with all their official credentials and honors, but in the eyes of BP, they were a little eccentric. It looked to BP like the administration had said one day, "Where are our experts?" and then rounded up anyone who did not flinch at the sight of a differential equation. Science, engineering, it was all the same. Send in the experts. Did BP really need a Nobel Laureate physicist like Steve Chu barging into the war room? The Obama folks were obviously in love with the *idea* of Chu—the notion of having an in-house Nobel Prize winner who could be dispatched, superhero-like to solve intractable problems with the power of his giant brain. And Chu's team? The freelance geniuses? They were an ad hoc addition to an already ad hoc process—ad hoc squared, ad hoc cubed.[3]

The problem was the illusion. A PhD does not an oil driller make. Part of the appeal of the oil-drilling business is, as Achenbach indicated, money and opportunity: "Even today, in a society that sniffs at a mere undergraduate degree, guys with only a high school diploma and maybe a little trade school under their belts can pull in six-figure salaries in the oil patch."[4]

In essence, the only people who could truly understand or solve this crisis were not the X-Men, but a bunch of blue-collar, hard-nosed, professional drillers.

The president pulled the talents from the national laboratories at Los Alamos, Sandia, and Lawrence Livermore. Their first idea? Blow it up. But what else should one expect from a group of nuclear physicists whose job it is to make things explode? This idea was dismissed quickly by more safety-conscious people. But even the famed Steven Chu floated ideas that did not smack of technological magic. In an e-mail between Chu and physicist Richard Garwin, Chu wrote, "Building on Dick Garwin's idea of mud balls in sausage casing, what about sending ball bearings in the choke and kill lines before trying a dynamic kill?" Even Achenbach was tongue-in-cheek; "The mud balls, or marbles, never actually made it from the whiteboard to the deep gulf, but the emails showed brilliant men fully engaged in the Macondo problem. The scientists were *on the job*."[5]

Part of the problem is the illusion that technology and advanced degrees create. Mud balls in sausage casings? The famed "junk shot" and "top kill" were nothing more than dumping a bunch of garbage on the leak and then covering it with mud and cement. This was not *Star Wars*. This was the sandbox in preschool stuff. Is this what PhDs—a team of the smartest men and women in the world—were talking about? Part of the evolving American culture is a new, awe-inspiring reverence for degrees conferred by colleges and universities. They have become symbols framed and mounted on our walls that announce to the world an inherent status as smarter, better, more advanced, more knowledgeable. But when faced with reality, the delusion fades. Smart men remain merely mortal.

Throughout the course of the BP oil leak, a major point of contention was the actual amount of oil that was being leaked from the Macondo well. The initial estimate put the leak at one thousand barrels a day. However, over the next eighty-seven days, the government would adjust the official estimate many times from five thousand barrels a day to seventy thousand. Truth was, nobody had any real way of knowing. Only when Chu performed an "experiment" by placing video of the oil plume on two laptops side by side—one showing the plume before crews had done any siphoning on the surface, and the other depicting the plume after the crews had begun to siphon twenty-two thousand barrels a day—did he come up with an equation to determine that the actual flow rate was nearly sixty-six thousand barrels a day, close to what BP estimated as a worst-case scenario.[6]

This was not scientific magic; this was eyeball guessing, and the public was starting to notice.

The other problem was the mistaken notion that people who are geniuses or highly credentialed should be able to solve *any* problem. Steven Chu was a physicist—not an engineer. He admitted before a congressional committee that he did not even own a car and he had never been a friend of the oil and coal industries.[7] He had been hired specifically to turn the United States toward alternative fuels. He admittedly looked for people who were not involved in the oil industry, hoping (perhaps rightfully so) that some minds thinking outside the box might be able to find an "answer."[8] But this did not materialize. The X-Men acted more as an oversight committee. The BP engineers—some who were PhDs and industry-level geniuses and others who had worked their way up in the industry—eventually solved the problem and closed the well. They had the experience, equipment, and know-how, and they worked around the clock those entire eighty-seven days. While it was popular to demonize the company, the men and women on the ground who faced a problem on an entirely new scale were able to adapt the technology, work together, and end a crisis.

The purpose of this work is not to denigrate the people who worked hard on ending the BP oil crisis. It is not to disparage those who have worked hard and attended years of schooling to become highly knowledgeable professionals in their respective fields and contribute greatly to the advancement of our society. The purpose of this work is to explore a belief that is part of our national culture and is the result of the intermingling of politics, media, science, philosophy, education, and a little bit of faith; it is the illusion of the "experts," one that Achenbach rightly titles "the X-Men." The danger that lies in this belief is that it has created a kind of cultural malaise, one in which society trusts what the "experts" and their various "studies" report in mass media daily without taking the time to think critically about the implications, motivations, and repercussions that result from the trust and authority which we grant to experts. We place trust and faith in the media to truthfully and objectively report scientific claims. We hear the term "expert" used daily by the news media to indicate that someone is worth listening to—the implication is that "this isn't just an ordinary housewife or Joe the plumber; this is an expert who has degrees and experience and is really, really smart." In other words, smarter and more knowledgeable than the general unwashed masses. It smacks of elitism but, more damagingly, it is an illusion. Moreover, as we will examine in this work, it is a fantasy born of ideology that those with advanced degrees conferred on them, those with the jargon and knowledge of mathematics, physics, and language, are more adept and able to direct our lives to create a better world. But what do those degrees really demonstrate? What does the knowledge of mathematics or economics have to do with governing a society and political policy? The answer may lie in the way in which we define ourselves and the world around us.

As the quote from Robert Musil's *The Man Without Qualities* indicates at the opening of this introduction, "the social sum total of everybody's little everyday efforts, especially when added together, doubtless releases far more energy into the world than do rare heroic feats." The media creates "heroes" out of our "experts" who are granted the title in recognition of some quality to which we are told we cannot aspire because it is just too much work or is too complicated for the average layperson. This is part of the illusion that this book will seek to dissolve. This is the pseudo-reality in which we now exist, one influenced through various forms of electronic news media and entertainment and the technology, science, and politics that are streamed to us twenty-four hours a day.

This pseudo-reality also occupies a large part of Musil's novel—a section he called "Pseudoreality Prevails." The story concerns a man named Ulrich—a man without qualities—and it follows him through an absurd satire of aristocratic life in Vienna 1913, a Vienna that was unknowingly on the verge of World War I, the resounding boom that marked the beginning of the modern era. Ulrich himself is a "modern man," one formed in the new (at the time), emerging science of relativity. He is a man without boundaries, who can adjust his intellectual position at will. Musil wrote, "And since the possession of qualities assumes a certain pleasure in their reality, we can see how a man who cannot summon up a sense of reality even in relation to himself may suddenly, one day, come to see himself as a man without qualities."[9]

In essence, those "qualities" which Ulrich lacks are a center of strength and belief by which an individual confronts reality. That center is a philosophy, a set of principles and virtues which anchor the individual in a complex, ever-changing world. The modern era, with its fracturing and breakdown of Old World traditions and morality, has resulted in a questioning of the very nature of reality.

Musil was ahead of his time, intuiting what the modern world would become a generation in the future, while critiquing the damage it had already inflicted. These issues were addressed subtly and satirically by Musil in the 1930s and then beaten over the head with a sledgehammer by Rand in the fifties: "Reason, my dear fellow, is the most naïve of all superstitions. That, at least, has been generally conceded in our age."[10] Still, these two voices could not calm a cultural storm.

But why should we concern ourselves with an obscure novel plotted in Vienna in 1913? What does that have to do with today? And what does a man without qualities have to do with modern science, experts, and the media?

The similarities between Vienna in 1913 and the United States in 2015 are eerie. Unknowingly on the brink of World War I, Vienna had become a bastion of Old World aristocracy in the Hapsburg Empire, but the economic separation between rich and poor had grown to a staggering level. The economic downturn had left millions in desperation. Frederic Morton, in his book *Thunder at Twilight*, opens his account with a description of a banker's party called "the Bankruptcy Ball" during the Carnival season:

A number of ladies appeared as balance sheets, displaying volup-
tuous debits curving from slender credits. Others came as collateral.
Their assets, ready to be garnished, were accented sometimes with a
décolletage, sometimes with a bustle. Thin men were costumed as
deposits, fat men as withdrawals. Sooner or later everybody ended up
at Debtors' Prison—the restaurant of the esceas on the Blumensaal
where the festivity was held. Here mortgage certificates served as
doilies for Sachertortes.[11]

Given the mortgage crisis and continuing housing collapse of 2008,
record bankruptcy filings and foreclosures mixed with bank bailouts,
this scene is strangely familiar.

Vienna was also beset with various terrorist attacks stemming from
its conflict with the Serbs who were rebelling against Austrian Empire
rule. The suicide rate had skyrocketed; "Over the Easter weekend,
Sunday March 23 and Monday, March 24, twenty-three people tried
to kill themselves, a majority of them in that unswept slum to the West;
seventeen of these drank concentrated lye. It was the cheapest poison
and therefore the most cost-effective means of suicide."[12] I'm sure that
the idea of terrorism in the name of combating an empire probably
needs no further elucidation. However, consider that recently the
number of deaths by suicide in the United States surpassed, for the first
time in history, the number of deaths due to car accidents. It is now the
number-one cause of injury-related death.[13]

There are numerous other similarities, and anyone looking to make a
socioeconomic critique of the United States would probably have a field
day with Vienna in 1913. But what of its importance to us today? As
Morton put it in the preface to his work, "Imperial Austria has become
a byword for melodious decay."[14] And, as indicated on the back cover
of *The Man Without Qualities*, it is "a maliciously acute portrayal of an
empire marching over a cliff."

This may all sound a little apocalyptic for a book that debates the
veracity of experts and studies that seek to determine whether or not
drinking coffee and talking on your cell phone simultaneously will give

you cancer. But the real point is not the studies or the experts themselves but rather the illusion of reality that they propagate. To this end, the media—newspapers, television, books, and the Internet—become not only the means by which these experts and studies reach the masses, but also the perpetrators of the myth. In an effort to dissolve this false notion, we will look critically at some of the studies and experts that are so prevalent in our modern media. However, the implications are that these various studies and the underlying cultural belief system can be seen—with a dose of fervor—as apocalyptic. This is not to suggest that we are on the verge of a culturally shattering world war (though I guess you never know; hindsight is 20/20), but rather, this apocalypse could be a nonviolent, cultural malaise in which the populace ceases to think critically. Perhaps a population that listens to the talking heads on the "walls" that show them different, incoherent pictures and messages, like Ray Bradbury's dystopia in *Fahrenheit 451*. Or perhaps it will be that society will take its cues from and put its faith in various "experts" whose knowledge does not match their influence and whose various competing studies leave us in a state of permanent fear and foreboding.

Maybe it will be the willful sacrifice of common sense for the three little letters *PhD* and the moniker of "expert."

But all is not lost. During the BP oil leak, not only were the experts working diligently as the nation waited with bated breath, but average citizens and professionals from many different realms of study were attempting to help as well. During the crisis, BP received more than three hundred thousand ideas from individuals all over the world who were trying to help solve the deep-sea plumbing problem. On July 15, when the well was finally stopped using the 3 ram capping stack and flange, Robert Bea, professor of engineering at Berkeley and former Shell executive, recognized something startling. Six weeks earlier, Bea had received a late-night phone call from an anonymous caller who then forwarded him a sketch and plans for a way to cap the oil gusher in the Gulf. "When Bea saw the design of the containment cap lowered onto the well last week, he marveled at its similarity to the sketches from the late-night caller whose humble refusal to give his name at the time nearly brought Bea to tears. 'The idea was using the top flange on the blowout preventer as an attachment point and then employing an internal seal against that flange surface,' says Bea. 'You can kind of see how a plumber thinks this way. That's how they have to plumb homes for sewage.'"[15]

Two days later the mystery plumber revealed himself: "His name is Joe Caldart, a married, forty-something blue-collar guy with five kids and three hound dogs living in St. Francis, Kan," wrote one newsmagazine. "Mr. Caldart has 907 Facebook friends. He likes the band Rednecks & Red Dirt, watches 'Family Guy' and cites the 1978 Burt Reynolds' flick 'Hooper' as one of his favorites."[16] In other words, Joe Caldart was just an average guy. He originally submitted his design on May 25, but received only a nondescript response from BP, basically saying that they were grateful, but no thanks. Joe then decided to start sending his design idea to experts and professors across the country in an effort to be heard. "I was thinking, well, if [Hollywood celebrities] Kevin Costner and James Cameron were having problems getting through, as famous as they are, I didn't have a chance," Caldart said in an interview. "A lot of people had a negative reaction to it [my design] and basically said, 'You're a plumber; plumbers don't know anything about science. If scientists with PhDs and all that can't fix it, then how can you?'"[17] Eventually he was able to reach Robert Bea, who then forwarded the design to BP with (hopefully) a little more influence to get the design considered. Six weeks later a strikingly similar design was lowered onto the Macondo well, and the eighty-seven-day crisis ended.

Joe Caldart never received anything for coming forward or for his efforts on the design. Indeed, BP would only state that they had used ideas from many different external sources, and their spokesman speculated that the design may have been in the works for weeks. Achenbach does not detail the idea and construction of the successful well cap in his book other than to say that BP had multiple different backup plans for everything they attempted. However, considering that Caldart made and submitted his design while some of the ideas being floated at the time were either blowing up the well, stuffing it with "mudballs in sausage casing," or a "junk shot" of garbage and debris, Caldart's idea alone seems remarkable. The fact that his design, whether directly influential or not, bore such similarity to the 3 ram that stopped the leak is reason enough for pause and consideration.

While politics has always been a matter of illusion (or "optics," as political strategists like to call it), the use of technology, experts, studies, and the media is relatively new, a development of the modern world that has a philosophical history that can be followed from the late 1800s. Furthermore, the veneration of academic credentials has exceeded previous generations by miles. More young people than ever attend college. College is more expensive than ever. More degrees are conferred each year than the year previous. Higher education rarely appears to be a choice these days, but more of a necessity—high school part two, if you will. But with all the degrees conferred and the numbers in academia soaring, it is prudent to examine not only what is being taught and how but also its effect on society and the culture. Perhaps Caldart's statement is indicative: "I also felt like people should know that here an average guy submitted something that maybe helped."[18] It is this notion of "average" as opposed to "expert" that is the underlying, fundamental problem and a stumbling block to societal progress. The fact that Caldart ultimately knew neither he nor his idea would be considered seriously without several letters following his name is troubling. Such assumptions can lead to the failure of a society to think critically about the information they are being fed under the assumption that the self-described experts have already analyzed the issue and are now saying, "This is important. Listen to this study; make these changes." It is a softening of the mind thanks to the razzle-dazzle of degrees conferred by universities that now seemingly hold the strings in determining what is relevant, what is serious, and what is to be ignored.

This is not an anti-intellectual work. Rather, it is a warning that critical and independent thinking needs resurgence in a society that is being lulled into intellectual complacency by relying on mass-media manipulation and the bureaucratization of knowledge. The real danger is that in the future a man like Joe Caldart may not even try; instead, he may just change the channel.

Like most books, this work, I suspect, was inspired by my day-to-day life. In essence this book is for Joe Caldart. It is for my father, who, with only a mechanic's training and a military background, worked his way to chief pilot of a Fortune 500 company. It is for the nurse's aide who said to me, "I always see you with a book. You must be smart because I know smart people read a lot" (not really). It is for one of the best and most knowledgeable nurses I have ever worked with who had to step down from a management position after ten years because she didn't have a bachelor's degree. It is for the union members who questioned the CEO of a hospital as to why she deserved such a large salary when the company was in the hole and laying people off, to which she answered, "because I'm highly educated." It is for my old neighbor who complained that he couldn't read very well but could fix anything in my crumbling house. It is for the people who look at a museum of "modern art" featuring Andreas Serrano's "Shit" collection and just don't get it.[19] It is for all who have been lulled into a feeling of inferiority through the illusion of advanced degrees, studies, experts, and intellectual narcissism.

It is, in effect, for the average Joe.

1

who are the "experts"?

Do you know, Francis, until this voyage, I honestly believed in the Open Polar Sea. I was quite sure Parliament was correct when it listened to predictions from the so-called polar experts—in the winter before we sailed, do you remember? It was in the Times—all about the thermobaric barrier, about the Gulf Stream flowing up under this ice to warm the Open Polar Sea, and the invisible continent that must be up here. They were so convinced it existed that they were proposing and passing laws to send inmates of Southgate and other prisons up here to shove the coal that must be in such plentitude just a few hundred miles from here on the North Polar Continent.

—dan simmons, *the terror*

Well, what would you say . . . you do here?

—bob slydell, *office space*

So who are the "experts"? As indicated before, this moniker is about an illusion meant to present ideology in the guise of science, and one that is much more easily defined by what it is not, rather than what it is. So in seeking a definition to assign to the "experts," we should first examine to whom we are *not* referring to when discussing their various proclamations and studies.

There exist, undoubtedly, men and women who are highly knowledgeable, skilled, experienced, and educated in their respective fields. These are people whose works have come to create much of the technological innovations and machinery that make society function. My brother-in-law, for example, is an expert engineer who works on helicopters for United Technologies, and he's the one to whom we as a family tend to turn when there is some sort of mechanical issue at hand—and he usually solves it with a few tools from his handy Swiss Army knife. Joe Caldart is an expert at plumbing, but no one was seeking him out during the BP oil leak. Experts exist in every facet of society. They are a combination of skill, education, experience and, sometimes, raw talent. But they are not the "experts" of which we speak, although they can occasionally be called upon as such. For the purposes of this work we shall henceforth refer to them not as experts, but as professionals, which also eliminates the need for any further snarky quotation marks around the word "experts." The term *experts* will henceforth refer to the illusion that we are dissecting. The professionals are the men and women whose motivation in their work is to produce a result: an actual, testable piece of hardware or a theory that can be proven empirically. The personnel working around the clock on the BP oil leak—the actual drillers who had been in the business for years—were the professionals; the government, for a display of optics, called in the experts. The professionals are, as Thomas Sowell puts it, subject to "external standards." "An engineer whose bridges or buildings collapse is ruined, as is a financier who goes broke. However plausible or admirable their ideas might have seemed to their fellow engineers or fellow financiers, the proof of the pudding is ultimately in the eating."[1]

The experts are also not synonymous with "intellectuals" and those who make their living in the realm of arts and humanities studies—writers, journalists, artists, and so forth, although lines do occasionally get crossed on both sides. There are many professional writers and artists that fail to become the elusive expert or the deified intellectual. However, it is the people in these fields that foster the illusion of the experts. Media journalists quote experts ad nauseam, often incorrectly or for pointless or political reasons, which we will examine later on. It is also the renowned "intellectual" that will often use the experts for scientific validation of various social theories.

Sowell wrote in his work *Intellectuals and Society*, "Here 'intellectuals' refers to an occupational category, people whose occupations deal primarily with ideas—writers, academics, and the like . . . An intellectual's work begins and ends with ideas, however influential those ideas may be on concrete things—in the hands of others."[2] In 1962, Richard Hofstadter wrote *Anti-Intellectualism in American Life*, in which he lamented the zealotry of McCarthyism and the presidential tenure of Eisenhower. While he did not give a working definition of *intellectuals*, he did provide a knowing differentiation between them and *professionals*: "Even in the sphere most immediately affected, that of education, the ruling passion of the public seemed to be for producing more Sputniks, not for developing more intellect, and some of the new rhetoric about education almost suggested that gifted children were to be regarded as resources in the cold war."[3] The implication here is that the ability to build a Sputnik is not the same as having intellect and thereby being an intellectual. This leads us to conclude that being an intellectual has less to do with ability in the sciences and more to do with thinking about the sciences and their wider implications in a philosophic context.

Politics is the natural manifestation of the intellectual pursuit. Ideas cohere into philosophies, and politics is, at its best, philosophy for the real world. Therefore, these battles of ideas will be played out. However, the term *intellectual* has taken on the veneer of left-wing political activism. Battles of ideas need to be fought; the battle between opposites influences and causes progress. However, there exists a problem when one side of that battle is not only winning on the intellectual front but also endorsing a myth that the general population accepts as being scientific or a matter of fact.

The word *expert* as it is used in media and pop culture is first and foremost a chimera, a construction presented by the media that offers a glimpse of reality without offering the real deal. The narrative through which we view the world is vital to our understanding of it. As technology has grown and developed—particularly television and the Internet—so has our scope of the events, trends, patterns, and life.

However, the lens through which we view these experiences is not a clear plate of glass. Rather it is, in effect, a prism; it breaks up reality into separate parts, and the ones we see are not only the ones we choose to see but also those that we are *told* to see because they are relevant and they will impact our lives. Sherry Seethaler wrote:

> Most of the messages that bombard us everyday [*sic*] are carefully selected to present just one of a kaleidoscope of possible perspectives on technological, environmental, economic, and health issues such as global warming, mad cow disease, nanotechnology, genetically engineered food, who should take cholesterol-lowering drugs and what are the merits of banning plastic bags. Oversimplified black-and-white perspectives of issues come from those who have a vested interest in convincing others of their point of view, or who are simply relaying information without thinking critically about it.[4]

Those slivers of reality, the media believes, need to be interpreted by experts so we can understand their full implications. Through their narrative we receive a piece of reality, although it is not the day-to-day reality in which we operate our average, ordinary, everyday lives. It is the reality of the world as a whole. Since the world is too big and too complex to fully explain, experts armed with credentials and studies are brought in to help. The experts lend scientific and supposedly objective verification of the narrative that the media produces.

It is not the professionals who ask for this attention, and in many cases, it is not even the professionals who are labeled the experts. The professionals will be misquoted, misunderstood, and misled for a four-hundred-word op-ed piece. Likewise, it is not the intellectuals who are labeled experts or who necessarily create the illusion, although often they are writing the script since they educate the future media and political personalities at the university level. The pundits, the papers, the Internet bloggers, the news anchors, the politicians, and the journalists are selling a story, and they use the experts to show us that their story is true and relevant to our lives. How else could we explain headlines such as these?

"Running farther, faster and longer can kill you."[5]

"Confirmed: He Who Sits Most Dies Soonest."[6]

"Marijuana Smoke Linked to Cancer."[7]

"Marijuana Cuts Lung Cancer Tumor Growth in Half, Study Shows."[8]

"Warning: Oil supplies running out fast."[9]

"The World Will Never Run out of Oil—Might its Price Tank?"[10]

"Climate Shift Tied to 150,000 Fatalities."[11]

"No Need to Panic About Global Warming."[12]

"Unhappy feet: Global warming and melting sea ice risk wiping out the Antarctic's Emperor penguins, scientists warn."[13]

"Antarctic Sea Ice Hits Record . . . High?"[14]

How can there be two opposite versions of the truth, both of which claim to have the backing of science and experts? Minus the experts, we could easily say to ourselves that one person is lying, mistaken, delusional, or has secret, nefarious motivations. However—and this is where the illusion of experts is fully manifest—it is the guise of science and expertise which the talking heads use to give their claims credibility and ultimately influence society.

Doctor and epidemiologist Ben Goldacre addresses many of these issues in his book *Bad Science: Quacks, Hacks, and Big Pharma Flacks*. Goldacre offers a virtual college course on the many tricks that researchers can use to produce the results they want for either research or marketing purposes or that fit a particular ideology or selling point. He reveals methodological flaws in research that can lead (and have already led) to more death and destruction than they were ever hoping to solve. It would not aid our discussion to review the different flaws and gimmicks that Goldacre outlines; suffice to say, it does not give one a pervading sense of security in scientists and researchers. They are, after all, only normal men and women, subject to the same inner attributes and faults as the rest of society. However, Goldacre reserves a good deal of criticism for the media and the sensationalizing of whatever research may fit a particular narrative in order to sell stories. In regard to the measles-mumps-rubella (MMR) vaccination scare that swept the UK (and is now enjoying some press in the United States), Goldacre points out that the very nature of modern journalism is to look for a narrative that falls into place with a preconceived notion of justice and power. "In some respects, this reflects changes in the environment for investigative journalism; this kind of work is expensive and risks expensive legal cases from the powerful people you investigate. Concocting a health scare is attractive, because it gives the appearance of challenging power and authority, but with none of the work, and none of the litigation risk if you're wrong."[15]

"At best the evidence of these 'experts' will be examined only in terms of who they are as people or perhaps whom they have worked for," he writes later in the book. "Journalists—and many campaigners—think that this is what it means to critically appraise a scientific argument and seem rather proud of themselves when they do it."[16] It is, as Goldacre says, a dumbing down of society, an excuse to dismiss arguments contrary to your own as not based on science when that very science has been corrupted and subverted by either the ones who conduct the study or the ones who report it.

In essence, the scientific or health-scare story is much easier for an investigative journalist because the onus of responsibility does not rest with the journalist; he or she is merely reporting the findings of experts and extrapolating from the evidence to create a headline-grabbing story. And, frankly, experts can be a dime a dozen. Seethaler outlines what she calls "stakeholders," those individuals and entities that have a stake in both the research being conducted and its presentation in the media. The obvious stakeholders are corporations, particularly the pharmaceuticals but also industries that may be interested in keeping certain legislation at bay by influencing public opinion. And, of course, there are the scientists and experts themselves who are employed by any number of interests for the sole purpose of developing a marketable product, regardless of whether or not it is effective. Such experts and scientists can employ a bevy of different statistical and methodological tricks in order to justify a product's effectiveness. Seethaler illustrates how marketing campaigns will find celebrity spokesmen such as Leonardo DiCaprio, Michael J. Fox, or Al Gore to market an issue to the public. "The media itself is a stakeholder because newspapers and magazines want to increase their circulation; radio and television programs want to improve their ratings; and Web sites want to increase their traffic. As a result, the media often fails to present what we should hear, but instead, presents what they think we want to hear."[17] However, as we shall discuss later, sometimes what is presented is what the media wants us to hear rather than merely what they think we want to hear.

Being an expert is nearly a job description in itself, and there exist websites with ready-made directories for journalists to find said experts. San Diego State University runs the SDSU News Center, which has the "Experts Directory." "This Experts Directory is a resource for working journalists seeking expert commentary on a variety of topics."[18] The website Allexperts.com allows people to directly ask questions that will, in turn, be answered by experts in whichever field applies within two to three days. The requirements to become an expert on Allexperts.com is to be able to type grammatically correct English, have an above-average knowledge of the subject material, be polite to questioners, and be able to respond to questions within two to three days.[19] With the availability of the Internet, journalists can find experts and experts can find journalists; they can advertise their credentials and their positions on a variety of subjects and can be cherry-picked by the media. It requires little effort on the journalist's part—just an e-mail or a phone call—to find an expert for nearly any and every story. An expert can be used to give the story both an air of scientific respectability and, in effect, to do the thinking that the public is apparently too lazy to do for themselves.

Chris Hedges, in his work *Empire of Illusion: The End of Literacy and the Triumph of Spectacle*, chronicles an intellectual road trip exploring some of the morass that have become the lesser points of American culture, including professional wrestling, pornography, and positive self-help gurus. He also brings his criticism to bear on higher education. While Hedges focuses on the illusion of celebrity culture rather than on the news media, his conclusion for the consequences of illusion is clear: "Corporate media control nearly everything we read, watch, or hear. They impose a bland uniformity of opinion. It diverts us with trivia and celebrity gossip. In classical totalitarian regimes, such as Nazi fascism or Soviet communism, economics was subordinate to politics."[20] Similarly, Mark Steyn wrote, "So, in government, in the dinosaur media, in the faculty lounge, in the community-organizing community, in the boardrooms of connected corporations, America's rulers are conformicrats. They have the same opinions, the same tastes, the same vocabulary. They think the same, and they expect you to do likewise."[21] Despite being on opposite sides of the political spectrum, both writers agree that the culture of illusion is one that threatens the very individuality and democracy that America claims as its birthright. Instead, we are being led by illusion into a form of soft fascism. Both writers cite Aldous Huxley's *Brave New World* as the current model of totalitarian government, and both cite higher education institutions, overreliance on technology, and corporate and media influence as leading America into this domination of illusion. While both writers obviously disagree on major points as to how we arrived at this position and where to go from here, the conclusion is the same: "a society that no longer recognizes that nature and human life have a sacred dimension, an intrinsic worth beyond monetary value, ultimately commits collective suicide. Such societies cannibalize themselves until they die."[22] The experts the media tout, which allow the citizenry to avoid thinking critically about a subject because it has already been packaged and delivered to them via expert opinion, are as much part of the illusion as any of the spectacles that Hedges and Steyn list in their works.

The second aspect of an expert as we are defining such an individual is that experts are given legitimacy primarily through the higher education system and only secondarily through media. Joe Caldart routed his idea through a PhD at a prestigious college, knowing full well that his lack of higher education would cause his idea to be either dismissed or ignored. These days we often define our experts by the number of letters following their names. The degrees conferred by colleges and universities offer a veneer of intellectual prowess, of education, of expertise. Society uses the higher education system as a form of litmus test as to whether or not someone's opinion, diagnosis, or thoughts should be given consideration. The more degrees conferred, the more deferment by the media, the more objective expertise we assign to that individual. Therefore, in examining what makes an expert, it is also necessary to examine the current state of higher education because its universities, academies, seminaries, and so forth are the so-called gatekeepers of expertise. But suffice it to say for now that the higher education system is largely responsible for whom we label an expert and why.

As we investigate the influence of the higher education system in determining whom we consider an expert, we must also explore the philosophical underpinnings of the current higher education system. While the public often believes that the monikers of *expert* and *science* mean that the findings are objective, factual, and correct, this is not the case. Many of the cited studies and experts often come from the realms of health, psychology, and social sciences, or new discoveries in the realms of physics and chemistry are used as "evidence" by which social theorists attempt to verify their beliefs. Because of the nature of his or her area of work, a physicist can theorize; but unless he or she is able to offer concrete proof, it remains merely theoretical. However, in psychology and social sciences, such proof is not required; all that is required is a theory that on the surface appears that it might work or somehow verifies preconceived notions. Studies conducted in these areas are hardly concrete and can easily be manipulated. These findings are more often highly suspect rather than informative. This is precisely because the realms that involve humanity are not subject to the same boundaries as physics or chemistry—they are far too complex to be treated as a hard science. Instead, they are given scientific veneers over what are beliefs about the way humanity *ought* to behave and the way society *should* be structured. Hence, much of this work is tainted with politics and philosophy.

As indicated at the beginning of this book, the reliance on experts and the journalists who cite their work at length results in a loss of critical thinking in the public. The experts are very often the men and women who lack the "qualities" described in Musil's novel in that they are willing to allow ideology, money, and fame to obscure and influence work that is supposed to be objective. The journalists and mass media are the same, allowing political pursuits and big-story sensationalism to cloud any true objectivity or critical judgment. Why? Because big, scary stories sell, and big, scary stories backed by smart-sounding experts sell even better by adding a level of scientific validation.

This leads to our third criterion in defining the expert: the transgression of the boundaries inherent in his or her respective field. Stephen Jay Gould, in his work *Rocks of Ages,* offers up the concept of Non-Overlapping Magisteria (NOMA), which he describes as a "respectful noninterference" between the realms of science and religion:

> I do not see how science and religion could be unified, or even synthesized, under any common scheme of explanation or analysis; but I also do not understand why the two enterprises should experience any conflict. Science tries to document the factual character of the natural world, and to develop theories that coordinate and explain these natural facts. Religion, on the other hand, operates in the equally important, but utterly different realm of human purposes, meanings, and values— subjects that the factual domain of science might illuminate, but can never resolve. Similarly, while scientists must operate with ethical principles, some specific to their practice, the validity of these principles can never be inferred from the factual discoveries of science.[23]

We are constantly reminded of organized religion's past and current intrusions into the realm of science, from the labeling of Galileo as a heretic to the battles in small Midwestern towns about whether or not to include the biblical story of creation in high school science books.

While these examples are told repeatedly throughout education and in polity, we have not yet come to recognize that the pendulum of time swings the other way as well. Science via experts is finding itself in greater and greater violation of NOMA, using tenuous findings and relativistic theories, end-of-the-world scenarios, and manipulated data to make judgments on human value systems, religion, morality, virtue, and even political beliefs.

Conservative journalist Jonah Goldberg cites journalist Chris Mooney, author of *The Republican Brain*, which offered looks at various studies that concluded that "conservatives are, literally by nature, more close-minded and resistant to change and facts. His evidence includes the fact that conservatives are less likely to buy into global warming, allegedly proving they are not only 'anti-science' but innately anti-fact, as well."[24] But don't just take Goldberg's word for it: "As I began to investigate the underlying causes for the conservative denial of reality that we see all around us," Mooney himself wrote in *Mother Jones*, "I found it impossible to ignore a mounting body of evidence—from political science, social psychology, evolutionary psychology, cognitive neuroscience, and genetics—that points to a key conclusion: political conservatives seem to be very different from political liberals at the level of psychology and personality. And inevitably, this influences the way the two groups argue and process information."[25] Neither of these men is a scientist. Rather, both are journalists, authors, columnists, and political pundits. However, there does remain a stark difference in their approach; while Goldberg is arguing Mooney's point using language and—although I'm sure Mooney would disagree—the logic of argument, Mooney is arguing using science, technology, and studies. This is where the trouble begins. If Mooney wanted to argue policy with Goldberg, they could undoubtedly each make a rational, poignant argument for their respective positions. However, using "science," studies, and supposed experts is avoiding an ethical, moral, or political argument. It imbues the realm of human ideals with the faulty notion that somehow chemical, biological, or physical sciences can offer an answer to the human condition. Mooney, almost admittedly, engages in pseudoscience by extrapolating rather minor data to produce major results. "We don't understand everything there is to know yet about the underlying reasons why conservatives and liberals are different," he confessed. "We don't know how all the puzzle pieces—cognitive styles, personality traits, psychological needs, moral intuitions, brain structures, and genes—fit together. And we know that the *environment* (or nurture) is at least as important as the *genes* (or nature). This means that what I'm saying applies at the level of large groups, but may founder in case of any particular individual. Still, we know enough to begin pooling together all the scientific evidence. And when you do—even if you provide all the caveats—there's a lot of consistency." What there is, in actuality, is a narrative of conclusions that Mooney is making. Mooney has a BA in English from Yale; he is adept at creating narrative and story, not so much in science and math, but to modern journalism this makes no difference. Goldacre laments the use of generalist reporters to cover scientific findings, especially those that may have profound social consequences: "Suddenly we were getting comment and advice on complex matters of immunology and epidemiology from people who would more usually have been telling us about a funny thing that happened with the au pair on the way to a dinner party."[26]

Mooney relies on scientific bloggers and anonymous experts to make the argument for him and explains that those inclined to vote Republican are in denial of reality due to the fact that they cannot filter facts and science through their belief systems. Never once does he question whether or not he may be doing the same thing, nor does he ask the bigger philosophical question as to whether or not science and belief can be separated (as we are doing with this work). Neither does he bother to question whether or not Republicans might distrust science because of these various studies that try to link beliefs or political affiliation to biological processes; he only reports that said Republicans are in "denial of reality." Some people might just be offended. Mooney, in almost every paragraph of his conclusion, continues to criticize the blindness and lack of "openness" of the political right without ever examining the implications that his argument makes against himself.

To go through every argument would take more time than it is worth for our purposes. Suffice it to say that one would hope for better from a "Yalie" who serves on several scientific boards. The point here was not necessarily a political one, although there are political implications in this work. This particular example was to illustrate the kind of science, media, and experts that are the subject of this work, and one can feel free to apply the same basic principles to his or her own political worldview. The point is not a political one; it is a question of ethics, illusion, and the ability for society to make cogent choices on matters of public importance and cultural values.

Mooney accuses the political right of not being able to differentiate its beliefs from reality, but as we shall see later in this work, such things have been major philosophical questions throughout the history of man; this is nothing new. Mooney's work also highlights the egregious use of science as a means to push a narrative or a political or personal agenda under the delusion that it is somehow objective. This allows for a rather cheap and easy way to avoid asking the bigger questions for which there are few if any definite answers.

To be fair, the political right employs its own experts at times in the matters of global warming and intelligent design, and there is even a book by a psychiatrist that argues that the political left is suffering from a form of mental illness. Despite having some experts to which it can turn, the political right is at a massive disadvantage due to the size, scope, and philosophical enterprise of current scientific trends; one is hard pressed to argue against evolution, relativity, or global climate change without being labeled a complete loon, regardless of the merits of his or her actual argument. The prevalence of media experts allows for a closing off of arguments that violate or even push the boundaries of these trends.

"There are few opinions so absurd that you couldn't find at least one person with a Ph.D. somewhere in the world to endorse them for you."[27] As if on cue, the website *Gawker* published an article entitled, "Born This Way: Sympathy and Science for Those Who Want to Have Sex with Children." The article begins with a rather graphic, stomach-churning account of a twenty-year-old methamphetamine addict having sex with his seven-year-old niece and then begins to discuss the science and neurology of pedophilia, making clear for the reader that this is a matter of sexual orientation rather than any deviant or predatory practice. The article primarily cites Dr. Van Gijseghem, who researches pedophilia; "Van Gjiseghem says what he and his colleagues mean by sexual orientation is a person's inborn and unalterable sexual preference, irrespective of whether that preference is harmful to others or not. Currently, there is no significant longitudinal evidence that pedophiles can be made to not be attracted to children, and thus it can be defined as their orientation. And if pedophilia is a sexual orientation, that also means it's futile to send pedophiles to prison in an effort to alter their attractions."[28] More recently, the *Guardian* had an article entitled "Paedophilia: Bringing Dark Desires to Light," disclosed that "not all experts are sure. A Dutch study published in 1987 found that a sample of boys in paedophilic relationships felt positively about them. And a major, if still controversial 1998–2000 meta-study suggests—as J. Michael Bailey of Northwestern University, Chicago, says—that such relationships, entered into voluntarily, are 'nearly uncorrelated with undesirable outcomes.'"[29]

What, however, is truly the point of these two articles? Both cite psychologists and experts who offer their informed opinion that pedophilia is different from molestation, and it may be that an individual is simply born with this particular sexual orientation; both suggest that perhaps pedophiles could be more effectively treated with behavior therapy similar to that given to alcoholics, whose condition is considered a disease rather than a character flaw or behavioral problem. The *Guardian* mentions that during the sixteenth century, child brides were common,

and the age of consent was ten years.* It paints a portrait of angry vil-
lagers marching through the streets, trying to purge society of those who
would have sex with children à la Frankenstein. While some dissenting
viewpoints are given, the narrative of both articles is clear: "The old
adage is that the true mark of a society is how it treats the weakest in its
ranks. Blacks, women, Latinos, gays and lesbians, and others are still in
no way on wholly equal footing in America. But they're also not nearly
as lowly and cursed as men attracted to children. One imagines that if
Jesus ever came to Earth, he'd embrace the poor, the blind, the lepers,
and, yes, the pedophiles."[30] Of course, the blinding hypocrisy of this
statement is the fact that the very same article began with the story of
a twenty-year-old man luring a seven-year-old girl into having sex with
him. Who exactly is the weakest of society's ranks in this case?

What these articles are really reporting or questioning is not a matter
of science but a matter of values—particularly societal values. They are
making moral arguments under the guise of science. The experts and
studies and doctors are being used as a means to question the validity
of societal norms, in these cases the seemingly normal societal revulsion
toward men who seek to have sex with children. Jefferson even draws
the comparison between consenting homosexual adults and pedophiles.
The multitude of horror stories that could be trotted out about the
victims of pedophilia, and the experts who state that this is a harmful
practice that merits punishment and removal from society, were not
broached. When we are told "Experts disagree," we are not told how
many of these experts disagree or even who these experts are. Is it just
Dr. Van Gijsegham, or is there a "consensus" of experts? How do these
sympathetic articles differ from those written about the Catholic priests
who abused children in their churches?

---

* It is curious to ask whether the author would prefer other social norms of the sixteenth century
to come back in vogue. Young girls were used as a form of property to be bought and traded for
dowries, often abused, and without any form of human rights.

This is perhaps the most important part of the definition of *expert* as it pertains to this work: an illusion of science that is meant to question, change, or deconstruct a value system that is inherently not a part of that expert's specialty. The desire for sex with children, while perhaps an interesting evaluative issue for psychiatrists, is ultimately a moral or value judgment determined by society and enforced by its justice system. The experts cited are being used in a narrative to alter the current moral or value system, which is executed through each respective country's judicial system; hence, pedophiles should not be jailed but given rehab similar to alcoholics.

In other words, an expert is someone who either makes a moral argument under the guise of science or, conversely, makes a moral argument out of scientific findings. A scientist will tell you what discovery of the Higgs boson particle means for science; an expert will tell you what the Higgs boson particle means for society or who you should vote for.

The modern era ushered in a new philosophy that eventually led to a relativism of truth—a belief that truth is a matter of perspective, culture, gender, and class. It has become a philosophy that has culminated with the postmodern era. The use of experts to question values is, in effect, the natural progression of the modern world. Social values form the psychological structure of a society by deeming what is and is not appropriate, acceptable, and legal. The belief that truth, ethics, values, and morals are relegated only to the individual or cultural perspective legitimizes nearly every viewpoint, belief, and action relative to the person who embraces it.

This relativism has caused a break with traditional notions of truth, justice, science, journalism, economics, ethics, and morality. It has become a license to never be proven wrong, no matter how the evidence stacks up against your position. Smart men and women—experts—can manipulate data and language in a number of ways, which Goldacre outlines in his work, that can uphold nearly any thesis. But the problem is more of a moral, ethical question. It is a question of *qualities*.

The experts, unlike professionals in similar fields and the media that use them, are men and women without qualities. They attempt to use science and expertise as a way to make moral and ethical arguments. However, the problem is that these very arguments *can* be understood by any rational average Joe or Jane. One need not have a PhD in applied physics to make a moral determination whether or not to drop the bomb on Hiroshima. Journalists who employ these experts attempt to use science and degreed authority as a way to overpower the moral and ethical questions. They do not take the time or have the heart to actually ferret out the real argument, and thus they violate NOMA in an effort to deconstruct the value system of a society and shape that society as they see fit.

This is not to say that these things are all necessarily new. Philosopher Gabriel Marcel lamented much the same while living in France during the post–World War II period:

> This work of reformation, in which each one of us in France is bound to lend a hand, in however humble a sphere his light may shine, consists above all in a restoration of values; we have to learn to grasp once more the distinction between the true and the false, the good and the evil, the just and the unjust—slowly and painfully, just as a paralytic who has recovered the use of his limbs learns slowly and painfully once more how to walk. . . . Nevertheless, the illusion which we must quite pitilessly proscribe is that the very word *freedom* can retain any meaning at all after the sense of human values has disappeared; and by the sense of values we must also understand the feeling that values are transcendent.[31]

And this is not necessarily a conservative lament, as Chris Hedges discusses very much the same loss of values in his work: "The moral nihilism embraced by elite universities would have terrified Adorno, a philosopher and outspoken critic of fascism and propaganda before and after World War II. He knew that radical evil was possible only with the collaboration of a timid, cowed, and confused population, a system of propaganda and mass media that offered little more than spectacle and entertainment, and an educational system that did not transmit transcendent values or nurture the capacity for individual conscience."[32]

The experts and the journalists who use and cite them may be smart people, but being intelligent does not equate with being wise. George Orwell wrote, "Implied in the demand for more scientific education is the claim that if one has been scientifically trained, one's approach to *all* subjects will be more intelligent than if one had had no such training. A scientist's political opinions, it is assumed, his opinions on sociological questions, on morals, on philosophy, perhaps even the arts, will be more valuable than those of a layman. The world, in other words, would be a better place if the scientists were in control of it."[33] He went on to dispute this idea by citing the scientists who "swallowed the monstrosity of 'racial science,'" during Nazi control of Germany. The expert is held up by the media as someone who stands above the masses based both on his experience and his education, but both those things are extremely limited. Even the smartest among us forget that fact.

As philosopher Gabriel Marcel wrote in a chastisement to his fellow philosophers, "Thus the very first duty of a philosopher is to have a clear sense of the limits of his or her own knowledge and to recognize that there are realms in which his lack of competence to make judgments is complete. Or, in other words, we may say that the philosopher should be perpetually on guard against making false claims that are incompatible with his true vocation."[34]

When journalists and experts work without acknowledged and accepted boundaries on the extent and nature of their occupation in an effort to form or reshape societal value systems, they are, in essence, acting as minor philosopher kings. They are dealing in the realm of ideas, morality, values, traditions, and the very basic questions as to man's place on Earth. These are subjects that are available to every thinking person, and thus expertise is irrelevant. This is not their role, this is not their job, and thus far they seem ill suited for the venture. Modern news media no longer even tries to keep a veneer of political and moral objectivity; opinion has replaced fact, and the smart individual or the wordsmith can wield his tools well—but to what end?

High on intellectual hubris, the smartest among us, those who have received the finest educations and been granted access to the highest institutions and serve as power players, deign to be Platonic philosopher kings. Plato knew that form of government could never exist, but he recognized the desire for it. The journalists and experts are failing to recognize their intellectual limitations, though perhaps this should be unsurprising for a generation that has more and more often been labeled narcissistic.

2

experts and media:
a call to impotent activism

Q: And you predict its ruin?

A: It is a prediction which is made by mathematics. I pass no moral judgments. Personally, I regret the prospect. Even if the Empire were admitted to be a bad thing (an admission I do not make), the state of anarchy which would follow its fall would be worse. It is a state of anarchy that I am pledged to fight.

—isaac asimov, foundation

Kent Brockman: Hordes of panicky people seem to be evacuating the town for some unknown reason. Professor, without knowing precisely what the danger is, would you say it's time for our viewers to crack each other's heads open and feast on the goo inside?

Professor: Yes I would, Kent.

—the simpsons

saac Asimov's science fiction series, Foundation, is the story of the collapse of a galactic civilization known as the Empire. The series is spread over the course of a thousand years and shows the various death throes of the Empire and the struggle to build a new civilization out of the anarchy, which is likened to the Dark Ages. The basis of Foundation, however, is the predictions and theories of a scientist named Hari Seldon, who appears in only the first fifty pages of the entire novel series, but whose legacy and scientific ability ensures the survival of civilization during its dark ages. He is continually present through his science (which ironically takes the guise of religion at one point), and he helps limit the destruction of civilization and hasten the building of a new and better society.

Seldon uses a form of science he developed called "psychohistory," which is defined as "that branch of mathematics which deals with the reactions of human conglomerates to fixed social and economic stimuli. . . . Implicit in all these definitions is the assumption that the human conglomerate being dealt with is sufficiently large for a valid statistical treatment."[1]

Asimov was a scientist. However, his work on the Foundation series is indicative of the true fiction of science—or perhaps we could call it the great hope of science—that with the right equation, with the right set of logical precepts and enough information, the future of humanity can be rightly predicted and, if need be, saved from imminent disaster. Hari Seldon is able to predict, with remarkable precision, the future of humanity for the next thirty thousand years. In effect, he was a prophet whose sole deity was science.

Likewise, this great hope of science is reflected in the predictions of various experts and promoted in the media. Their predictions are often of disaster and are future oriented, based on statistical trends, psychology, and history. But how are we to interpret these various predictions?

The *New York Times Opinionator* blog hosts a forum titled The Stone, for "contemporary philosophers on issues both timely and timeless." Gary Gutting, professor of philosophy at Notre Dame, has offered several articles focusing on the use of science and media in society. In his article "On Experts and Global Warming," he opens with "Experts have always posed a problem for democracies. Plato scorned democracy, rating it the worst form of government short of tyranny, largely because it gave power to the ignorant many rather than to knowledgeable experts (philosophers, as he saw it). But, if, as we insist, the people must ultimately decide, the question remains: How can we, nonexperts, take account of expert opinion when it is relevant to decisions about public policy?"[2]

Power to the ignorant . . . ouch for us. Gutting goes on to posit a consensus among climatologists that anthropogenic global warming is a reality, and several times asserts that, "nonexperts are in no position to argue against the consensus of scientific experts."[3] Dismissing the arrogance of the piece, we should take a moment to dissect Gutting's argument for the authority of the experts, as it figures strongly in this chapter's analysis of experts throughout history.

First, Gutting cites Plato's argument in *Republic* that democracy is the worst form of government because it leaves leadership in the hands of the uneducated masses. Plato believed that the best form of government is a monarchy presided over by a philosopher king, which Gutting substitutes with experts. But this isn't just any ordinary monarchy; in fact, it resembles versions of fascism and totalitarianism from the twentieth century. Plato's idea of a benevolent and wise leader sounds nice on the surface, but when his idealist society is given a critical eye, it begins to show its true colors. The ideal Platonic state is one in which individual rights and liberties are determined by the philosopher king and the individual is seen as an organ or tool of the state.

In Plato's society children are raised by a collective of mothers who are determined to be best suited for the role of child rearing. In fact, Plato's idea of the perfect society has been a model on which many so-called great societies were built but which devolved into mass murder, war, totalitarianism, and collapse. Consider Bertrand Russell's take:

> [Plato] was a pupil of Socrates, for whom he had a profound affection and respect; and Socrates was put to death by the democracy. It is not, therefore, surprising that he should turn to Sparta for an adumbration of his ideal commonwealth. Plato possessed the art to dress up illiberal suggestions in such a way that they deceived future ages which admired the Republic without ever becoming aware of what was involved in its proposals. It has always been correct to praise Plato, but not to understand him. This is the common fate of great men. My object is the opposite. I wish to understand him, but to treat

him with as little reverence as if he were a contemporary English or American advocate of totalitarianism.[4]

Plato's utopia is totalitarian in the extreme: marriages are arranged based on eugenic principles, there is no private property, and craftsmen and artisans are allowed to create and construct only "beautiful" things. The idea is that a man who is wise enough can order society in a perfect way so as to eliminate the uncertainty and inequities of humanity as it has traditionally formed itself. However, this inevitably leads to a form of tyranny and totalitarianism. As Russell states in his overall assessment, "Would anybody advocate entrusting the government to university graduates, or even to doctors of divinity? Or to men who, having been born poor, have made great fortunes? It is clear that no legally definable selection of citizens is likely to be wiser, in practice, than the whole body."[5]

Gutting's rationale is that society and policy should be shaped around those whom we determine to be experts; however, this is a very nebulous and subjective term. The thought of trying to differentiate classes of experts in a subject as vast and complex as global warming presents such a myriad of difficulties as to render the whole enterprise pointless. Does a geologist count as an expert in global warming? A meteorologist? A marine biologist?

Furthermore, his contention that it should be a consensus of experts that ignore the few voices of dissent presents probably the greatest argument against his thesis. As we shall see in this chapter, it is often the dissenting voices that ultimately prove true and the consensus of experts that typically represent only the current trends in thought. They are unable or unwilling to think outside the most recent scientific and social theories. Copernicus and Galileo were the dissenting voices during their time. Einstein became a dissenting voice in quantum mechanics.

Implicit in Gutting's argument is the notion that society should be propelled forward regardless of actual truth because truth and reality are created rather than objectively existing. It is the base of postmodern theory, and one that has proven a failure over and over again. Gutting's ultimate position on global warming is that action must be taken regardless of its reality.

Another difficulty in Plato's and Gutting's proposals is defining who is and who is not an expert. Following the logic of Gutting's article, this is not done by strength of argument or through new and original ideas, but rather through (presumably) some sort of accreditation system such as we have in colleges and universities whose sole purpose is to indoctrinate students into the current paradigm of thought. Thus, there would be no room for the uncredentialed geniuses that so often create the technology and devices that fuel and change our society. It certainly would not have left room for Joe Caldart, which is why he felt the need to anonymously route his idea through a professor at a university.

When we attempt to define who and what are considered experts, both in Gutting's article and Plato's *Republic*, we end up with a static society rather than a dynamic one. Stasis is when there is the least uncertainty and, perhaps, the least inequality, but it is also the very spiritual and philosophical morass that was mentioned in the first chapter. In essence, "progress" as defined in Gutting's assessment of the need for experts, results in no progress whatsoever. This push for progress is, rather, a form of impotent activism, a need to do something—anything—in the face of nothing. It is a need for action even though that action may be misguided, unnecessary, or based on false predictions. It is a car spinning its tires full speed while suspended in the air. It goes nowhere and uses a lot of gas.

The experts and their subsequent predictions present the case for a culture of crisis in which experts' predictions of crisis are echoed in the media and lead to a state of public panic that justifies government intervention, expanded public policy, and the disregarding of normal rules of law. It was a genuine piece of Machiavellian truth when Rahm Emanuel uttered the words, "Never let a serious crisis go to waste."[6] A burgeoning crisis such as global warming puts an educated elite of experts in the position of Hari Seldon, warning society that its continued course will result in disaster. However, far too often the experts are deceived by their own statistics, political inclinations, opportunism, and sense of impending doom.

In his 2011 book, *Future Babble: Why Expert Predictions Are Next to Worthless and You Can Do Better*, Dan Gardner has written, "The inaccuracy of predictions isn't limited to pessimists or optimists, liberals or conservatives. It's also not about a few deluded individuals. Over and over in the history of predictions, it's not one expert who tries and fails to predict the future, it's whole legions of experts."[7] Similarly, in 2010, David H. Freedman published *Wrong: Why Experts Keep Failing Us and How We Can Know When Not to Trust Them*. Both of these works cite the financial and housing collapse that left the United States in financial ruin. While there were a few individuals who claimed to have seen the collapse of the financial markets coming, by and large, the belief persisted among experts and the media talking heads that all would be smooth sailing throughout 2008 and beyond. They literally missed the big one, though none of the experts lost their jobs and indeed, even the men and women who brought about the collapse—the heads of the major financial corporations—did not suffer castigation but were granted a bailout by the U.S. government.

These two authors offer two different approaches to examining the role and influence of experts in society: Freedman takes a more scientific approach, similar to that of Ben Goldacre, and lists the various ways that scientists botch their findings either erroneously or on purpose or sometimes because of peer pressure. In fact, Freedman's work offers such a dismal look at the world of science—one to which there is assigned an ideal of objectivity in society—that halfway through the book one starts to wonder if there is such a thing as science.

Dan Gardner, on the other hand, offers psychological reasons for both the assurances made by experts and our willingness to believe them time and time again in spite of their failures. To a great extent, Gardner takes the view that the human brain is brilliant yet flawed on an evolutionary scale, and at times it seems he may actually be guilty of the very certitude that he decries in the experts he profiles by using the theory of evolution to explain nearly every human foible.

Both men, however, take aim at the media—sometimes presenting them as lazy and easily excited by scientific baubles and other times as quite dishonest and treacherous, willingly spreading hysteria that is based on lousy science without ever offering a critical eye.

And both men also cite Philip Tetlock, author of the most extensive study ever of expert predictions, the findings of which he put forth in a book titled *Expert Political Judgment: How Good Is It? How Can We Know?* Tetlock's study was conducted over seven years, interviewing 284 experts in the field of political science. When we say "political judgment," we are not necessarily talking about predicting who will win the next presidential election, but rather, major questions of political importance the world over: Will the USSR collapse? Will a nuclear-armed Pakistan mean war with India? Will turmoil in the Middle East cause rebellion?

Turn on your cable news channel anytime and you will see experts saying what some world event means and how it will turn out. The recent revolutionary movements in Egypt and Libya come to mind as examples. Tetlock's findings are not encouraging, and he even sets the bar pretty low, seeing how expert judgment stacks up against a "chimp throwing darts." Tetlock made one observation that indicated some experts may be more adept at prediction than others and that there was a difference in how various experts thought about problems. Tetlock divided the experts into two different classes, labeling one hedgehogs and the other foxes, the difference being that a fox knows many little things whereas a hedgehog knows one big thing. In essence, an expert that is framed as a hedgehog has a worldview or a theory into which he or she can and will cram every piece of evidence; the hedgehog knows one big thing into which all other data is absorbed.

Hedgehogs appear everywhere in the media. They are the most fun to watch. They are sure that they have the answer; they know what is going on, and they are passing on that specialized information to their viewers like a priest dispensing God's love to his congregation.

Hedgehogs come in all shapes and sizes and political leanings. They are aggressive in debates, dismissive of counterarguments, and often quite charismatic. "The intellectually aggressive hedgehogs knew one big thing and sought, under the banner of parsimony, to expand the explanatory power of that one big thing to 'cover' new cases."[8]

An expert that labels himself as something—for instance, a free market capitalist—will parlay that idea to incorporate any number of instances of contradicting information. He does this partially because he probably truly believes what he is saying, but also because it is a matter of pride, of saving face and not admitting that in some instance he may be wrong. It is a failure of humility in favor of arrogance, and a belief that there is an "answer" to be had, that the seemingly chaotic manifestations of our complex world can be summarized through a worldview and a form of secret knowledge. An intelligent person has the ability to quickly rationalize any new information through logic, statistics, rhetoric, and diversion to meet his or her standard worldview, which offers an answer based on that worldview. It is a rare thing to have a hedgehog admit that he or she has been wrong or ever will be.

A perfect example is Paul Ehrlich and his 1968 book *The Population Bomb*. Ehrlich asserted in his work that the world would not be able to sustain its rate of population growth and its ability to feed people. He predicted mass starvation, war, and overall cataclysm if something was not done immediately. Ehrlich became the face of this movement, and he was only one of a vast number of other experts making similar claims and writing similar books. For whatever reason, Ehrlich was made the sacrificial lamb when nothing happened that he and many other experts had foretold. The world is vastly more populated than they ever anticipated and has more than enough food to go around (providing for adequate distribution and willing governments). Thus Ehrlich has been excoriated in books like Gardner's and Freedman's and in the press. However, the fact that he was wrong is not what is at issue. Everyone is wrong most of the time. The issue was the surety with which he presented his idea, the fact that his warning was taken very seriously and many people were affected, and the fact that even today he does not admit that he was mistaken. In 2011, in an interview with the *Guardian*, Ehrlich repeated his warnings from over thirty years ago: "The next two billion people, should we get them, will put more and more pressure on environmental systems that are struggling today. Each individual has to have food from more marginal land . . . materials from poorer ores, we're going to use more oil so we have to drill deeper: we're past the point of diminishing returns."[9]

While Ehrlich admits that his previous predictions did not materialize, he is unwilling to admit that he was wrong, just that he had underestimated the impact of new technology on food production (referred to popularly as the "Green Revolution") and that his predictions will still manifest in the future. What is even more interesting is the fact that his beliefs continue to be shared by a large segment of people. They remain entrenched in the environmental movements, global warming efforts, and population control advocates of the present day.

However, there is something more telling in Ehrlich's comments to the *Guardian*, particularly this passage: "We could support a lot more people on the planet if humans were willing to share equally, but they don't: we want to design a world where everybody can lead a decent life without everybody being fair." It is not the science that sustains his admirers and his theories; rather, it is his ideology: the belief that a better society can be created on earth through a sustained effort of population control and equal distribution of limited goods. It is a belief system that stands up in the face of what was clearly a wrong hypothesis he made thirty years ago and is incorporated into the modern environmental movement. It is a matter of consumption and distribution according to the idea of fairness and equality. Without this idea, Ehrlich's pronouncements would just be the ramblings of another false prophet, but instead they are still celebrated and given strength (and a whole lot of awards as well) by people who believe in the same basic ideas.

Hedgehogs do not sell science. They sell ideology in the guise of science. It is also important to remember that Ehrlich was not one lone voice warning of the impending doom; rather, he was part of the legion of experts who continue to forecast disaster due to overpopulation. What is truly frightening is not the prospect of what will happen in the future if Ehrlich's warnings pan out, but rather what has already happened because of the legion of experts' warnings, which author Fred Pearce outlines in his book *The Coming Population Crash* (and yes, I realize that this is just as scurrilous a thesis as is *The Population Bomb*, but we will focus on his research of the past rather than his predictions of the future).

In 1970 Sanjay Gandhi began to systematically sterilize men in India. After their initial efforts to recruit men voluntarily for vasectomies, Gandhi took a heavy-handed approach, declaring a national state of emergency due to population fears. "Sterilization became a condition of receiving everything from rickshaw licenses to medical care, and irrigation water to ration cards," Pearce recounted. "All across the country, state governments began jailing people with three or more children who refused sterilization. During the two years of emergency, more than nineteen million sterilizations were carried out in India, three quarters of them on men. . . . The coercive policy was a tragic mistake. Thousands died from botched sterilizations during the Indian emergency. And the semi-educated masses proved far from docile. Newspapers were banned from reporting either the deaths or the widespread demonstrations against the sterilization program."[10]

China's one-child policy began in the late 1970s in response to a perceived population bomb. While the true history of Chinese families had largely been one of restraint, Mao, during his rule, encouraged large families, and the birthrate skyrocketed. Following Mao's death, however, fears of the rising cost of the population resulted in the one-child policy, which then devolved into a program of forced sterilization and abortions.[11]

This, of course, is not Paul Ehrlich's fault. It is the fault of brutal governments and politicians with a poverty of moral conscience. The consensus of the experts during the early 1970s warned of impending doom due to the population bomb. The media reported this fatalistic warning without question and thus provided the governments with impetus and cause to act, to declare states of emergency, and to use false crises as an excuse to exercise greater control of their populations. That is the danger of the illusion of experts in media. The illusion promotes various nonexistent crises, which are used to change a culture and control its people and shape them to different beliefs and ideologies. We are told that the best and brightest among us are forecasting doom unless we change our ways and adopt values and practices that are contrary to those currently at work in our culture. When those warnings are accepted by the public, they are then enforced through the strengthening and expansion of government.

These crises serve a purpose. They give a veneer of science and rationality to a belief system. In this particular case it is the idea of equality and fairness, the belief that there are too many people and not enough resources to enable mankind to be fair toward one another. It is not a new belief, for all its intellectual posturing. It is, in fact, rather primitive. Furthermore, such beliefs disguised as science often manifest themselves in terms of political affiliations.

Another inherent danger in this kind of pseudoscience is that the irrational belief system trumps any rational argument against it. Often the force of this belief sweeps other, possibly skeptical scientists up in its tide, thereby creating a majority consensus and stifling any dissenting voices. The great value that we place on the sciences is their supposed adherence to objectivity, facts, and placing limits on their knowledge. Unfortunately, much of this has been washed over in our media-saturated age of illusion; science was supposed to give us reality but is now being used to supply something different.

Experts predicted cataclysmic war and death during the Cold War, which obviously never occurred, and then failed to foresee the collapse of the Soviet Union. Indeed, experts had a difficult time even perceiving what was in front of their noses when the Soviet Union was in its darkest days. Following the Great Depression in the United States, the idea of communism as a better alternative to capitalism took hold among the political elite. In subsequent trips and pilgrimages to Stalin's Russia, the supposed best and brightest of us were easily fooled by obvious frauds. H. G. Wells, ambassador Joseph E. Davies, and physicist J. D. Bernal were just a few of the elite that heaped praises on Stalin's new country. "Self-delusion was obviously the biggest single factor in the presentation of an unsuccessful despotism as a Utopia in the making. But there was also a conscious deception by men and women who thought of themselves as idealists and who, at the time, honestly believed they were serving a higher human purpose by systematic misrepresentation."[12] Naturally, the praise of these admiring intellectuals and experts for a system of government that seemed like an answer to the chaos of capitalism was presented in the media. It was an effort in the name of fairness and equality, something that communism and many other totalitarian movements falsely promised.

The same thing occurred with Mussolini's Italian Fascist state, Hitler's Germany, and Mao's China. Taking these regimes at face value and unwilling to see the larger implications, experts and reporters, intellectuals and statesmen allow their irrational convictions to overwhelm their critical faculties and, unfortunately, give power and influence to awful political movements.

One of the theses of this book is that the illusion of experts put forth in the media has more to do with pushing ideology than with putting forth science, and nowhere is this more evident than in political reporting, because politics is inherently an ideological judgment. It is almost entirely subjective to irrational, nonscientific emotions and preconceived notions, and therefore any claim of a political system that is "scientific" (such as Karl Marx's communism) is contradictory. Reporters often fail to take critical, hard looks at political ideologies that appeal to their own belief systems. This is a particularly dangerous situation for all political parties on the right or left of the political spectrum. A lack of critical thinking and analysis, a dismissal of objectivity in favor of blatant rhetoric in journalistic endeavors, is dangerous to society no matter its political implications. It is a violation of journalistic principles and most of all integrity, a quality that is innately transcendental and part of what we expect from those who supposedly inform us of our world.

While politics is a murky area of experts and media due to its intrinsic subjectivity, surely hard science cannot be so influenced and manipulated in such ways—or can it? Well, this depends on what is considered "hard science"—a bit of a buzzword in itself.

One would think that offering up numbers and statistics, averages and medians, would be a form of solid, objective math and science. But that is hardly the case; in fact, it is massively misleading and reductionist and somehow manages to garner media attention constantly. The problem is that, presented with enough information in the form of statistical measurements, scientists can make any number of ridiculous conclusions merely by using the words "related to," "indicative of," "linked to," and other misleading phrases to insinuate that one trait inherently causes or is caused by another, when in fact no such relationship exists. Freedman cites a particularly humorous example: "Researchers at the University of New Mexico compared the tips received by lap dancers on a birth control pill with those amassed by dancers during their fertile periods. The latter tips were larger on average, leading the researchers to conclude that men are more attracted to fertile women."[13] This study finds a supposed "link" between fertile women and larger tips for lap dances at your local strip club and ignores the myriad other possible factors that might seep into a man's decision of how much to tip his beloved stripper. This is a reductionist "link" that uses numbers to show some form of relationship that explains absolutely nothing. It sounds interesting but, in fact, is pointless; and reporting of this "fact" amounts to nothing other than taking up space in the "science" section of your newspaper. Of course, the science writer, starved for attention perhaps, still feels it necessary to print the information.

Similarly, various studies that reported finding an increase in the risk of death due to, per se, sitting at your office desk for eight hours a day, are invariably skewed and reductionist. Survival studies are long, drawn out, and complex and not suited to quick reporting of facts and statistics. For instance, if we say that people who eat an apple a day live longer than those who do not, we leave out a vast array of human complexities that also factor into a person's life span.

Many studies report findings based on animal testing and then extrapolate from the animals to deduce that humans would react in the same way because, after all, we share a large amount of genetic traits with lab mice. However, as David Freedman points out, "human moms tend to prefer clean rooms, whereas rat moms often eat their young after their cages have been cleaned, as one researcher warned in a journal article. And yet mice, rats, and other tiny scurrying mammals are widely used to inform our understanding of human thought and emotion, and especially for testing psychiatric drugs."[14]

Another study that comes to mind was based on a theory developed by Martin Seligman and Steve Maier. They conducted a test on dogs to determine their response to shocks; one set of dogs received no shock, a second set of dogs received a shock but were able to press a lever that eliminated the shock, and a third set of dogs received the same shock as group two but had no lever to stop the pain. Group three's shock ended when the dogs in group two pressed the lever, thereby, giving the dogs in the third group no control over their painful situation. When the same sets of dogs were placed in a box where they would receive a shock but had a means to escape, the dogs from the third group would merely lie down and whine, while the other sets would simply remove themselves from the pain. These findings were extrapolated to factor in human behavior, particularly in the realm of depression, and named "learned helplessness." In their book by the same name, Seligman and Maier concluded that someone who was constantly met with difficulty or pain would simply give up. The theory was further extrapolated to include economic conditions, racism, and social conditions; was trumpeted in further studies and blogs, in pseudo-scholarly journalism, and by media talking heads, and eventually helped fuel a culture of victimization. The idea is that individuals cannot overcome their life situations due to the unavoidable physiological and psychological phenomenon of learned helplessness, thus requiring a measure of social activism and, naturally, government and expert intervention.

Once again, this science results in the effect of impotent activism, in which money, effort, and general goodwill fuel a movement generated by psychological testing on animals and extrapolating the findings to include humans. Subsequent studies were conducted on humans but were generally very limited and used the theory of learned helplessness as their base prediction. Indeed, learned helplessness became a prism by which other studies were conducted and interpreted. It became the paradigm of thought in psychological studies, something that the authors even admit in their defense of the concept: "Since its beginnings in the mid-1960s, learned helplessness has been a center of debate. We believe that there have been several sources of controversy. Most generally, as already pointed out, the concept has been overused. Sometimes we have been guilty of this ourselves, using our learned helplessness hammer to treat everything we encounter as a nail."[15]

The authors also acknowledge that their theory has wider social applications that may overreach the boundaries of their findings. That being said, in the very same book the authors trample over the subtleties and complexities of their own theory in order to posit a form of morality. "More profoundly, we should inculcate an orientation to the common good in our society. We need to make the interdependence of people something that we value. Only when we start to take other people's welfare seriously will they start to do so for us." This is a call to activism, although one that is, at best, impotent. "This sounds like a moral argument, but we have arrived at it from our research. Our only assumption is that depression,[*] demoralization, underachievement, and illness are bad. We think the lack of an orientation to the commons— the incredible selfishness that so abounds in our country—is in no small way responsible for these ills."[16]

---

[*] On a side note, the authors of *Learned Helplessness* spend an entire chapter demonstrating that depressed people have a firmer grasp of reality than nondepressed people. Thus, by saying that depression is "bad" are we to assume that self-delusion is, in fact, good?

Thus, laid before us is the actual process of "science" in the hands of experts transitioning into a moral argument, one that cannot be disputed by "non-experts" because it is backed up with data, studies, and degrees.

In actuality, the findings were most likely born from the mixing of data with preconceived moral convictions held by the men and women conducting the studies. But instead of questioning the nature of their findings, the authors indicate they arrived at this conclusion only through their research . . . the research of shocking dogs without ever questioning the moral validity of studies that involve shocking dogs. Physician (or psychiatrist), heal thyself.

Psychology itself, dealing almost exclusively with the enigma of human consciousness, can never really be considered "hard science" because it deals in generalizations and assumptions rather than in the laws and equations that guide fields such as physics and chemistry. Either way, the assumption that mankind is just another animal, subject to the same controls and thought processes as a Labrador, is an ideology that has its roots in secularism and does not account for instances of human endeavor that have overcome amazing odds, both physical, emotional, and spiritual. It reduces the individual human condition to a matter of social and psychological conditioning.

One of the authors of the original study, Martin Seligman, segued his work into self-help books titled *Authentic Happiness* and *Learned Optimism*, and suddenly there was a legion of other experts capitalizing on the theory of learned helplessness and insisting that they could offer change for their patients. He was, in essence, offering a cure based on his grand theory of humanity. It is an interesting sign of the social power that an expert can suddenly have when he or she develops a theory for life through which nearly every facet of the human condition can be viewed. It became a movement embedded in a belief system.

Other studies that deal in so-called hard science and offer "facts" are merely confirmations of the obvious. Ben Goldacre wrote, "You can take a perfectly sensible intervention, like a glass of water and an exercise break, but add nonsense, make it sound more technical, and make yourself sound clever. This will eliminate the placebo effect, but you might also wonder whether or not the primary goal is something more cynical and lucrative: to make common sense copyrightable, unique, patented, and owned."[17] We often come across studies that essentially affirm "scientifically" what we already know or that common sense would deem unnecessary for study by our best and brightest.

There is virtually no end to the studies that seem to tell us what we already know. Here are a couple of gems that made it into peer-reviewed studies: "Reality TV skews reality"; "Bad relationships depress people"; "Umbrellas protect you from the sun"; "Cheating men have strong sexual urges"; and "Racists are close-minded."[18] These are rather benign findings in the world of science and ones for which our society will be no better off. It is difficult to understand why such studies are even being conducted, but there is an inherent desire to do something—anything—if it can possibly help us establish some kind of order to the world, even if that study and the order it supposes are rather incidental, fleeting, or even nonexistent. "This process of professionalizing the obvious fosters a sense of mystery around science and health advice that is unnecessary and destructive," Goldacre concluded. "More than the unnecessary ownership of the obvious, it is disempowering. All too often this spurious privatization of common sense is happening in areas where we could be taking control, doing it ourselves, feeling our own potency and our ability to make sensible decisions; instead, we are fostering our dependence on expensive outside systems and people."[19]

Moving beyond the trivial, there are very real-world consequences for experts' findings, predictions, and the attention they amass in the media. Dan Gardner takes special aim at President Jimmy Carter's persistent warning of the coming oil crisis when, in fact, there was nothing of the sort. Oil prices plummeted during the 1980s and '90s. President Carter was not shooting from the hip. He had a bevy of experts telling him that the world was on the verge of a collapse of oil supplies, and he was trying to prepare the American people. Gardner also discusses social experts who thought that divorces made easier would increase societal happiness. "No change better represented the dual-edged nature of the fast-moving reality then the no-fault divorce, a legal innovation that swept the Western world in the 1960s," he wrote. "It made splitting up easy, and the 'Me Generation'—Tom Wolfe's coinage—did it with abandon. At first this was widely believed to be to everyone's benefit because ex-spouses would be happier, and happier mothers and fathers would make for happier children, but it didn't take long for people to realize this was naïve."[20]

In their book *Freakonomics*, Steven Levitt and Stephen Dubner discuss a Senate hearing regarding homelessness during which an expert stated that forty-five homeless people died every second in the United States. The figure was staggering and led to public and political outcry for legislation. No one did the math, however, to realize that that rate would equate to 1.4 billion dead homeless people every year. Quite impossible, but it did not matter. The media ran with the numbers, and legislative and action committees were crafted.

The Y2K panic, which made headlines around the world leading up to the new millennium, forecast all kinds of terrible disasters, and it was all accounted for in Michael S. Hyatt's book *The Millennium Bug*. Capitalizing on a rather subtle sense of unease about the role of technology in society and making the unspoken recommendation that it was time to step back from technology and embrace the primitive self, it had a little bit of appeal for nearly everyone. Preachers issued dire apocalyptic warnings about it. Experts predicted it. Facts and figures backed it up. Doomsday preppers prepared for it, but it never came. The true absurd beauty of *The Millennium Bug* is that Hyatt was an experienced publisher rather than, say, an expert in computers and technology, though he did claim that he used their input in his work. In essence, a voice of authority need only be an authoritative voice.

Many companies spent millions if not billions in preparation for the change-over. True to form, the discredited experts who predicted ruin managed to rationalize the estimated $600 billion spent on updating computer systems. Peter de Jager, self-proclaimed expert on the influence of technology and one of the guiding forces for the Y2K panic, said, "The truth of the matter is this. All the hype, including some of the more ludicrous statements, forced companies to do one thing and one thing only. It forced competent managers round the globe to examine their systems with the single-minded goal of answering a simple question: did this thing called Y2K pose a threat to their computer systems? If the answer was yes, then they took appropriate action. If the answer was no, then they rightfully ignored it."[21] He was, in effect, not conceding that he was wrong but saying that he was right and that all the money and worry was money and time well spent. De Jager's website is presented with a moral statement; "We must accept that rapid accelerated change is going to be an ongoing and inescapable feature of our lives, one of the very few certainties in a world characterized by monumental uncertainties."[22] In other words, he offers answers to the uncertainty of the world through nothing more than an authoritative voice.

Even more recently there has been a new-old crisis of "hunger" in America. Feedingamerica.org runs ads on radio with sad, lonely piano keys reminiscent of Sarah McLachlan's ASPCA ads. Woeful voices inform listeners that someone they work with or are standing next to in the elevator or even a neighbor is "dealing with hunger." Supposedly, one out of six people in America is dealing with hunger. How could we have missed this? We hadn't though. There was nothing to miss. The ads oddly occurred alongside the constant drone from the very same media sources saying that we were experiencing an "epidemic of obesity." In fact, everywhere you looked, Michelle Obama, nutritionists, and the media were imploring us to eat right and stop being so fat. There was even an award-winning documentary championed and narrated by Jeff Bridges, called *A Place at the Table*, telling us of the hunger epidemic that strangely coincided with the obesity epidemic.

However, things are not as they seem. The USDA definition of hunger is in fact "food insecurity," a weak buzz phrase that covers a range of different nutritional situations, from having not known where your next meal would come from once in the past three months to feeling that you hadn't eaten enough to not being able to eat as nutritionally as you would like.[23] According to a report from National Academies Press, *Food Insecurity in the United States: An Assessment of the Measure*:

> The broad conceptual definitions of food security and insecurity developed by the expert panel convened in 1989 by the Life Sciences Research Office (LSRO) have served as the basis for the standardized operational definitions used for estimating food security in the United States. *Food security* according to the LSRO definition means access to enough food for an active, healthy life. It includes at a minimum (a) the ready availability of nutritionally adequate and safe foods and (b) an assured ability to acquire acceptable foods in socially acceptable ways (e.g., without resorting to emergency food supplies, scavenging, stealing, or other coping strategies). Food insecurity exists whenever the availability of nutritionally adequate and safe foods or the ability to acquire acceptable foods in socially acceptable ways is limited or uncertain.[24]

By this definition I was one out of six who was "dealing with hunger." And I had no idea.

The film *A Place at the Table* was dismantled in a review by Graeme Wood: "A social advocate from a century ago would stand in slack jawed amazement at the fact that we worry about how fat poor people are. . . . After the Clinton welfare reforms of the mid-1990s, food-stamp qualification became more onerous, and by 2000, only 17 million people participated. But the standards were loosened, and now almost 50 million Americans use food stamps, a 194 percent jump in a single decade. As Jeff Bridges reminds us, the last decade has seen no progress in eliminating the remaining food insecurity in this country. Weirdly, giving people food does not seem to make them less food-insecure."[25]

This is not third-world hunger. This is a first-world illusion of a problem, a world in which, bewilderingly, hunger and obesity coexist and are, in some cases, the same. Being obese does not mean that you are food secure; in fact, it may mean the complete opposite. According to figures, the state of Mississippi is both highest in obesity and food insecurity simultaneously.[26] This is not absolute hunger; this is relative hunger, and only in a nation so focused on itself could someone possibly be thought of as being obese and "dealing with hunger" at the same time. More than simply a deception of numbers and statistics calculated by experts in an effort to change a society's political leanings, it is, above all, a moral failure. It is a failure to recognize absolute reality in favor of one that is relative to statistical manipulation. It is a failure of personal and collective moral constitution to look at ourselves as a nation and posit that there is a problem with hunger. It is a purposeful blindness to true suffering in favor of imagined suffering. Its root cause is arrogance, and its goal is not humanitarian, but rather a call to impotent social activism and government empowerment.

The nonprofit organization Feeding America is blatantly political, and its Web site headlines warn of the many people who would go hungry if the Supplemental Nutrition Access Plan (food stamps) were cut. In their "Advocating Against Hunger" section (as if anyone advocates *for* hunger), they state, "To achieve our vision of a hunger-free America, we must build partnerships across the public and private sectors. Everyone can play a role. No other organization or individual can do more to help put food on the table for people in need than our federal government. Feeding America works to educate elected officials about the impact of food insecurity in their communities and identify and advance policy solutions to put struggling families on the road to healthy, hunger-free lives."[27]

Similar filters and modifications of definition occur throughout the media, the government, and the bevy of experts. The unemployment rate gets put through a variety of filters, including no longer counting people as unemployed who have given up looking for work. While the media, experts, and government were touting unemployment rates around 8 percent in 2013, the actual unemployment rate, if it were measured by the same filters used during the Great Depression, would have been closer to 15 percent.[28] The definition of poverty in America has been altered over the years to reflect a relative poverty rather than an absolute poverty. According to *Measuring Poverty* from the National Academies Press, "Like other important indicators, the poverty measure should be evaluated periodically to determine if it is still serving its intended purposes and whether it can be improved."[29] However, we are never made aware of what those purposes are. Clearly, eliminating poverty would be a purpose of a study on poverty, but what would be the purpose of redefining poverty? Currently the government definition of poverty includes people with homes and cars and televisions. It is not absolute poverty in the way that an individual in the developing world may live without clean water or food; it is poverty relative to the standard of living in the United States, which is vastly better than the rest of the world. It is this redefinition of poverty that fuels activists to seek "economic equality" through any number of government interventions.

This is a moral failure as much as it is a deception under the guise of science, experts, and charity. It is meant to create crisis where none exists, and in a crisis society turns to the experts and the government that easily employs them, supposedly for the benefit of all. However, this is a self-replicating cycle. The experts set the parameters and definitions for studies that suddenly tell us that we are not experiencing an obesity epidemic but are, in fact, dealing with hunger on a vast scale, and the only solution is to grant more money to the federal government in order to pay the experts to figure out how to solve the problem using more studies. The media either comply out of laziness or because they agree with the underlying belief in the role of government. We are given a narrative by the media and respond with charitable donations, volunteer work, or just a general sense of unease that promotes desire for some kind of government security blanket.

The cover of the June 20, 2013, issue of *Rolling Stone* magazine, which included a special section titled "The New Stoned Age," featured four actors known for portraying potheads in many high-grossing comedy movies. The banner proudly declared that the "War on Pot" was over following Colorado's decriminalizing of marijuana. Between the covers was a celebration of pot, with articles by Bill Maher and glorious profiles of Jonah Hill and James Franco. *Rolling Stone* is supposed to represent the youth, though I wonder if the glorification of teenagers' ability to remove themselves from reality is really in their best interest. However, what intrigued me was a small subtitle that read "Plus: Is It Bad for You?" This led to a single page devoted to "Debunking the Myths," complete with experts telling us that there is nothing negative about smoking pot, and any thoughts or fears otherwise are completely unfounded in science. While the article incorporated single sentences from three experts, the main focus was on Carl Hart, neuroscientist and professor at Columbia University. Hart states near the opening to the article, "Much of what we believe in this society about drugs is bullshit. . . . And we as scientists have been complicit."[30] Without delving into the research at all, it should be noted that saying that scientists have been complicit in propagating a belief that is bullshit, in and of itself, damages his own work. He is already stating between the lines that science is guided by factors outside of objective experiment, study, and conclusion. His denigration of the complicity of scientists in bullshit beliefs automatically calls into question his own work as being guided by belief, bullshit or otherwise.

Though a quick look at Hart's previous work shows that he has built his career on the activism of decriminalization of drugs, his own history has influenced his work. He grew up poor in Miami and used and sold drugs like many other inner city youths, but he was able to turn his life around through the military and hard work. He went on to get his PhD from the University of Wyoming and wrote his memoir/drug activist book, *High Price: A Neuroscientist's Journey of Self-Discovery That Challenges Everything You Know About Drugs and Society*. As one of his talking points, he cites a study with rats offered drug-laced water in two different environments, one which was in poor environment and another that was more active and fun. The rats in the poor environment drank the drug-laced water more often than those in the rat playpen, leading him to conclude that drug use is more closely associated with environment than with addiction . . . at least in rats anyway.

However, Hart's true intention has little to do with discussing drugs and their effects on individuals' lives; he has loftier goals in mind:

I often testify as an expert witness to help women who have used marijuana while pregnant to keep their children. Case after case is a black woman. Security in the court is all black; the judges are all white; and the lawyers are young and white, building careers. It's just slavery all over again.

When you have a group that's already identified as an "other," or a villified [*sic*] group that is a minority, it's easier to associate a behavior with them. But people don't see black people as being fully human. That's what happens in the US, although people won't tell you that.

Because when we think about Trayvon Martin, when we think about Ramarley Graham, Sean Bell, these black kids who were killed at the hands of some security or law enforcement person—that almost never happens with white kids. If it did, it would be a national crises [*sic*]. But it's not a national crises [*sic*] because we really don't value black men and boys in the same way we value white boys and men. We don't see them as being equal.

I look at how people behave, and it's clear. As long as you view this group that way, you can continue to put [a] large percentage of law enforcement resources in those communities, but not so much to make them better. If you want to make it better, you give people jobs. Instead, we put police in those communities to pretend that they care, to pretend that you're doing something. But that's not helping.

Whereas drug reactions are predictable, interactions with police are not and too often become deadly. As a parent of a black youth, I'd much rather my kids interact with drugs than [with] law enforcement. White people don't need to think about that. Police officers too often see young, black boys as less than human. It creates a mentality where black kids are supposed to "know your place," and it affects your psyche. Indignities become part of who you are."[31]

Hart's ultimate goal through his push for the "decriminalization of all drugs" is racial economic equality, not helping addicts and their families or attempting to understand why people continually and on such massive levels try to alter their realities. Thus, his work, his science, is a means to an end rather than an end in and of itself. The science is subject to the ultimate goal.

Rolling Stone's lack of any journalistic integrity in their piece on "weed" is astounding. The writer, Simon Vozick-Levinson, cites Norwegian economist Ole Rogeberg, who questioned the methodology of a study that purportedly found a link between marijuana use and lowered IQs. "Do the authors believe that cannabis is the only thing that could affect your IQ between the ages of 13 and 38?" Rogeberg asked. He could have just asked the scientists, but instead he was asking a nameless teenage reader. He also criticized the study in another article (not in *Rolling Stone*), stating that the lower IQ was more likely tied to socioeconomic factors, such as poverty, which do not allow people the same access to education (although education and IQ are not necessarily related). The authors of the study responded to Rogeberg's criticism indicating that they had controlled for socioeconomic conditions and that, no, they didn't believe that marijuana use was the only contributing factor, but just a big one. "In their original analysis, [researcher Madeleine H.] Meier says, she and her colleagues controlled for socioeconomic status and found that in all socioeconomic categories, the IQs of children who were not heavy users remained unchanged from adolescence to adulthood. Therefore, she says, socioeconomic status does not influence IQ decline."[32]

Of course, *Rolling Stone* could have asked Hart's own colleagues at Columbia for their actual opinion. They quote Meg Haney as saying, "If somebody is smoking one or two joints a week the consequences are probably going to be very, very, very minimal."[33] However, Haney states in a separate interview:

> Smoking is simply not good for the lungs, and marijuana has more tar than cigarettes, and is smoked in a way that may increase the likelihood of cancer-causing effects: People inhale deeply and hold

marijuana smoke in their lungs longer than they do cigarettes. I'm not certain of data showing that it is worse than cigarettes (people generally smoke less marijuana per day than cigarettes). Most marijuana smokers also smoke cigarettes so it is difficult to separate the effects of the two drugs, yet marijuana smokers perform worse than non-smokers on tests of respiratory function. There is also evidence that marijuana can worsen performance on cognitive tasks (e.g., memory and learning). The good news is that when frequent smokers abstain from marijuana for several weeks, their performance often improves to the level of non-marijuana smokers.[34]

In this piece that she posted at Columbia's very own Ask the Experts web page, she wrote:

The vast majority of people who smoke marijuana do not develop psychosis. However, recent research has shown that individuals with a certain set of genes are vulnerable to the effects of marijuana on mental health. Specifically, individuals with a variation of a gene regulating brain dopamine levels who smoked marijuana as adolescents (by age fifteen) were much more likely to develop psychosis as adults than (a) individuals without this genetic vulnerability, or (b) individuals who had the genetic vulnerability but who did not smoke marijuana as adolescents.

It is not clear why marijuana affects this vulnerable population in this way, but it is likely due to marijuana's effects on dopamine regulation. Schizophrenia is associated with disturbances in brain dopamine. During adolescence, the brain is developing rapidly. It may be that for a vulnerable group, a drug of abuse like marijuana has more profound effects on the regulation of dopamine during this time of development than in later years.[35]

Rolling Stone, however, decided to stick with Hart's commentary regarding any link between marijuana use and mental illness: "Give me a break. . . . You look at these studies and see how they determine psychosis—it's a joke."[36]

Another of Hart's colleagues, Dr. Richard N. Rosenthal, chairman of psychiatry at St. Luke's–Roosevelt Hospital in Manhattan and professor of clinical psychiatry at Columbia, also offers a differing opinion. "The people who become chronic users don't have the same lives and the same achievements as people who don't use chronically."[37]

Within a one-page myth-debunking article, *Rolling Stone* has managed to gloss over, ignore, or sidestep various contradictions. Hart contradicts his own work by indicating that his science is guided by the goal of social equality. The information that contradicts Rogeberg's criticisms is ignored; Dr. Haney's statements and work contradict both Hart's conclusions and Guillermo Velasco's, who states that THC has a "powerful tumor shrinking effect in rodents with breast, liver, pancreatic and brain cancers."[38]

I found all this information in one hour on my smartphone while on a work break. This isn't difficult work, but *Rolling Stone* makes it sound as if the conclusions are all in and it's a slam dunk for "The Stoned Age." What we are actually left with, however, is a moral decision to make, not a scientific one. Think of it like this: If you present your expert saying one thing and I present another expert saying the opposite, we are at a standstill. Each of our experts contradicts the other, and therefore we cannot craft social policy based on the science. Now we have a value judgment to make. What do we value as a society? Is there greater good in greater freedom of choice, decriminalization of a popular drug, and less incarceration? Or is it society's job to try to prevent young, impressionable minds from becoming lost in a hazy smoke of indifference and laziness? These are the ultimate questions that have to be answered, but science cannot answer them, as much as Carl Hart would like it to. Hart states that drug use is the "symptom of a broken society" and I couldn't agree more, but in what way does he believe that it is broken? His work and his stated goals appear to indicate that he believes society's economic system is broken, not its spiritual or moral underpinning. This ignores the past during which there was more poverty and fewer social safety nets, but less drug use. His ultimate goals call into question his research and his conclusions. His work includes paying addicts $950 to smoke crack or methamphetamine in a laboratory and monitoring the effects on the brain. He doesn't appear to be trying to help these individuals make better lives for themselves, but rather to validate what they do as harmless and the fault of society. His work is the means to an end, and unfortunately the men and women he studies are merely the means rather than the end. They are not helped in his quest, and the negative effects of drug use are ignored.

It is difficult to imagine what Hart's ultimate goals would look like. He wants the decriminalization of all drugs because, by his own admission, the world was already bad when drugs like crack showed up in the urban areas of the United States. Hart's solution, however, appears as a form of surrender. He is not advocating changing people's behavior but changing the laws. It's not a matter of lifting the person out of his or her situation but making the situation common to everyone. He is, in effect, taking a drug problem and calling it a drug solution; nothing changes but the vocabulary. Rather than encouraging people to pull themselves out of the muck of drug use and cure the symptoms of the "broken society," Hart encourages society to tune out and settle into the comfort of a modern-day opium den.

Similarly, *Rolling Stone* either considers its readers too dumb (or possibly too high) or not deserving of the truth. In their tacit belief that their readers are unable to make an informed moral judgment for themselves, they do not offer up the whole picture. They wouldn't even have had to leave the staff lounge at Columbia University to get a fuller picture of the questions surrounding this issue, but instead they cherry-picked experts from around the world and gave them each one line in a one-page article, all to uphold their preconceived ideology. It is non-journalism, and it is pathetic and patronizing to their readers.

Our small world of experience is overcome by the "disempowering" and "the privatization of common sense"—to use Ben Goldacre's terms. What is essentially being told to us is that our personal world is too small for us to possibly comprehend. Thus, the media with its limitless global access and the experts with limitless amounts of data are the only ones in a position to inform us of crises and appropriate actions. Plato's *Republic* indeed.

It is the same belief that allows Paul Ehrlich to continue preaching the same message and allows people to keep insisting that he is right. If there is no right and wrong, then who is to say Ehrlich was wrong in his prediction? It's really just a matter of perspective. Keep waiting for his prediction to come true and keep believing in the ideal of fairness and equality, and even if it doesn't happen in your lifetime, you can rest assured that at some point in the future your beliefs will be validated and Ehrlich's predictions will manifest.

There exists an image of a scientist in the public's mind: white lab coat, glasses, possibly a German accent, thin, neat, and a teetotaler. But genuine experts and scientists are normal, average people, not beyond reproach and not immune to mistakes, ideology, or good old-fashioned greed. They have jobs that pay them money, and they support themselves through the research they conduct; one doesn't get paid much these days for constantly turning up negative findings, so an effort is made to find *something*. "Most of us don't think of scientists and other academic researchers as cheaters. I certainly don't," Freeman admitted in *Wrong: Why Experts Keep Failing Us*. "What could motivate such surprisingly nontrivial apparent levels of dishonesty? The answer turns out to be pretty simple: researchers need to publish impressive findings to keep their careers alive, and some seem unable to come up with findings via honest work. Bear in mind that researchers who don't publish well-regarded work typically don't get tenure and are forced out of their institutions."[39] A little data-managing can form that "link" or "relationship" between two essentially foreign things, such as mortality rate and time spent in the sun, and a little moral relativism can tell you that it's okay to do so.

Furthermore, there are inherent differences in various types of science. Physics, chemistry, and mathematics can be boiled down to equations that are provable and falsifiable. However, this is not so for the realm of social sciences, such as sociology, psychology, politics, health, and medicine. There are no guiding laws. In comparison with human interaction and consciousness, advanced physics is relatively simple. There is no equation for the complexity of the human condition. Yet that is precisely what people search for in science—an explanation of the human condition through the most reliable medium that we know of and one that can be agreed upon the world over. But the human condition is not gravity or evolution or the big bang. Gardner wrote similarly, "More than three centuries have passed since Newton published the *Principia*, and we have indeed learned a great deal and can predict much that we once could not, but the smooth equation between growing knowledge and advancing predictive ability has not been borne out."[40] Gardner cited chaos theory and nonlinear equations that form a world that is far too complex to make accurate predictions. Furthermore, if you factor in human consciousness, then all bets are off; better hire that dart-throwing chimp that Philip Tetlock had working behind the scenes.

Scientists and experts are not immune to preconceived notions; rather, it is often what drives their exploration. Those notions and ideologies can often cause battles in the scientific community. I am personally reminded of the back-and-forth battle between two of the twentieth century's top geniuses, Albert Einstein and Niels Bohr, regarding quantum mechanics and the true nature of the universe. Neither ever proved his point, but the intellectual battle helped make great strides forward in quantum mechanics due to Einstein constantly challenging the beliefs of the quantum physicists. Indeed, toward the end of his life, Einstein was more of an outsider looking in, anchored in his gut belief that there must be a grand theory that would combine relativity and quantum mechanics—what is now known as a unified field theory and which theoretical physicists and cosmologists are currently debating. There you have it—the two smartest guys ever and even they couldn't agree. What hope is there for us?

The illusion of experts need not be limited to pseudo-activist socialist issues that seek to expand government intervention and make people feel more secure. In 2013 the nation was shocked to learn that the National Security Administration had been monitoring phone calls, texts, e-mails, and Internet activity for years as a means of guarding against possible terrorist activities. The revelations were made by twenty-nine-year-old Edward Snowden, who immediately sought asylum, first in China and then in Russia. Obviously, this was distressing news, but probably what was just as distressing was captured by a headline in the satiric news website and tabloid *The Onion*: "Nation Mostly Alarmed That Government's Top Programs Handled by 29-Year-Olds." Humorous, but also indicative of a certain disappointment when the illusion of experts is momentarily interrupted. It was the national security equivalent of "sausage-cased mud balls." Snowden was a high school dropout who rose through the ranks by starting in the military and showing a predilection for computer work. He was then moved to security at the CIA. Eventually, he became an analyst and then found himself living in Hawaii making well over one hundred thousand dollars a year working for the NSA and monitoring vast amounts of data. Not bad for a dropout. However, the lack of educational degrees does not mean that Snowden was unintelligent. In fact, based on the manner in which he planned and carried out his revelation, he would appear to be quite bright indeed. That he had risen through the ranks quickly and was young for such an elevated position (I had a master's degree and was bartending at his age) shows that a lack of formal education does not mean one is unintelligent. The veil of experts had been temporarily lifted, and there was Edward Snowden.

Second, in the face of Snowden's revelation of massive data collection that could be "mined" for signs of terrorist activity was the fact that the United States had recently experienced several terrorist attempts; two were carried out successfully, namely the Fort Hood shooting and the Boston Marathon bombings. While laden with data on phone calls, texts, and Internet searches, the NSA, CIA, FBI, and local law enforcement were unable to stop some very rudimentary bombs and unsophisticated terrorists. On May 1, 2010, a T-shirt vendor in Times Square discovered a bomb set by Faisal Shahzad. The "Underwear Bomber," Umar Farouk Abdumutallab, was spotted and subdued by the passengers of the airliner on which he was flying. The Fort Hood shooter, Maj. Nadal Hasan, had been exchanging e-mails for weeks with radicalized imams in the Middle East; his activities were known but nothing was made of it. Boston Marathon bomber Tamerlan Tsarnaev was known to authorities previously. He had recently traveled to Dagestan for several months. The Russian government had warned the US intelligence agencies twice that he was a person to be watched for possible terrorist activity. Nonetheless, he returned to the United States unnoticed, detonated bombs made out of pressure cookers (not exactly high-tech movie stuff), and then could not be identified or found for days. The experts in government claim that the massive data accumulation of the NSA is necessary for identifying and tracking down terrorists, but apparently a phone call from a major foreign power was not enough of a warning.

The data revealed nothing in all of these cases. What was revealed was the limits of experts and technology. The government and society in general had placed more faith in equipment and expertise than they had in common sense, and the results were devastating. It was a civilian who finally located the second Boston Marathon bomber, not the police engaged in one of the largest manhunts in history.

The list of failed predictions, data-laden intelligence failures, false crises, and doomsday warnings from experts are literally too numerous to list. They tend to capitalize on some sense of unease in society whether it be terrorist fears, health concerns, economic instability, racial or social tensions, school shootings, or a sense of fear generated by a twenty-four-hour media cycle that reports every instance of chaos across the globe. This unease is then used to create a false crisis in order to push a particular agenda that is, on the surface, supposed to make everyone more comfortable. But the effect is the opposite. It is not so much a vicious circle as it is a downward spiral.

We began this look at experts by examining Tetlock's conclusions and discussing the hedgehogs of the expert world, who have one big idea into which they form fit the rest of reality. They are confident media darlings, and they make us feel as if we are privy to some kind of insider knowledge. But there is another form of expert he encountered: the fox. Foxes know many small things; they take bits of information from various sources, analyze them for what they are rather than trying to fit them into a preconceived framework, and humbly admit that they are most probably wrong. And most of the time they are, but they are right far more often than the hedgehogs. However, since their predictions do not hold the force and glamour of those made by hedgehogs, the foxes are passed over by media in favor of the always-wrong-but-always-sure hedgehogs.

Still, the blame does not lie entirely with the experts or the media that hawk them like wares at a bazaar. There is a deeply personal and human need to feel that there is some form of order to the universe. In modern times science has tried to give us that order, and often it has, by uncovering some of the intricacies of life and the laws of the universe. But science has not been able to do so in the realm of humanity. People still hunger for an explanation that will make the chaos of the human condition more reasonable and bearable. Tetlock wrote, "A balanced apportionment of blame should acknowledge that learning is hard because even seasoned professionals are ill-equipped to cope with the complexity, ambiguity, and dissonance inherent in assessing causation in history. Life throws up a lot of puzzling events that thoughtful observers feel impelled to explain because the policy stakes are so high. However, just because we want an explanation does not mean that one is within reach."[41]

We look for an order to the universe and for a way to understand our existence. This was traditionally the realm of religion but has now become the forte of science. Hence, we have hedgehogs, draped in arrogance and attesting to godlike knowledge, to whom the media clamber for answers and prophecies. Having been fully birthed into the modern world of science and technology, we hope and yearn for an equation, a law, an Einstein that will explain it all, but we have continually come up short. This also explains the need for hedgehogs to force everything into a single framework; they are looking for that unified field theory to explain why conscious men and women are here on this rock floating at the edge of a rather average solar system. We grab hold of a theory—scientific, social, philosophical—and then try to form fit our society to that theory through heavy-handed government intervention. In our effort to form a more perfect and unified world, we accomplish the exact opposite. Our existence doesn't make a whole lot of sense, and when we try to explain the interactions of humanity—the chaos of the world, the laws of the universe, good and evil—with one overarching theory, we are unable to make it work. There are no Hari Seldons as in Asimov's Foundation series. As Tetlock said, just because we want an explanation does not mean that one is in reach.

For this reason, the idea of a consensus of experts guiding the course of humanity is not a reasonable expectation or cause to action. Experts and the media create a paradigm of thought based on available knowledge and current trends and theories, but this does not make them correct. The ability to manipulate data and rhetoric in order to meet preconceived paradigms of thought is what creates the danger of illusion, and the lack of humility in the face of an infinite universe leads mankind down dangerous roads. Throughout all the false panics and incorrect predictions and disastrous policies, there have always been the dissenters, those whose voices were raised, but not above the din of the consensus. This is not about being merely contrarian; it is about having all your bases covered. Indeed, when everyone—the consensus—is all looking in one direction, the wisest choice may be to look in the other direction and examine the potentialities and repercussions of a different form of action or, perhaps, no action at all. It seems that often in the matters of experts, media, and government, the most important minds are the ones that are left behind.

3

culture of crisis

There even seemed to be a privileged proportion of this mixture that got furthest on in the world; just the right pinch of makeshift to bring out the genius in genius and make talent look like a white hope, as a pinch of chicory, according to some people, brings out the right coffee flavor in coffee. Suddenly all the prominent and important positions in the intellectual world were filled by such people, and all decisions went their way. There is nothing one can hold responsible for this, nor can one say how it came about. There are no persons or ideas or specific phenomena that one can fight against. There is no lack of talent or goodwill or even of strong personalities. There is just something missing in everything, though you can't put your finger on it, as if there had been a change of blood or in the air; a mysterious disease has eaten away the previous period's seeds of genius, but everything sparkles with novelty, and finally one has no way of knowing whether the world has really grown worse, or oneself merely older.

—robert musil

We're the middle children of history, man; no purpose or place. We have no Great War, no Great Depression. Our Great War is a spiritual war. Our Great Depression is our lives.

—tyler durden, *fight club*

during the Reign of Terror of the French Revolution, when thousands upon thousands of French aristocrats and commoners were killed at the guillotine, a new belief system took hold in the nation of France—one intended to replace Christianity. It was known as the "Cult of Reason." Christopher Hibbert wrote in his *Days of the French Revolution*:

> A few days before the Commune ordered the closure of all the churches in the city, a grand Festival of Reason was celebrated in Notre Dame. A young actress was carried into the cathedral by four citizens to represent the Goddess of Reason. Clothed in white drapery with a blue cloak over her shoulders and a red cap of liberty crowning her long hair, she was accompanied by a troupe of girls also dressed in white with roses on their heads. She sat on an ivy-covered chair while speeches were made, songs were sung, and soldiers paraded about the aisles carrying busts of Marat, Lepeletier and other martyrs of the Revolution. . . . From Paris the de-Christianization movement spread all over France.

Hibbert went on to record how street names were changed, people named their children after revolutionaries rather than the traditional saints, clergy married or renounced their beliefs, and churches were turned into Temples of Reason. Amid all this celebration of reason, said witness Sebastien Mercier, "the men wore no breeches; and the necks and breasts of the women were bare. In their wild whirling they imitated those whirlwinds, which, foreshadowing tempests, ravage and destroy all within their path. In the darkness of the sacristy they satisfied those abominable desires that had been aroused in them."[1]

The American and the French Revolutions were both inspired by the Enlightenment, a period (approximately 1690–1800) during which humanity quickly turned from a religious worldview to a scientific one. It was the time of Galileo, Isaac Newton, and the philosophers John Locke and Baruch Spinoza. The Enlightenment was a time of science, when men began to question long-held religious beliefs and traditions and discover the scientific laws and principles that would guide humanity into the twentieth century. The American and French Revolutions were both rebellions against a monarchy and the belief that a king was granted his power through God. The scientific breakthroughs of this time led to a belief in the individual rights of man, so described in the Declaration of Independence and the French Declaration of the Rights of Man and of the Citizen. The Enlightenment brought us a form of rational, scientific inquiry that called into question previously held beliefs and traditions, and it was through this rationalism that the American colonies and the French people began to question governmental authority and rebel against it. Both revolutions were violent. However, the French Revolution descended into a form of chaos that has only been seen in the most brutal regimes in history. Whereas in the American Revolution the colonists fought and killed the British, the French turned on each other and began to kill one another during the Reign of Terror. What happened? A people who had set up Temples of Reason descended into insanity and some of the most unreasonable actions the world has ever seen in the name of "justice" and "equality." What made the champions of rational thought so irrational?

Beginning with Copernicus in the mid-seventeenth century, the old beliefs based on tradition, Christianity, and papal authority began to rapidly erode. Copernicus and Galileo demonstrated that the earth was not the center of the universe. Newton developed modern physics, describing the laws that, for the most part, guide the universe. Suddenly, it was not the hand of God guiding the course of the universe, but rather a set of mathematical equations deciphered, interpreted, and wielded by man. This was the beginning of scientific inquiry and the end of religious authority concerning the natural world. The next century would see religious belief systems further demystified with the theories of Karl Marx, Charles Darwin, and finally, Friedrich Nietzsche, who made the telling observation that "God is dead" in his work *The Gay Science* (note the word "science"). It was the time of the industrial and scientific revolutions, when masses left the farms and the countryside to work in factories, sometimes under brutal conditions. This time also saw the rise of capitalism in some of its ugliest forms. Within approximately 150 years, the world had been massively transformed, and the people were left reeling. As poet William Butler Yeats wrote in his poem "The Second Coming" (note the religious reference):

Turning and turning in the widening gyre

The falcon cannot hear the falconer;

Things fall apart; the centre cannot hold;

Mere anarchy is loosed upon the world,

The blood-dimmed tide is loosed, and everywhere

The ceremony of innocence is drowned;

The best lack all conviction, while the worst

Are full of passionate intensity.[2]

The "centre" that cannot hold was the common worldview that man had held throughout the past millennium, the belief that the hand of God guided the universe and bestowed authority on kings and popes. During this time Western humanity generally shared the same beliefs, traditions, and values. However, the progress of science changed society. Paul Johnson opened his work *Modern Times* with an account of the confirmation of Einstein's general theory of relativity. He wrote:

The emergence of Einstein as a world figure in 1919 is a striking illustration of the dual impact of great scientific innovators on mankind. They change our perception of the physical world and increase our mastery of it. But they also change our ideas. The second effect is often more radical than the first. The scientific genius impinges on humanity, for good or ill, far more than any statesman or warlord. Galileo's empiricism created the ferment of natural philosophy in the seventeenth century which adumbrated the scientific and industrial revolutions. Newtonian physics formed the framework of the eighteenth century Enlightenment, and so helped to bring modern nationalism and revolutionary politics to birth. Darwin's notion of the survival of the fittest was a key element both in the Marxist concept of class warfare and of the racial philosophies which shaped Hitlerism. Indeed the political and social consequences of Darwinian ideas have yet to work themselves out. . . . So, too, the public response to relativity was one of the principal formative influences on the course of twentieth-century history. It formed a knife, inadvertently wielded by its author, to help cut society adrift from its traditional moorings in the faith and morals of Judeo-Christian culture.[3]

Science has cultural impact. Not on purpose or by design, of course, but the simple fact is that we form our ideas and our culture around what we can say is fact, aka science. When science changes, so does mankind and so does our perception of our place in this universe.

It was not an intentional change; Isaac Newton and Charles Darwin did not set out to "kill" God. However, from their findings, philosophers and laity alike found that the previous world had been rocked and rendered strange. In essence, the Enlightenment, this period of intense change and scientific development, left mankind in a state of perpetual crisis. It was not a crisis of an economic nature or the BP oil leak, but rather, a crisis of a spiritual nature. Questioning previous beliefs, man began to turn to himself and his own reason as the source of authority and power. The Temples of Reason during the French Revolution were symbolic in many ways; they represented the destruction of the old belief system in God and the values and authority handed down by God, and the beginning of man's believing in himself as god. Eric Voegelin referred to this as "the apocalypse of man" and Albert Camus referred to it as a "metaphysical rebellion." It was humanity's revolt against God. It was a spiritual crisis, and it continues to define our culture today.

Voegelin wrote, "A society is by definition in a state of crisis when its remedial forces, while perhaps present, are socially ineffective. The social problems that urgently would require a solution cannot be solved because the spiritual and moral strength for the task is lacking in the ruling group."[4] In essence, the qualities of the ruling group are either absent or too weak to be effective.

What does this have to do with experts, and how does this answer the question of how men and women of reason became so unreasonable and irrational?

It is simply this: when the Enlightenment called into question the authority of the church and of God, it also called into question the belief in what are called *transcendental principles*, or principles that are timeless and not just creations of mankind or culture. For instance, integrity: if God is not real, then the belief that mankind must be honest and practice integrity is called into question. If there is no God, if there is no eternity, and if there is no true right and true wrong, then "integrity" is just an idea of man, nothing more. And if integrity was developed by man and then turned into a principle through culture, then man can just as easily violate or undo this principle in favor of something else. In essence, without God, or at the very least a belief in some form of eternal right and wrong, something such as integrity is merely a man-made construct, the result of conditioning over millennia of evolution (Darwin), or a means by which the ruling class or ruling race can keep others in line (Marx).

It should be noted, however, that the argument here is not necessarily a religious one. An atheist can also recognize the need for right and wrong because without it society cannot function properly and effectively, and this is the crux of my argument later in the book. For the time being, however, we will focus on what was lost through the Enlightenment and the spiritual crisis that followed. While the Enlightenment enabled man, through the scientific process, to achieve magnificent, godlike abilities, it also caused something to be lost, some unnamable idea that caused him to question everything. As Musil wrote in the chapter quote, "There is just something missing in everything, though you can't put your finger on it, as if there had been a change of blood or in the air; a mysterious disease has eaten away the previous period's seeds of genius, but everything sparkles with novelty, and finally one has no way of knowing whether the world has really grown worse, or oneself merely older." What was lost was any notion of underlying or guiding principles by which men and women were supposed to live their lives. "For the first time in history, and with growing confidence and audacity, men arose to assert that they could diagnose the ills of society and cure them with their own unaided intellects: more, that they could devise formulae whereby not merely the structure of society but the fundamental habits of human beings could be transformed for the better."[5] God was dead, as Nietzsche said, and with Him everything that had previously been held sacred. Thus, during the French Revolution, every effort was made to desecrate churches and symbols of the previous age. Sacrilege reigned supreme, and with it the Terror.

With the idea of God gone or, at the very least, called into serious question, humanity looked to science and its rationality for answers to questions previously answered by religion. In science there appeared to be reason, order, and most of all, laws by which we could understand the complexities and chaos of modern life. These scientists, philosophers, and politicians were the very first experts, using science as a hammer to nail down the mysteries of life and thus offer a replacement for religion. There was, however, a problem; if man was now the master of his own universe, then he was not subject to any law greater than his own. This implied that laws and principles could be molded and shaped by man to suit his own needs. On the surface this sounds fine, *if* we assume that mankind is reasonable and rational. Part of the reason that experts are idolized in our society is because we assume they are the most reasonable and rational among us and, therefore, the best equipped to guide our lives and answer the mysteries. However, as we shall discover, this is not the case. Our definition of an expert is one who either makes a moral argument from science or portrays a moral argument as science. We shall begin with the latter and examine some of the most influential examples of experts and then determine whether or not humans are truly rational and reasonable.

I would argue that Karl Marx, along with Nietzsche and Charles Darwin, is still one of the most influential thinkers of modern time and perhaps the most influential in affecting our world at the dawn of the twenty-first century. Marx was an economist and, along with Friedrich Engels, began the communist movement in the mid-1800s. Marx's work was a reaction to the dramatically swift and often brutal industrialization of Europe. He focused largely on England, as it was the most developed and also the most mired in unrestrained capitalism at the time. To be sure, his work is often brilliant and, indeed, has played a necessary and good role in history by aiding in the elimination of terrible work conditions, child labor, sixteen-hour workdays, and unionizing workers so they could advocate for themselves. His work on the influence of economics on politics and culture was and still is very insightful and was quite radical at the time as he argued against what many capitalists called the "natural" mode of economics.

Marx claimed that his work was "scientific," giving it a veneer of objectivity and rational inquiry. However, the core of Marx's work is a moral argument, and a highly emotional one at that. Consider the wording in this piece from his economic work *Capital*: "We have seen, too, how this antagonism vents its rage in the creation of that monstrosity, an industrial reserve army, kept in misery in order to be always at the disposal of capital; in the incessant human sacrifices from among the working-class, in the most reckless squandering of labour-power, and in the devastation caused by a social anarchy which turns every economic progress into social calamity."[6]

Robert C. Tucker, professor and scholar on Marx, indicates that very same moral argument in his preface to Friedrich Engels's *On Morality*: "Value judgments resting on moral convictions abound in Marx and Engels. Thus they not only analyze exploitation and the division of labour in society, but morally condemn these phenomena as evil. Yet, there is no abstract discussion of ethics in their voluminous writings."[7] Marx and Engels were both rabid atheists; a discussion of ethics and morality (with the small exception of *On Morality*, a very, very short piece) would have led them down a path where science was pushed aside and philosophical and religious argument would have appeared.

Thus, in maintaining that their work was scientific and devoid of the traditional religious beliefs in God, they managed to cloak their moral and ideological argument in the veil of science.

To be sure, Marx's analysis of capitalism is scientific in that it closely examines working conditions at the time as well as the historical, social, technological, and economic causes of these conditions and how they affected at least a part of the population. However, just because the inquiry is scientific in nature does not mean that it is a science or that its conclusions are necessarily scientific. "These two great discoveries, the materialist conception of history and the revelation of the secret of capitalistic production through surplus value, we owe to Marx. With these discoveries socialism became a science."[8] Unfortunately, Marx's vision of the future and his calls for revolution turned out to be anything but scientific and rational. The revolutions and regimes that his philosophy inspired inherently turned out to be brutal and bloody, short-lived and devastating for the very people he wished to save from capitalism (Russia, China, and Cuba). Also, the way these countries functioned was the exact opposite of scientific; they were downright irrational. Russia, under Stalin, performed mock trials that ended in execution, very similar to the trial of traitors to the people during the French Revolution, and Maoist China burned books in the streets; in all cases, religious belief was expunged from society and the churches destroyed. Adolf Hitler began his career as a socialist (National Socialist Worker's Party, aka Nazi), and Benito Mussolini was an outspoken communist before becoming a fascist. In every one of these instances, the system conceived by Marx and Engels and argued as "scientific" fell victim to irrationalism, murder, and dictatorship. Marx's and Engels's works may have been scientific in analysis, but they were, at their base, moral arguments. A moral argument for the restraint of capitalism is fine in and of itself. People make moral arguments all the time. The problem, however, was the denial of morality and ethics in their work and their claim of Marxism and communism being a science that led to the ultimate deception when their theories became reality.

This is a pattern we will see recycled again and again. The denial of morals, ethics, and principles in the name of science can lead to irrationalism, devastation, and totalitarianism. Science, logic, and technology are tools—a means to an end—but not an end in and of themselves.

Marx represents a moral argument that calls itself a science. Now let's examine its inverse—science turned into a moral argument. Charles Darwin's work *On the Origin of Species* was one of the most revolutionary scientific works in history, and its social repercussions were just as enormous. The theory of evolution was not unique to Darwin but had been in the general realm of science for some time. However, Darwin developed the theory of natural selection as the means by which life evolved into its current state. It was a theory that was brilliant and simple, and unfortunately, one that transferred quite easily into an ideology that regarded human life as disposable. Evolution through natural selection, whether Darwin approved or not, was one of the final nails in the coffin for the Old World and the belief in God as the creator and mover of life. The notion that we had evolved from "lower" forms of life relegated man to a big-brained monkey, no better or more sacred than any other animal. Man was no longer God's special creation; he was now nothing more than the accumulated desires and manifestations of millions of years of animal survival. Man's very nature and even his universal desire to worship a higher being were now the result of genetic mutations, chemistry, and pure blind luck. The philosophical and moral implications were enormous.

The evidence of this cataclysmic discovery is still very much in evidence, as some towns and cities face board of education battles about what is to be taught in science classrooms regarding evolution. The latest manifestation of this debate is the intelligent design theory, which posits that the complexity of life is such that it could only have had a creator. Scientists such as William A. Dembski and Michael J. Behe have made many a strong argument against the typical atheistic implications of Darwinian evolution. I would be remiss if I did not point out that ultimately they fall under the class of experts in that their ultimate argument comes down to an ideology and a moral argument for the existence of God based on science. To be sure, they are not scientific hacks, and they do offer very interesting questions and criticisms of evolutionary theory as it is perceived by the public at large. All of this, of course, is somewhat beside the point but serves to illustrate that we are still very much in the throes of the spiritual crisis spurred by the Enlightenment.

The theory of evolution by natural selection was shanghaied by philosophers, politicians, and activists as a means to not only understand the world but to control and influence it for the better; to affect the next evolution of humanity. Sadly, that didn't work out. What happened was the exact opposite. Indeed, the theory of natural selection is inherently in the subtext of arguments concerning overpopulation, environmentalism, birth control, and fairness in society. Thomas Malthus first posited the theory that the world could not sustain a large population of people, and thus the herd would need to be culled through disease, famine, and catastrophe.[9] Darwin had read Malthus's work and was greatly influenced by it, as were many others at the time. Indeed, if Malthus's theory proved correct, only the "fittest"* of society would survive; this would invariably be the wealthy and highly educated, who could insulate themselves from said disasters. The "weak" of the herd of humanity—the poor—would die off through a form of natural selection.

Darwin's concept of a struggle for existence was seized upon by socialists and liberals at the time as a means of beating down capitalism and laissez-faire economics. The argument, in essence, said that the rich were trying to rid society of the poor through exploitation, progressive taxation, socialism, and so forth. These charges have continued into the current times and have involved politicians such as former president Ronald Reagan and the UK's Margaret Thatcher, who are often attacked as social Darwinists, willing to allow the poor to die off in favor of the

---

* It should be noted that the term "survival of the fittest" was coined by Herbert Spencer regarding Darwin's theory of natural selection. Spencer became one of the best-known and most controversial social Darwinists of the day.

rich. In his work *Social Darwinism: Science and Myth in Anglo-American Social Thought*, Robert C. Bannister opens his introduction with this: "Social Darwinism, as almost everyone knows, is a Bad Thing."[10] Using the new science of survival of the fittest and evolution as a moral cudgel, politicians and activists tried to beat down their opponents with accusations that they were willfully ignoring the poor and weak in an effort to rid the world of them. However, the truth of the matter was quite different. Those making the accusations were, in fact, using this new science as a means to expand governmental control in an effort to control the chaos of nature that leads to natural selection. "Although effective in debate, this tactic was ironical in view of the fact that the reformers, not their laissez faire opponents, were the Darwinians in any precise meaning of the term," Bannister observed. "Acceptance of the evolutionary framework meant, not simply that ideas and institutions must adapt to new circumstances (as stressed in older accounts of reform Darwinism), but that the situation demanded measures to control an increasingly chaotic 'natural' order. This perception of disorder was a common thread in the otherwise apparently disparate reforms of the progressive era—from the regulation of monopoly, to eugenics and Jim Crow. Pre-Darwinian evolutionists, cherishing the Enlightenment faith in beneficent laws of nature continued to argue that society ought best be left to develop without central direction or controls. But to those who saw nature through Darwinian lenses, this option seemed intolerable."[11]

As to the reality of social Darwinism, the theory of survival of the fittest could be molded to fit nearly any preconceived moral framework. It was a moral argument disguised as science. It became a way to sidestep moral issues through the invocation of science, which was viewed as objective and rational.

The theory of survival of the fittest was taken to its Malthusian conclusion in the work of eugenics. Eugenics is the attempt to improve the human race through promoting the breeding of people with desirable traits and inhibiting the breeding of people with lesser traits. It is, on the surface, a perfectly rational idea that, when put into practice, results in horrifying irrationalism comparable to the French Revolution's Terror. "Malthusian ideas gave birth to eugenics. The line runs through Charles Darwin, who said that his own theory of natural selection grew from reading Malthus's predictions about the effect of a 'grand crush' in human populations."[12] Darwin's half cousin, Francis Galton, developed eugenics. It is a "science" that incorporates the "dark side" of evolution; namely, that a species, such as man, could regress into more primitive states due to the survival and population of "lesser" peoples. It was a mere hop, skip, and jump to such modern atrocities as Hitler's attempt to craft the Aryan race and eliminate Jews, minorities, the mentally ill, and the handicapped in Germany.

The founder of what eventually became Planned Parenthood, Margaret Sanger, was also an unapologetic eugenicist who believed that the upper classes should breed more and the lower classes and races should be prevented from childbearing. "As an advocate of Birth Control, I wish to . . . point out that the unbalance between the birth rate of the 'unfit' and the 'fit,' admittedly the greatest present menace to civilization, can never be rectified by the inauguration of a cradle competition between these two classes," she wrote. "In this matter, the example of the inferior classes, the fertility of the feeble-minded, the mentally defective, the poverty-stricken classes, should not be held up for emulation to the mentally and physically fit though less fertile parents of the educated and well-to-do classes. On the contrary, the most urgent problem today is how to limit and discourage the over-fertility of the mentally and physically defective. Birth Control is not advanced as a panacea by which past and present evils of dysgenic breeding can be magically eliminated. Possibly drastic and Spartan methods may be forced upon society if it continues complacently to encourage the chance and chaotic breeding that has resulted from our stupidly cruel sentimentalism."[13]

Thus, Darwin's theory of natural selection was combined with the population theories of Malthus and the politics of control to come to completely irrational conclusions, namely, the forced sterilization and genocide that highlighted some of this past century's worst eras. The science of evolution by natural selection was used to advance causes that were not scientific, but rather political and ultimately moral causes. Socialists used the chaotic and brutal aspects of survival of the fittest as an argument against capitalists and free market economists as well as to accuse the wealthy of ignoring the plight of the poor and working class. Eugenicists used natural selection as a reason to control the populations of the poor and working class in an effort to better all of humanity through planned reproduction of the "fittest." Both ignored the moral implications of these ideas and, instead of arguing their causes based on what they really were, attempted to sidestep the moral issue by using objective science and saying, "Case closed." "The few who best understood the new theory studiously avoided applying concepts of struggle and selection to contemporary society. In contrast to older natural-law theorists. . . . Darwin, Huxley, and Wallace insisted that men must find guides to social policy elsewhere than in nature."[14]

That being said, the religious-like belief in Darwinian evolution as an answer for all of man's problems is still very much in evidence. From crime to philanthropy, experts declare that there are simple, evolutionary causes for all of it. There is no evidence, but rather an evolutionary framework for their educated minds to work with. If I choose to believe that everything has an evolutionary cause, then it is easy to rationalize any form of behavior to suit that belief. In her essay "Darwin Meets the Berenstain Bears: Evolution as a Total Worldview," Nancy Pearcey discusses the book *A Natural History of Rape* by biologist Randy Thornhill and anthropologist Craig T. Palmer in which they argue that the act of rape has an evolutionary basis. "The book aroused considerable public controversy, which the authors say took them by surprise," she reported. "After all, it is simple logic that any behavior that survives today must have conferred some evolutionary advantage—otherwise it would have been weeded out by natural selection. . . . Finally he [Thornhill] said, in essence, that the logic is inescapable: for if evolution is true, then it must also be true that 'every feature of every living thing, including human beings, has an underlying evolutionary background. That's not a debatable matter.'"[15] This would be a dangerous way to shape public policy, and, to be sure, their theory was met with outcry from other scientists and psychologists.

What is particularly interesting in highlighting these major scientific and sociological trends is the confluence of Darwin, Marx, and Nietzsche, whose call for the "superman" was viewed as a form of social Darwinism. Bannister wrote, "Wedded to the assumptions that ideas were ultimately plans for action, the progressive generation too easily translated Nietzsche's analysis of the creative potential of intellect into political reactionism and thus rejected it. The presence in his work of such terms as *ubermensch*, *slave*, and *aristocracy*—each with overwhelmingly negative connotations—encouraged this translation. Only with the migration of a later generation of European intellectuals could Americans fully appreciate the tender or existentialist Nietzsche"[16] All of these theories and their subsequent experts occurred during the mid- to late-1800s and were a massive influence on future generations and the philosophies that followed. As I said before, these three men, Darwin, Marx, and Nietzsche, though dead, are the most influential thinkers at work today. What they all held in common was an adherence to atheism, a denial of anything greater than man's intellect.

But this still leaves our question unanswered: How do rational men fall victim to such irrationality when supposedly following science? How does a Temple of Reason become the Terror? It is not just a matter of deceit and politics, but something deeper, something that the philosopher Søren Kierkegaard addressed during this very same era when he dissected the biblical story of Abraham and Isaac. Abraham was asked to do the unthinkable: sacrifice his son Isaac to God. God's command presented Abraham with a serious moral dilemma, to obey God and kill his only son, or to defy God and save his son's life. It is nearly an impossible quandary. Ultimately, Abraham took Isaac to be sacrificed, but an angel interceded and halted the sacrifice. Abraham was allowed to sacrifice a goat and keep his son as reward for his faith. But Kierkegaard focused on the internal dilemma that Abraham faced during the several days' travel to Moriah for the sacrifice. What he found is that at man's core there exists a paradox between faith and the rational world. And faith always wins. Abraham, without faith, would have been merely a murderer. However, the fact that he was willing to make this sacrifice as matter of faith in God renders his story timeless. According to Charles Guignon and Derek Pereboom in their work *Existentialism: Basic Writings*, "In Kierkegaard's view, then, there is a dimension of humanity, expressed in an individual relationship with God, that is independent of one's relationships and obligations to humanity, and that cannot be rationally comprehended but only passionately appropriated. And thus . . . life does not become meaningful through rational acceptance of a coherent system of ethical principles. Rather, it becomes meaningful through a passionate struggle to live in accord with the fundamental and irresolvable paradox that lies at the heart of human existence."[17]

In other words, faith and belief lie at the very heart of men and women. They are a form of irrationality that cannot be explained through science, technology, or psychology, and they are why humanity cannot be reduced to a science or an equation. Science presents us with a dilemma: the ability to understand the physical world around us through mathematics and laws of science but the inability to understand ourselves. It is a dilemma that desperate men and women try to solve by supposing their beliefs to be science or science to be their beliefs.

While the physical world around us is one of rational functioning through physics and chemistry and various other sciences, the human heart is ultimately an irrational one that is not provable or subject to an equation like Newton's laws. That is the paradox, and that is why rational men of reason descend into irrationality and horror so easily. The beliefs of Marx and Engels led them to try to create a science based on their beliefs, but they failed. Likewise, others tried to develop a moral theory from the rational science of evolution and ended up causing more damage than good. It doesn't work, and it won't work. Even atheists believe in their atheism even though it is not ultimately provable.

The problem of the Enlightenment and the death of God is that man no longer placed faith in God at the center of his being, but instead put his faith in man's reason. Because humanity is, at its core, irrational—relying on faith rather than reason, placing such faith in man's own reason inherently becomes problematic. Rather than breeding a world of reason, this misplaced faith has created the exact opposite. It is also why certain political and "scientific" movements are actually matters of faith in the guise of science. It is why experts see everything through the lens of their own theories. They think they have replaced faith with reason only to find that they have been fooled. Faith breeds humility and a knowledge of one's limitations. Believing that you are the ultimate arbiter of what is reasonable leads to arrogance, irrationality, and failure.

Friedrich Nietzsche recognized this change when he observed that "God is dead." The evidence that traditional values, principles, and the authority of the church had been superseded was all around him: the numerous revolts and revolutions of 1849 throughout Europe, the rapid industrialization that suddenly caused the populations of cities to sky-rocket, and the rapid accumulation of wealth by newly minted industri-alists. The living conditions were terrible; that, combined with increased poverty, led to higher crime rates. Everywhere there was evidence of a change, not only in man's technology and environment, but in his soul. Nietzsche celebrated this change and called for man to become his own god, and thus the pendulum of history swung from the rationalism of the Enlightenment to the irrationalism of the Victorian age. "Even the most harmful people are perhaps the most useful of all, as regards the preservation of the species, for they maintain in themselves, or by their effect on others, drives without which humanity would long ago have become sluggish or decayed. Hatred, malicious gloating, the ambition to rob and rule, and anything else called evil belongs to the amazing economy of the preservation of the species. . . . Indulge your best or your worst desires, and even do yourself in! In either case, you are probably still furthering and benefiting humanity somehow, and are entitled to your eulogists—and your mockers, too!"[18] These are frightening words from a man who would become the Nazi's patron philosopher-saint and even more frightening considering that Nietzsche's philosophy is alive and well in American universities, as will be demonstrated shortly.*

To be certain, these times and changes are never fixed dates in history. To use a metaphor, the change from white to black passes through all the shades of gray. It is interesting to note, however, that the rationalism of the Enlightenment logically led to the irrationalism of the Victorian era and onward to World War I. The logic of this "progression" is evident in the philosophers from René Descartes to Nietzsche; they each built off the other and used their abilities of reason to reach an understanding of the world that became quite unreasonable in the horrors of the two world wars.

As a final example, let us look at the career of Robert McNamara, John F. Kennedy's secretary of defense, during America's own descent into insanity (aside of this present one), the Vietnam War. McNamara had graduated from Harvard and was president of the Ford Motor Company in 1960 when Kennedy was elected. He was studious, a mathematical wizard, and had little patience for probing the ethical and philosophical discussions of life. David Halberstam's brilliant *The Best and the Brightest* paints a picture of McNamara, who was considered the best of Kennedy's best and brightest. "If the body was tense and driven, the mind was mathematical, analytical, bringing order and reason out of chaos. Always reason. And reason supported by facts, by statistics—he could prove his rationality with facts, intimidate others."[19] Also, "He was a man of force, moving, pushing, getting things done, *Bob got things done*, the can-do man in the can-do society, in the can-do era."[20]

Following the victory in World War II, America had moved to the head of the world stage. A never-before-seen superpower, both economically and technologically, it largely experienced an era of peace and

---

* It has been amply demonstrated that the Nazis were using a perverted form of Nietzsche's work that was supplied to them by his sister who was a Nazi sympathizer and sought to gain influence in the movement. Nietzsche was dead long before Nazi Germany. However, this is good evidence that philosophy has consequences and can be a rallying cry for horror, misunderstood or not.

prosperity. It seemed, at the time, that anything was possible; the flying cars were just right around the corner. America had become infatuated with science and reason and rationality, and the election of John F. Kennedy and his cabinet of intellectual superheroes seemed destined for greatness. However, the outcome was vastly different. These learned men from the finest institutions lacked qualities—principles to which they were subject. They thought themselves gods among men and, using their great intellects, believed that they could shape the world through facts, statistics, and analysis. They were proven very wrong.

Eisenhower had originally considered entering the fray of Vietnam; however, when he consulted with one of his Army chiefs of staff, Matthew Ridgeway, who had sent a survey team to Indochina, he decided that it would be a grave error. "The answers were chilling: minimal five divisions and up to ten divisions if we wanted to clear out the enemy (as opposed to six divisions in Korea), plus fifty-five engineering battalions, between 500,000 and 1,000,000 men, plus enormous construction costs."[21] Eisenhower passed on the venture, even with mounting political and international pressure.

However, when Kennedy's best and brightest took the reins, they did some calculations and determined that they could win this war largely through air power, in other words, superior technology. Kennedy and McNamara believed that a small commitment of troops and air power would be enough to handle the Vietnam issue, so they moved forward with the troop deployment, believing "in the capacity of rational men to control irrational commitments." They believed themselves smart enough to do with a few troops and air power what the French could not do with 300,000 men and ten years. After Kennedy was assassinated and Johnson became president, McNamara remained secretary of defense, and things went from bad to worse.

The real issue at hand was that McNamara believed that by manipulating numbers and statistics, he could, in effect, change the reality on the ground in Vietnam. He pressured generals to report numbers that met his expectations rather than the numbers as they truly were. He believed that by mastering an illusion, he could master reality. Such arrogance and rationalization of the truth begins small, but like a snowball, becomes bigger and bigger as it rolls downhill. Eventually, they found themselves in an impossible position and heading a war that would nearly break America's back. There had been a change from the Eisenhower administration to the Kennedy/Johnson tenure. It was a change in the qualities of integrity, humility, and respect for the truth. "Whereas Eisenhower genuinely consulted the Congress, Johnson paid lip service to the real consultation and manipulated Congress. Eisenhower's chief of staff had made a tough-minded, detailed estimate of what the cost of the war would be; eleven years later an all-out effort was made by almost everyone concerned to avoid determining and forecasting what the reality of intervention meant. Johnson and McNamara would carefully shield accurate troop projections not only from the press and the Congress but from their own budgetary experts."[22]

Theirs were small rationalizations that had enormous repercussions. Reality cannot be denied and it is not subjective. McNamara and many others thought that the truth could be manipulated, created or destroyed, and bent to their unrivaled minds. They were wrong.

The problem with illusion is that it presents itself as reality, but it is not reality. And when that illusion is discovered, we are left with cold, stark reality. For McNamara, "when the mathematical version of sanity did not work out, when it turned out that the computer had not fed back the right answers and had underestimated those funny little far-off men in their raggedy pajamas, he would be stricken with a profound sense of failure, and he would be, at least briefly, a shattered man."[23]

McNamara went on from his position as secretary of defense to become the president of World Bank in 1968. He was the one who was consulted by various Malthusian fearmongers who prophesied the coming catastrophe of the "population bomb," and it was he who began to distribute funds to developing countries based on their effectiveness of population control, such as the forced sterilization in India. "McNamara swiftly declared that in the future, aid for health care would be tied to population control. Death control, he said, was not acceptable without birth control."[24]

When men and women no longer recognize that at their very core is an irrational form of faith, and instead take themselves to be the ultimate arbiters of what is reasonable, they find themselves in a very poor position. Principles, morals and ethics provide a limitation on that irrationality, but they can do so only when they are believed to be eternal. Even Nietzsche recognized that if mankind were not subject to some kind of eternal standard, then the world would be thrust into ethical chaos. For this reason, he developed his idea of "the eternal recurrence of the same" in which he challenges people to question the choices they would make if their lives were to be relived again and again for eternity. "It seems that what Nietzsche is suggesting here is that if we were to will that our lives be repeated innumerable times exactly as they are, with no embellishments or changes, then this would give a kind of 'weight' to our existence."[25] Even the world's foremost atheist understood that an idea of the eternal was necessary.

What should be held at the core of humanity is a belief in some kind of eternal principles that we are subject to, rather than principles being subject to our whims. Whether that faith is manifested in God or some other kind of guiding principles is up to the individual. Reality is guided by reason and the physical laws of the universe, but humanity is guided by belief and emotion. When we come to believe that we can actually control reality through our own reason, we are, in effect, trying to make gods of ourselves. We are tearing down the cathedrals and erecting Temples of Reason, all the while basking in a form of insanity that our belief is actually a science.

In his magnificent book *The Rebel*, Albert Camus (an atheist none-theless) urged that man must practice restraint and place limits on how much he is willing to violate transcendental principles. He concludes with these haunting words, "Denying the real grandeur of life, they have had to stake all on their own excellence. For want of something better to do, they deified themselves and their misfortunes began; these gods have had their eyes put out. Kaliayev, and his brothers throughout the entire world, refuse, on the contrary, to be deified in that they refuse the unlimited power of death. They choose, and give us as an example the only original rule of life today: to learn to live and die, and, in order to be man, to refuse to be a god."[26]

On Christmas Day of 2013, in the High Cathedral of St. Peter in Cologne, Germany, a twenty-year-old philosophy student named Josephine Witt stormed the altar. Witt was an activist with FEMEN, a feminist group, which proclaims its ideology is "sextremism, atheism, and feminism." She was topless, and on her chest were written the words *I AM GOD*. She climbed atop the altar, faced the congregation, and made a triumphant *V* with her arms extended in the air, lording over the entire congregation. It was a scene reminiscent of the French Revolution's Goddess of Reason making her triumphant entry into the Notre Dame cathedral.[27]

4

higher learning and
the credentialed age

The true edge is not where you choose to live but where they situate you against your will. This event is infinitely deeper and more electrifying than anything you might elect to do with your own life. You know what this is? This is twenty-six guys from Harvard deciding our fate. . . . Dig it. These are the guys from the eating clubs and the secret societies. They have fraternity handshakes so complicated it takes three full minutes to do all the moves. One missed digit you're f----d for life. Resign from the country club, forget about the stock options and the executive retreat, watch your wife disappear in a haze of secret drinking. You have to be hip to stay connected. These guys wear boxer shorts with geometric designs that contain the escape routes they've been assigned when the missiles start flying. . . . We're all gonna die!

—don delillo, *underworld*

I can't give you a brain, but I can give you a diploma.

—the wizard of oz

In 2009, author and journalist Walter Kirn released his memoir of his time at Princeton. The book, titled *Lost in the Meritocracy: The Undereducation of an Overachiever*, is a devastating and frighteningly candid remembrance about the disintegration of both our society and the elite who deign to rule it. Kirn aced the SAT and left his Midwestern town for Princeton, where he became enmeshed in the "meritocracy," as he refers to it. He was surrounded by the supposedly "best and brightest" (and wealthiest) that American society had to offer. Suffice to say that if the people he met at Princeton during the 1970s are the same ones who are running our largest corporations, educating our college students, and running our government today, we are all doomed.

What Kirn realized in his recollection is that one cannot deconstruct reality without deconstructing oneself. Where once there was a person, there is now nothing but a vacuum. During his time at Princeton, Kirn essentially became a man without qualities, and the nature of the elite university system not only encouraged him but rewarded him with access to the upper echelons of society. And he wasn't the only one; in fact, according to his depiction of his peers and friends, they were just as vacuous, if not insane:

> A few of my club mates scare me. I avoid them. One, a reputed physics prodigy, is catatonic from LSD, which he takes by placing the tabs on his bare eyeballs. On weekends he engages in pinball marathons that sometimes last ten hours. Strike a match an inch from his face and he won't even flinch—his pupils won't even contract. Then there's the girl in the neck brace whom we call Anna, after the heroine of Tolstoy's novel. A comp-lit student, pale and heavyset, she told Adam one night at dinner that they were destined to be married. . . . When Adam asked the girl to go away, she flung herself off a third-floor metal railing in the atrium of his dormitory. She survived, by some miracle, and ever since Adam has been her guilty slave.[1]

His entire time at Princeton was a drug-fueled orgy, but of more concern is that he appears to have graduated Princeton as an English major without having learned anything. Even the critical "deconstruction theory" was nothing but gibberish to him, devoid of any actual understanding of the texts. "I relied on my gift for mimicking authority figures and playing back to them their own ideas as though they were conclusions I reached myself. . . . To me imitation and education were different words for the same thing, anyway. What was learning but a form of borrowing? And what was intelligence but borrowing slyly?" This kind of thinking could explain a lot of the problems with our current culture. Further, he admitted, "I sought the company of other frauds. We recognized each other instantly. We toted around books by Roland Barthes, Hans-Georg Gadamer, and Walter Benjamin. We spoke of 'playfulness' and 'textuality' and concluded before we'd read even a hundredth of it that the Western canon was 'illegitimate,' a veiled expression of powerful group interests that it was our duty to subvert. In our rush to adopt the latest attitudes and please the younger and hipper of our instructors . . . we skipped straight from ignorance to revisionism, deconstructing a body of literary knowledge that we'd never constructed in the first place."[2]

It was not knowledge that Kirn possessed at that time; it was only the illusion of it. Yet it was all that was needed to have a degree conferred upon him. Kirn eventually recognized the hollowness of his education and sought to educate himself, but the implications of such a story are frightening. Students were not thinking; they were imitating. And what they were imitating was subversive to Western tradition and our own country.

What is most apparent and disturbing in Kirn's memoir, a fact that he openly acknowledges, was the lack of a moral, spiritual, and ethical base in his education. Kirn describes his earliest education as the time he spent with a retired Navy admiral who took him under his wing. Looking back, Kirn realizes that this was ultimately the best education he received and states that "just because something isn't completely solid does not mean you cannot stand on it." He reminded readers that all objects are not solid on an atomic level, but still they support the weight of the world.

Allan Bloom addressed the dearth of principles and morality in 1987 when he wrote *The Closing of the American Mind*. It was a philosophical treatise on the disintegration of true education in the university system, particularly with regard to the big questions and beliefs upon which one can truly build a life, such as, What is a good life? What is good?

What is a good society? Until recently, these were the questions that concerned philosophers. What changed was the philosophical foundation upon which much of higher education based itself, namely, the influence of Nietzsche. Bloom credits this influence in large part to the importation of German thought.

Nietzsche's philosophy refuted Socrates, Plato, and Aristotle; he rejected reason and rationalism in favor of irrationalism, thereby refuting any claim to universal principles or values. Thus, the university system has become ground zero for deconstructing what few values students may arrive with and supplanting them with the very same impotent activism that we examined in chapter 2. According to Bloom, "Since values are not rational and not grounded in the natures of those subject to them, they must be imposed. They must defeat opposing values. Rational persuasion cannot make them believed, so struggle is necessary. Producing values and believing in them are acts of the will. Lack of will, not lack of understanding, becomes the crucial defect. Commitment is the moral virtue because it indicates the seriousness of the agent. Commitment is the equivalent of faith when the living God has been supplanted by self-provided values."[3]

Western civilization is defined by its philosophical tradition of reason; however, modern academia no longer thinks this quality has value and believes instead that it has caused many of the world's problems, from slavery and colonialism to poverty and racism.

One of the main points of Bloom's work is that while German philosophers such as Nietzsche and Heidegger refuted the ancient Greeks, they had studied those original thinkers and were thus able to reach their own conclusions. Modern students are not expected to study the philosophies and thinkers that have made their present lives and conditions possible; they are taught only to dismiss them. This is very similar to Kirn stating that he and his fellow students "skipped straight from ignorance to revisionism, deconstructing a body of literary knowledge that we'd never constructed in the first place."

Perhaps the most damning aspects of the influence of German

thought in American schools is that Nietzsche was hailed as a national hero by the Nazis, and Heidegger was their official national philosopher. Nazism was not a rational or reasoned philosophy or political body. In fact, it was the exact opposite; it was built on the "rationality" of a madman and brought to power by appealing to an imaginary German *Volk*. One has only to watch the videos of Hitler's speeches before his fellow Germans to see that what was being celebrated was a faith, not a rational political system and certainly not a science. Focusing only on the irrational and subjective, and forming values and morals from only that center, is dangerous.

Experts, as we are defining them, are given legitimacy primarily through the higher education system and only secondarily through media. According to *Time* magazine, college enrollment in four-year schools in 2011 was approximately 10.6 million students, up from 5.1 million in 1970.[4] With more and more people attending higher education institutions and more and more degrees conferred by those institutions, it is imperative that we ask what effect, either positive or negative, this may have on a society. While furthering one's education always sounds positive in principle, we should look critically at whether that education results in greater opportunity, knowledge, or the ability to competently handle any number of complex issues that may arise in society. That very same *Time* article indicates that, as a whole, a college education still results in higher income, but at a much higher cost. Four-year public university program tuitions rose from approximately $2,500 in 1980 to $8,200 in the 2011–2012 education year. Private school four-year programs rose from $10,000 to $28,500 in that same time period, and a graduate's average debt was $26,600. By 2020 it is projected that 65 percent of all jobs will require some college education, as opposed to 28 percent in 1973.

Furthermore, the increased number of students and the current educational paradigm have resulted in more specialty degrees, often in the area of humanities. This is reflected in the trend toward a greater number of degrees conferred at all costs. The University of Connecticut offers undergraduate and graduate degrees in puppeteering; Michigan State offers a major in packaging à la UPS; and Kansas State offers bakery science and management. While these are some of the more unusual majors, the very nature of specialization in both academia and the professional world has rendered higher education subject to whims, fads, and trends. It makes nearly any job worthy of degree conferment. Does someone who loves and wants to bake need a degree in bakery science? Probably not. The higher education system has become an industry unto itself. It is rarely portrayed as an option for high school students, but rather as a requirement—in essence, high school part 2— where the student is merely learning a specific skill set for a career rather than developing an exclusive higher education. In other words, much of what is learned in colleges and universities could be learned on the job rather than spending the time and money on that advanced education. However, society has come to value the degree conferred rather than the nature of the education itself. Does one need a degree in plumbing in order to solve the BP oil crisis? Apparently not.

The specialization of degree conferment is one tine in Bloom's two-pronged critique of the university system; he submits that degree specialization caters to the market and social forces rather than to the propagation of knowledge. Bloom expects that the university should be above and outside the realm of influence of economy and mass culture. "No public career these days—not doctor nor lawyer nor politician nor journalist nor businessman nor entertainer—has much to do with humane learning. An education, other than purely professional or technical, can even seem an impediment."[5] University learning has been streamlined for a production economy and has shrugged off much of what was previously considered essential learning—trying to answer the big universal questions through understanding the thinkers who built society as we know it. This is remarkably similar to Christopher Hedges's contention that "the elite universities disdain honest intellectual inquiry, which is by its nature distrustful of authority, fiercely independent, and often subversive. They organize learning around minutely specialized disciplines, narrow answers, and rigid structures designed to produce such answers."[6] Questioning the leading opinion of the day in the higher education system can have dire consequences for those in the system.

A recent scandal involved a blogger who lost her position with the *Chronicle of Higher Education* for criticizing a number of PhD dissertations that were coming out of the black studies departments. She labeled the dissertations as "irrelevant" due to the highly specialized nature of the dissertations, such as black midwifery in history.[7] It is not the existence of ethnically specific studies or cultural studies in general that is the problem; what is alarming is that someone can be fired for offering an opinion that might, at worst, have been seen as politically incorrect.

This is the inherent concern with academia and why uncritically accepting someone's opinion simply because he or she has a PhD and is deemed an expert can be dangerous. The expert in question has been promoted through a system that abhors the questioning of its very authority, regardless of the merit of the argument or so-called academic freedom.

This brings us to our first question regarding higher education: does the higher education system and its subsequent degree conferment actually warrant our perceived authority of experts?

Our first lesson: A degree does not make one intelligent. As the Wizard of Oz said to the Scarecrow, "I can't give you a brain, but I can give you a diploma." The university system has become a business, and its products are degrees. A university would probably not last long if its students were not graduating with degrees. Therefore, it is in their economic interest to ensure enrollment and graduation. This, for the most part, is to be expected; however, it is necessary to examine the cost inherent in the economics of education. Students, parents, individuals, the government, donors—all pay for the typical university to churn out students with degrees. The assumption is that a college education will ensure a better-paying job and a happier population. This would seem to make sense except that when the majority of the population suddenly has bachelor's degrees, they become the equivalent of high school diplomas. So the go-getter pursues his or her master's degree, which is specialized, and while it implies greater learning and effort, it also lessens its practical application in society. The more specialized the degree, the more subject it becomes to the whims of the economy, and the more people who have it, the less valuable it becomes. Suddenly you have three hundred applicants with master's degrees competing for an assistant's position. Our current economic situation readily confirms this. We have more young people with higher education degrees than ever before, but the economy itself is failing and jobs are scarce, and the recent college grads are the ones having difficulty getting work because they have no experience. So a degree does not necessarily guarantee a better job (or any job for that matter).

It should also be noted that higher education cannot replace drive and hard work. In his book *Outliers*, Malcolm Gladwell profiled people and personalities that lie outside the norm, but who, by the very qualities that separate them from the masses, have had great success. He profiled the coming-of-age of Bill Gates, who was lucky enough to gain access to a computer in 1968. He began working on the Teletype as much as possible. When that computer was no longer available, Gates and his buddies began hanging around the University of Washington and were able to gain access to a computer in exchange for working on a piece of software for the university. "In one seven-month period in 1971, Gates and his cohorts ran up 1,575 hours of computer time on the ISI mainframe, which averages out to eight hours a day, seven days a week."[8] It was not Gates's education that led to his success; it was his work ethic. It is not necessarily a matter of talent or IQ. Indeed, some of our richest and most successful people have not taken the "usual" route to success; Bill Gates, Mark Zuckerberg, and Steve Jobs all skipped higher education in order to pursue their passions and start their companies. This was much more common in the past; the major companies that developed before the push toward higher education were born out of a population that today would be considered uneducated.

However, Gladwell makes an argument against the idea that only hard work equals success and offers qualifiers to those stories of hard work. "You have to have parents who encourage and support you. You can't be poor, because if you have to hold down a part-time job on the side to help make ends meet, there won't be enough time left in the day to practice enough."[9] Gladwell illustrates this thought with his profile of Christopher Langan, the man with the highest IQ ever recorded but who failed in higher education largely because his background of poverty and a broken family did not lend itself well to the confines of higher education institutions. He ended up spending much of his life as a bouncer for a bar and now lives on a farm, reading voraciously and working on his "Cognitive Theoretic Model of the Universe."[10]

Gladwell's point is that success and ascent into a position of power do not necessarily mean that someone is smarter or has worked harder, but that he or she has had a more qualitative cultural element. In essence, Langan's upbringing precluded him from inclusion in the elite universities that would have mainstreamed him into a position of influence. It is reminiscent of philosopher Eric Hoffer, who never attended a higher education institution and worked, most famously, as a longshoreman. He lived in poverty his whole life but was eventually given an honorary doctorate from Berkeley for his works, such as *True Believer*.

In 2011, Richard Arum and Josipa Roska released their book, *Academically Adrift: Limited Learning on College Campuses*. Their book was the result of a large study and survey taken of undergraduate students, faculty, and administration on college campuses. It assessed the difference in students' abilities in "critical thinking, complex reasoning, and writing skills," between their freshman and senior years. Their findings were disturbing. "With a large sample of more than 2,300 students, we observe no statistically significant gains in critical thinking, complex reasoning, and writing skills for at least 45 percent of the students in our study. An astounding proportion of students are progressing through higher education today without measurable gains in general skills . . . While they may be acquiring subject-specific knowledge or greater self-awareness on their journeys through college, many students are not improving their skills in critical thinking, complex reasoning, and writing."[11] While the university professes a desire to help students "think critically," they are really only encouraging them to engage in a form of groupthink where stepping outside the bounds of authority is met with banishment, as the *Higher Education* blogger found out the hard way.

Consider the case of Steve Roggenbuck, "Internet Poet," "Vegan Blogger," who wants to "Boost the World." He runs a blog titled *Live My Lief* [*sic*] and was formerly a master's of fine arts (MFA) student at Columbia, which means he already had an undergraduate degree. Steve dropped out of Columbia and then took to the Internet to explain why—much of which had to do with the fact that his professors did not seem to understand his work. (In an effort to save time, please understand that all the following misspellings and grammatical errors are on Steve's part; this way I don't have to write *sic* after every word.)

> *professor #3*: she was all about writing from pain, and in 2011 i just wasn't interested in that at all. i wanted to make people smile and laugh with my poems. she talked about how poems are the most "honest" when they explore deep pain that is difficult to write about— tragedy and loss and stuff. that was valuable for many class members, but i wasn't at all receptive to that message at that time, and it just frustrated me that she dismissed other posibilities of good writing. this was also the teacher who didn't understand my misspellings at all. she wanted there to be a logical reason or justification for each specific misspelling. once in class she said, "as someone who doesn't really use the internet or texting, what does this poem do for *ME*?" and in my sassiest in-class moment of all time, i jus responded, "maybe it's not for you !! maybe you're not my audience !!"[12]

Roggenbuck has apparently taken it upon himself to deconstruct the English language without any point or "justification." One wonders, however, if he has taken the initiative to learn the language in the first place. Here is a piece of Roggenbuck's poetry from his online poetry collection, *i am like october when i'm dead*:

i dont care about reading a poem

who do you think i am, robert frost?

i have never been in the woods and i hate walking[13]

I don't necessarily mean to pick on Roggenbuck, except that he so perfectly encapsulates the main point being made here, namely, that students no longer believe that learning, knowledge, and education are things of value. Instead, they revert to a narcissistic view of themselves as "artists" entitled to our adoration. His mocking reference to Robert Frost is the icing on the cake; he feels no need to learn from the poet, only to defy him. The fact that he was accepted into the MFA program of a very prestigious university gives us pause.

The authors of *Academically Adrift* also cite a change in the way our culture sees higher education as part of the problem; namely, as a place that offers a gateway to better jobs and as a way to bring greater equality to people through education. The authors refer to this as a "college for all mentality," though I'm still partial to "high school part 2." However, this idea has proven to be largely untrue. In fact, college has been shown to exacerbate inequalities precisely because higher education has given up on the moral cultivation of its students, opting instead for a hands-off approach toward morality and ethics. "Children from upper-class families acquire 'linguistic and cultural competence' and 'familiarity with [the dominant, upper- and middle-class] culture.' These skills and predispositions are in turn rewarded in school, granting children from more privileged families higher grades, better course placements, and other positive educational outcomes. Since schools expect but do not teach these cultural competencies, children from less advantaged families are left to fend for themselves, and in the process they typically reproduce their class location."[14]

Students from families and situations that did not provide them with an education in morals and principles continue through school never learning these values or how to apply them to their lives. Reason and principles are attainable by anyone, which is why they are universal and why they are the basis for Western society. Denying that knowledge to students in favor of subjective reasoning is doing them a vast disservice.

When it comes to the sciences and engineering, there are often more job opportunities because of the specialized nature of the work in technical sciences. Do you need to go to college to be a chemical engineer? Yes, you do. Therefore, the university system has been streamlined to jettison students with those interests through their education and into the workforce. Thus, we find Richard Hofstadter's criticism to be true, that higher education is primarily designed for creating more Sputniks, not necessarily for fostering intelligence. Hedges, Hofstadter, and Bloom all offer the same criticism of higher education; by jettisoning students into the workforce, it has ceased to study the great thinkers that came before them and made their work possible. They no longer have to ask the deeper questions about life in their effort to quickly join the workforce.

Thus, while they have ability, they are not necessarily left with the knowledge as to what that ability entails. Science built the nuclear weapon, but whether or not to use it came down to arguments outside the realm of hard science and mathematics. Einstein was perhaps one of the last scientists to examine the greater philosophical implications of science (although there has been a resurgence with the popularization of cosmology and theoretical physics), while his rival, Niels Bohr, thought such questions were superfluous and pointless. But it was this base belief in the bigger questions that led Einstein to continually challenge Bohr's interpretation of quantum physics.

Throughout much of history philosophers and scientists were considered one and the same. Isaac Newton was, perhaps, one of the greatest scientists in history but was also well-read in philosophy, religion, and history. His ideas and his accomplishments were born out of that knowledge. It was the nature of inquiry, both scientific and philosophical, that led to the Enlightenment. Copernicus and Galileo were not only astronomers and mathematicians but thinkers who reflected on the bigger questions of life, our place in the universe, and the truth.

Current academia and scientific studies, satisfied that we have estab-lished certain unquestionable laws and theories of science, including our exact location in the universe, have not found it necessary to continue with such inquiries.

Philosophy and science have divorced in academia, but historically they were bound together. This presents an inherent problem when an expert, be it an engineer, physicist, chemist, or mathematician, comes forward to proclaim that his or her findings determine how society should be ordered or how people should live. For the most part, these are the experts who will try to transform a moral argument into a scien-tific theory, feeling that they can justify their irrational convictions with rational science. These are also the experts who often offer doomsday predictions based on their findings and calculations, predictions which are merely a means to serve their greater moral ends.

Our second question regards the philosophy (if it can be called that) at work in the university system, namely, does the rejection of traditional philosophy based on reason and rationalism in favor of subjective beliefs actually lessen the ability of experts to make authoritative judgments in our society?

The current philosophical trends that are inherent in the university system most often manifest themselves in the realm of the humanities and social sciences—subjects such as literature, psychology, political science, journalism, law, and sociology. Indeed, these fields of study produce most of the media experts that we hear from today as they envision themselves to be scientists of humanity, and therefore have no ethical restraints on making sweeping proclamations about how society and people should order themselves. These experts draw largely from science to form moral arguments, recognizing that their own professions and educations do not offer the assurance of objectivity and falsification that the hard sciences do in order to gain acceptance. Indeed, these are often the people who will tell us that the Higgs boson particle means that we should raise taxes and be fairer to one another.

It is true that these "social sciences" do not offer the objectivity and confirmation that the hard sciences provide. Their theories are not falsifiable, and their failure can be excused through any number of semantic gymnastics without ever having to fess up that they were wrong, or worse, that they lied. Indeed, you will probably never hear an expert in any of these fields admit such a heinous thing. Therefore, they often cite breakthroughs in science or, as those become rarer, studies that confirm their irrational beliefs, offering ideology and morality in the guise of science. However, there is an underlying philosophy that overwhelms current humanity studies. It goes by many names: *deconstruction* or *post-structuralism* in English and literature, *multiculturalism* in sociology, *historicism* in history, and often just plain old *relativism*. For our purposes we will stick with *postmodernism*. Despite its many names and variations, postmodernism has one overarching theme—refutation of the Enlightenment.

The Enlightenment, with its reason, is seen as the cause of many, if not all, the world's ills due to its Eurocentric origins, the development of industry and colonialism, and the imposition of European values onto other civilizations through the spread of religion and commerce. Objectivity in both science and journalism is also regarded as part of the Enlightenment and thus is subject to attack and accusations of racism and bias and of contributing to the "white power structure" in Western civilization. America is largely the focal point of this battle of ideas because it remains the greatest success of Enlightenment thinking.

The United States is based on philosophy rather than ethnicity, religion, or race, which means that it can be changed or subverted through philosophy and education. A French person is French by heritage, ethnicity, and shared history; however, anybody can become an American by adopting the way of thinking outlined in the Declaration of Independence. Hence, America's ability to be changed lies not in its ethnic or historical makeup, but rather, in its shared philosophy. Change the philosophy and you change the nation. While the Constitution provides a bulwark against such ideas, it has not been able to successfully prevent continuous reinterpretation. Thus, the United States is apparently up for grabs to prevailing social philosophies.

The most popular manifestations of postmodernism are the ideas of tolerance and equality. While they may sound nice on the surface and, indeed, have their roots in the Enlightenment and in the founding of this country, these ideas have come to represent their exact opposites. In the name of tolerance and equality, any criticism against a perceived minority group is grounds for accusations of racism and intolerance and even dismissal. It should also be noted that in the postmodern paradigm, a minority need not be merely a numerical issue, but rather a matter of social and economic power. Since much of the world's power and wealth supposedly rests in the hands of rich white Christian men, anyone who is not a part of that group can automatically be granted "minority" status due to the historical sins of the group in power. Thus, while women make up more than 50 percent of the world's population, they constitute a minority group because historically they were denied certain rights. Similarly, while Islam is the largest religion in the world, it is considered a minority group because power supposedly rests in the hands of Christians.

Postmodernism is, in effect, a philosophy of revolution. It seeks to undermine power structures, traditions, religions, philosophies, and economies. Unfortunately, it offers nothing to replace those things with and often leaves believers in this petty faith at a dead end, at which point they latch on to some other cause and take to the streets again. Postmodernism was born from the combined philosophies of Marx and Nietzsche, which were transferred to the United States through French and Belgian intellectuals such as Michel Foucault, Jacques Derrida, and Paul de Man, who, interestingly enough, wrote for a Nazi publication during the Nazis' rise to power. The intellectual history of postmodernism has a bit of a problem in that its originators and thinkers have for the most part had love affairs with the brutal regimes of fascism and communism.

Dr. Edward Hagan, professor of English and literature at Western Connecticut State University (and one of my old professors), remarked on postmodernism:

> I've been out of sympathy with Foucault and all these French . . .
> and truth be told, the French have long since stopped with Derrida

and company. Americans are still hot and heavy with it but the French have long since decided that it was, in some cases, outright tomfoolery. Deconstruction is always suspicious and looking at the subtext. It implies that the author is a dummy but the critic is really telling the truth because the writer is encoding mysticisms into the text of the book that awaits the deconstructive abilities of the critic to show how race, class, and gender, or the powers that be, are messages hidden in there, which makes writers into complete idiots and critics into geniuses.

Dr. Hagan argues that postmodern philosophy is a form of reductionism, with everything being whittled down to a matter of race, class, and gender. This same reductionism is to be found in the sciences as well. "There are a lot of reductive scientists," he says, "and what reductive scientists are, I would argue, are people who think, *The universe is a problem, but we're working on it.*"[15] This, to date, is one of the finest summations of the problem of experts I have come across. While those in the hard sciences may seek to answer the problem of the universe through reductive theories, the humanities and social sciences reduce the human world to a matter of race, class, and gender to fit their personal predilections. It can be thought of as a stereotyping of knowledge and experience.

Stephen R. C. Hicks, professor of philosophy and author of *Nietzsche and the Nazis* and *Explaining Postmodernism*, wrote, "Postmodernism rejects the reason and the individualism that the entire Enlightenment world depends upon. And so it ends up attacking all of the consequences of the Enlightenment philosophy, from capitalism and liberal forms of government to science and technology."[16] Thus, there is the attack on the "Western canon" of literature, Christianity, traditional morality as conceived in the Judeo-Christian tradition, and the philosophy of reason and rationality.

Postmodernism is not considered a dirty little secret at the universities today; in fact, not following the postmodern spirit is the easiest way to find yourself kicked out of academia. Lawrence Summer was forced to resign as president of Harvard after "he proposed that innate genetic differences between the sexes may be one explanation for why fewer women succeed in math and science careers."[17] He was dismissed by his own faculty. Summers was later considered for the position of chair of the Federal Reserve by President Obama and news of his consideration brought out the old allegations of sexism. The communist publication *Daily Kos* ran the headline, "Notorious sexist with notoriously bad judgment is reportedly top candidate for Fed chair."[18] Despite his apologies and the rather inane nature of his original comments, any deviation from the idea of "tolerance" and multiculturalism results in vigorous and prolonged moral outrage and backlash.

Intellectual historian Richard Wolin wrote:

> Riding the wave of academic postmodernism, the politics of difference has managed to entrench itself as a new intellectual orthodoxy. Although cultural differences must be respected, it is but a short step from the uncritical glorification of difference to a new intellectual tribalism. . . . The politics of difference is relativist—all differences and standpoints should be treated equally—but only up to a point. The one standpoint undeserving of equal treatment is "Eurocentrism," the culture that gave us both Reason and the horrors of colonialism, the political corollary of Reason's endemic intolerance. Such intellectual tendencies—their glib denunciations of reason, their instinctual rejections of political liberalism as a sinister plot to level differences (on the basis of precepts such as "tolerance" and "equality before the law") are troubling indeed.[19]

The postmodern idea of tolerance is, indeed, intolerant of philosophies, religions, and ideas that are not in complete agreement with its own message.

This is one of the many logical fallacies that postmodernism runs into as it devolves into a circular form of irrational emotion and moral indignation. It is actually the exact opposite of knowledge and intelligence because it does not allow for disagreement and debate in an effort to reach the truth. It denies the truth and declares that the debate is over. It does not require thought, only action without purpose or goal—impotent activism. Ask your average college activist what his or her goal is, and you will probably get an answer like "equality" or "fairness." Ask the student what that means, and you will get a stumbling, rambling, incoherent mishmash of old Marxist dogmas and possibly a tirade about corporations and the military-industrial complex—echoes of the '60s counterculture, which was the triumphant announcement of American postmodernism.

Today's universities are designed to promote either soulless professionalism or impotent activism through the postmodern structure. Allan Bloom believes the turning point came in 1969 when he was a professor at Cornell, which was being held hostage by armed black separatists who demanded the dismissal of professors who were deemed unsympathetic to their cause. The university acquiesced; they fired professors, accepted resignations, and established new, more "open" and "inclusive" courses centering on "black studies" and other racially motivated topics. Of course, whether or not the professors and administrators in question actually were racist was never questioned or even broached. Instead, the force of subjectivity—the irrationalism of a new form of faith that considered its own belief as truth—asserted its force of commitment through the threat of violence. Thus began the failure of the university system and the adoption of the postmodern paradigm where everyone's subjective truth is treated with equal value and any notion of actual objective truth is dismissed out of hand as racist, misogynistic, or oppressive.

With these issues confronting the university system, it is fair to be skeptical of its credentialed graduates and whether they are really in a position to make recommendations as to the function of society—its values, social standards, and traditions. They have been taught to tear down these "social constructs" with little regard for why they were "constructed" in the first place. They are being inculcated into an authoritative form of groupthink that denies reason, rationality, and ethics and promotes forms of separatism, Marxism, and hedonism. Have a look at some higher education all-stars as they make the headlines with fevered, irrational proclamations that testify to anything but rational, reasoned inquiry:

An Oregon adjunct law professor threatened students demonstrating for immigration and began pushing them. He said, "Start a f***ing war! Stop being pussies. Start a war, get a gun, shoot me first. I'm right here." The professor was removed from his position after the video went viral.[20]

The University of Minnesota hosted a program to teach female students how to achieve orgasm, in an effort to promote "an underlying message of sexual health and women's empowerment."[21]

Yale hosted a workshop titled "Sex: Am I Normal," which discussed such desires as bestiality and incest, among sadomasochistic desires. It was part of Sex Weekend, which is a shortened version of their annual Sex Week. "At Saturday's workshop, multiple student-submitted discussions topics were about sexual fantasies involving family members. When students shared their thoughts on incest, three responses were related to fantasies about fathers."[22]

A Michigan State University professor of creative writing told his class that "Republicans are old people with 'dead skin cells washing off them' who raped the United States to get 'everything out of it they possibly could.'" He went on to say, "I am a college professor. If I find out you are a closet racist, I am coming after you." The rant was caught on video and led to his suspension with pay.[23]

A Kansas State University associate professor of journalism chastised members of the NRA following the Navy Yard shooting by a mentally ill man. "The blood is on the hands of the #NRA," he tweeted. "Next time, let it be YOUR sons and daughters. Shame on you. May God damn you." He was placed on administrative leave.[24]

A Florida Atlantic University professor had her students write the name "Jesus" on a piece of paper and then instructed them to throw it on the ground and stomp on it in an effort to show the power of words. The University president issued an apology (the irony does not go unnoticed).[25]

Another Florida Atlantic University professor claimed that the Sandy Hook school shooting, in which twenty-six children were gunned down, was actually a hoax; he wrote on his blog, "While it sounds like an outrageous claim, one is left to inquire whether the Sandy Hook shooting ever took place—at least in the way law enforcement authorities and the nation's news media have described." He believed it was a conspiracy hatched by the Obama administration to push a gun-control agenda.[26]

A professor of English at Montclair State University, in response to a question from the audience concerning the people murdered under the Stalin regime, asserted, "What you said is bullshit!" He went on to claim that all of history is falsified, but none more than that of the Soviet Union. "I have yet to find one crime, yet to find one crime that Stalin committed." One must wonder what he used for research since everything is so falsified.[27]

For the most part I limited all these examples to the year 2013, except for that last one. My reason for including it was that the video shows the level of discourse and rationality that many professors of the humanities have devolved to and also shows the face of postmodern historicism. What is more disturbing, perhaps, is the round of applause the professor received for making claims that should have been considered complete lunacy.

These are only a fraction of the stories that have made headlines, in large part because students came forward with video or audio recordings and then provided them to media outlets. How many times do things like this happen where the students simply agree or just shrug their shoulders and repeat back to the professor what he or she wants to hear? How often do the students take this to be the prevailing "right" thought and incorporate these ideas into their own worldview, thus perpetuating the illusion of enlightened knowledge?

As we discussed in the previous chapter, there exists a duality between man and nature, in that humans, at their core, are faith-based, irrational beings. However, nature, the earth, and the universe are not. They all function on basic laws, precepts, logic, and rationality. Humans' ability to reason and think in order to understand the natural world is what sets us apart. It is that very ability to reason, to seek truth, that has allowed for the establishment and building up of society to the point at which it exists today. However, doing away with rationality in favor of subjective irrationality is ultimately destructive to that very society. The belief in truth and reason outside of individual subjective views is what enables every individual, regardless of race, class, or gender, to gain knowledge and wisdom. Conversely, if reason is subjective, then we can never agree or come to the same knowledge as one another. It is a fracturing of society, an alienation of people from one another, and an excuse to not even try to gain insight into life.

Using the irrational, subjective experience of man as the guiding principal for society, whether expressed in politics, activism, law, language, or science, is to create a society based on spirit rather than reason, and spirit does not allow for the individual thinker. "Deprived of its rational foundation, the democratic principle becomes exclusively dependent on the so-called interests of the people," wrote philosopher Max Horkheimer, "and these are functions of blind or all too conscious economic forces. They do not offer any guarantee against tyranny."[28]

Philosophers Gabriel Marcel and Max Horkheimer were both writing in the aftermath of World War II and were trying to come to terms with what they had witnessed in Germany. The term *Nazi* is thrown around (too much) in politics and protests, and often by college students as they shout down a speaker whose views they disagree with. The reason for this is that the Nazi regime is one of the few manifestations that nearly everyone in the world can point to and say, "That was evil." In essence, it is agreed upon nearly the world over; Nazism was bad, and it's one of the few points of agreement left. This statement obviously excludes small cadres of neo-Nazis in both the United States and Europe as well as some terrorist organizations that are trying to emulate the movement, but by and large it is an accepted truth that Nazism was bad. People who argue otherwise or deny it are usually ignored out of hand, which is a good thing, but it is also why the term carries so much weight and is used as a cudgel in political battles. The reason I am using Nazism in this work is twofold. First, it was and remains a political system built on irrationalism and whose chief philosophers—Nietzsche and Heiddegger—rejected reason and rationalism in the name of spirit. Unfortunately, those are the two philosophers whose thinking largely remains in vogue in the higher education system. Second, I wish to point out that giving over to the idea of spirit and rejecting reason, truth, and rationalism is dangerous. It breeds a mob-like mentality that shakes loose any principles, values, or traditions that previously held society in balance.

Marcel wrote, "Do not let us seek to persuade ourselves that an education of the masses is possible: that is a contradiction in terms. What is educable is only an individual, or more exactly a person. Everywhere else, there is no scope for anything but a training."[29] Without individuality and the philosophy that embraced it, there is no room for education, but only inculcation into a form of groupthink. Clearly, no Western nation is marching people off to concentration camps. That era is (hopefully) permanently behind us, but what remains is still the belief in a unifying spirit that binds the nation together into one "people," for whom the individual is just one egg to be cracked to make the omelet. When we regard the ends as greater than the means, when we fashion our own personal truth in the form of some social cause, such as justice and equality, and see men and women only as means to achieve those truths, then we are walking on dangerous ground. But this is precisely what is being taught in college classrooms.

So then, what is the danger in current society? Precisely this: the studies most profoundly changed by postmodern theory—law, journalism, English, sociology, and political science—are the majors most politicians and media talking heads use to begin their careers in Washington, DC, and New York. Why? Because that is where the money, power, and influence reside. Thus, since the Kennedy administration—the "Best and Brightest" administration—Richard Nixon, Gerald Ford, George H. W. Bush, Bill Clinton, George W. Bush, and Barack Obama have all had Ivy League educations, not to mention that they all attended nearly the same universities: George H. W. Bush attended Yale; Bill Clinton attended Georgetown, Oxford, and Yale; George W. Bush attended Yale and Harvard; and Barack Obama attended Columbia University and Harvard. All of them received their degrees in law. This would seem to indicate, if not a conformity of thought, at least a conformity of education.

Robert C. Post is the head of the Yale School of Law and has been since his predecessor, Harold Koh, left the university to take a position as legal counsel in the State Department. He authored the book *Democracy, Expertise and Academic Freedom*, in which he wrote, "During the major part of the nineteenth century, the objective of most American colleges was to instruct young men in received truths, both spiritual and material. It is only when American scholars became infected with the German ideal of *Wissenschaft*, with the idea of systematizing and expanding knowledge, that universities began to transform their mission."[30] Post explained this *new* idea as creating a "sociology of knowledge," which basically amounts to knowledge by consensus through which universities can judge whom or what is brought into the higher education fold. "We expect scholars to create new knowledge," he wrote. "Universities cannot expand knowledge if faculty merely reproduce already existing knowledge." However, universities are not expanding knowledge but are rather replacing knowledge. They are abandoning the old, discarding it as if it hadn't directly formed the world as we know it in favor of a new, ad hoc knowledge that is based solely on race, class, and gender. How can knowledge be expanded if there is no truth?

Inherent in the phrase "sociology of knowledge" is the idea that knowledge or truth is formed by society rather than preexisting the social body. While this may be true in some cases regarding issues that are a part of social acceptance, it is not the case in the large questions of right and wrong, good and evil, as explored by the classical Western philosophers and the rationalist tradition. For better or worse, the social science practices are subject to social currents and must be understood in that context. It must also be recognized that, barring some major shift in cultural thinking, the current postmodern philosophy is deeply entrenched in the higher education system and it will be difficult to remove. A professor is not likely to get a job making arguments against the current "sociology of knowledge" protected in the realm of higher education.

During a conversation/debate with a friend on the nature of right and wrong, I asked him if he thought that a woman being stoned in Iran for infidelity was right or wrong. He answered that he understood why that culture might think it was right. But understanding is not intelligence; intelligence is being able to discriminate, discern, and make a judgment. Understanding is a way of not having to exercise any discernment or discrimination and instead saying, "While I may disagree with it, I understand it." It is a way of shutting off the brain, saying that right and wrong are relative to culture, and decrying anyone who does otherwise as being racist, which essentially ends the discussion. But aren't debate and discussion the essence of critical thinking? Isn't part of critical thinking the ability to criticize? More and more it seems that so-called critical thinkers on college campuses can only spout the party line, the spirit of the time, the zeitgeist, which dismisses critical thought in favor of action in the name of some higher ideal.

Undergraduate students are generally between eighteen and twenty-two years old. They are fresh out of the high school culture, on their own for the first time, and trying to find themselves. Thus, they remain generally pliable and subject to peer pressure, adolescent rebellion, and ideology. They are looking for something to believe in and new ways to view the world. However, postmodern theory delivers none of this and, instead, replaces that need for understanding and knowledge with a confused morality based on perceived offenses and self-righteous indignation. Pulitzer Prize–winning screenwriter

David Mamet recalled a course that he guest taught at Columbia University on playwriting. During the course of the class, Mamet made the mistake of suggesting that the heroine of a particular story be kidnapped by Arab terrorists, whereupon the class descended into a vigorous debate over whether or not such an idea is racist. "But the class had ticked over into what I recognized was a usual stage of progression," he wrote. "Someone had taken the high ground and shouted 'racist,' or 'homophobe,' first and loudest, and all who did not wish to be so branded must submit to his dominance, for did he not speak in the name of all the Good? . . . They were and are the children of privilege—in some the privilege is inherited, and the cost of college meaningless, in some the cost is huge, and families suffer; but in all cases, the privilege taught, learned, and imbibed, in a 'liberal arts education' is the privilege to indict. . . . They have learned to be shrill, and that their indictment, on the economy, on sex, on race, on the environment, though based on no experience other than hearsay, must trump any discourse, let alone opposition."[31]

The fact that this irrationalism has infected both mainstream media and politics is overwhelmingly evident, particularly in the area of language, race relations, justice and criminal law, gender identity issues, and international politics. Political correctness is probably the most evident example of postmodernism coming to roost in popular culture, as it rearranges language to create a moral cudgel based on real or perceived past grievances and then uses it as a means to take the moral high ground. Of course, these moral rules apply only to the social power structure, leaving certain "victim" groups with the ability to assert a moral dominance where none, in fact, may exist. The latest incarnation of political correctness run amok is the use of the term *microaggressions* to describe instances in which members of minority or victim groups are made to feel ostracized because of the unintentional use of a word or phrase which, through an obsessive game of word association, somehow is racist or prejudiced. For instance, the vice president of the Students' Society of McGill University (SSMU) was forced to make a public apology when he sent out an e-mail that said, "Honestly, mid-terms get out of here," and had a video clip of President Obama kicking a press conference door open. Obviously the video clip was not real; in fact, it was part of a skit aired on the *Tonight Show* with Jay Leno. Nevertheless, the student wrote in his public apology, "The image in question was an extension of the cultural, historical and living legacy surrounding people of colour—particularly young men—being portrayed as violent in contemporary culture and media." Similarly, and perhaps even more disturbing, is the professor at the University of California–Los Angeles who was accused of microaggression for correcting grammar and spelling mistakes on students' papers, or the professor who was accused of enacting sharia law by forbidding cell phones in his classroom.[32] The complete lack of any rational, moral, or ethical responsibility inherent in these accusations is disturbing. It is the evidence of a generation of narcissistic youth that have been served a wicked diet of moral relativism and racial hypersensitivity, though the irony of professors now having to reap what they have sown is not without its humor.

Frankly, the list of inane (if not insane) demands for "justice" and "equality" and their lists of imaginary grievances that have made the news are just too numerous to mention, but here are a couple. A *Harvard Crimson* columnist recently asserted that a more rigorous standard of "academic justice" should discontinue any research that promotes or justifies oppression.[33] And an anonymous petition at Dartmouth listed one hundred student demands, one of which involved an announcement at every school function that the land they were on was originally Abenaki land and threatened "physical action" if their demands were not met.[34]

Postmodernism has ushered into the university system a totalitarian mind-set that is completely at odds with American freedom and liberalism. While trying to break the perceived oppressions of modern American society—which the postmodern movement has been doing for the past forty years with apparently no success because they never stop finding more versions of oppression—these young, pseudo-intelligent minds have fostered even more oppression.

Mamet's critique is withering, but he poses a question that I would like to answer for him. He asks, "On leaving the university, what would these Young Stalinists do? . . . In what society could they live?"

The answer is simple, Mr. Mamet: they will live and work in Washington, DC, the news media, and of course, the higher education system.

5

quantum confusion:
a postmodern science?

The LORD came down to see the city and the tower which the sons of men had built. The LORD said, "Behold, they are one people, and they all have the same language. And this is what they began to do, and now nothing which they purpose to do will be impossible for them. Come, let Us go down and there confuse their language, so that they will not understand one another's speech."
—genesis 11:5–7

The years passed, mankind became stupider at a frightening rate. Some had high hopes that genetic engineering would correct this trend in evolution, but sadly the greatest minds and resources were focused on conquering hair loss and prolonging erections.
—*idiocracy* (2006)

The impact of postmodernism in the liberal arts and social sciences—literature, law, sociology, psychology, and so forth—is easy to discern and has a proven track record of being wrong, misguided, and just plain dumb at times, especially when espoused by professors who lack any ethical restraint and are unleashed by modern irrationalism. But has this trend extended to the hard sciences, such as physics, biology, astronomy, chemistry, and mathematics? Has the postmodern influence on scientists affected their ability to function and work and be effective in this world? Is it possible that someone outside academia may be better equipped to deal with the challenges posed to humanity than a university-educated expert—someone not schooled in relativist beliefs and a denial of truth? The answer is much more nuanced, and for that reason I have divided this chapter into sections to properly highlight the distinctions.

First, a simple clarification: the processes of the physical world do not change and science seeks to discover those processes; that is why it is science and that is why we base our lives around it. Gravity does not cease to work just because we no longer believe that it works or because we assign it a different label or malign it as being misogynistic. As Shakespeare wrote, "A rose by any other name would smell as sweet." Science is reality, and postmodernism, as much as it would like to, cannot change reality. It can certainly try to conceive reality differently, but the postmodern adherents' belief that conceiving something differently changes its nature is wrong. Hence, postmodernism continually bumps up against reality, only to look foolish.

The effects of postmodernism can better be seen in science as an industry—one that is subject to political, economic, and cultural factors. It is in the interaction of science with the mass culture where postmodernism has had its strongest effect, particularly in the realm of ethics and the value of objectivity that is the hallmark of good science. A philosophy inherent in the higher education system which denies truth and reality and believes that logic and ethics are man-made creations that embody a white-male power structure will inevitably affect those trained in the universities. As we discussed in the previous chapter, higher education has given up on teaching morality, values, ethics, and the Western tradition of rationalism. So what is to prevent scientists from engaging in the very same deconstruction as their liberal arts peers? In effect, can we trust that their proclamations are based on objective science, or are they attempting to influence society based on their personal goals? Earlier we discussed Dr. Carl Hart of Columbia University, who uses his research into the effects of illegal drugs on the human brain as a gateway toward drug legalization and social justice.

Are such practices widespread, and how can we know? Can we believe the experts, or has science been corrupted by the political?

Following Allan Bloom's *The Closing of the American Mind* in 1987 and Roger Kimball's follow-up in 1990, *Tenured Radicals*, a new kind of resistance to postmodernism reared its head in the 1990s in the form of *Higher Superstition: The Academic Left and Its Quarrels with Science*, by Paul R. Gross and Norman Levitt. This was followed in 1998 by Alan Sokal and Jean Bricmont's *Fashionable Nonsense: Postmodern Intellectuals' Abuse of Science*, and that same year, *A House Built of Sand: Exposing Postmodernist Myths about Science*, which was a collection of essays from across the scientific spectrum that refuted postmodernism. Apparently, individuals who work in the sciences and deal with logic, objectivity, and rationalism don't like being called racist, misogynistic, homophobic perpetrators of Western imperialism. Moreover, scientists tend to be a little picky about ideas that refute long-standing science, whether it be creationism pushed by fundamental evangelists or a push for "feminist science" by the postmodern, multicultural academy. Sokal and Bricmont commented, "Vast sectors of the humanities and social sciences seem to have adopted a philosophy that we shall call, for want of a better term, 'postmodernism': an intellectual current characterized by the more-or-less explicit rejection of the rationalist tradition of the Enlightenment, by theoretical discourses disconnected from any empirical test, and by a cognitive and cultural relativism that regards science as nothing more than a 'narration', a 'myth' or a social construction among many others."[1] And Gross and Levitt wrote, "The academic left's critiques of science have come to exert a remarkable influence. The primary reason for the success is not that they put forward sound arguments, but rather that they resort constantly and shamelessly to moral one-upmanship. If you decry the feminist critique of science, you are guilty of trying to preserve science as an old-boy's network."[2]

The writers of all these works are careful to separate their science and arguments from politics. Gross and Levitt go to strenuous lengths to separate their term "Left" from any political notion of the term.

Sokal and Bricmont insist that they are sympathetic with the political left of the spectrum but are forced to mount their defense for the sake of science, completely separate from political orientation. This is the essence of professionalism. These are not experts as we have defined them in this work. Their defense of science does not seek to impose their own political and social ideologies on their readers; rather, they seek to defend objectivity and logic devoid of such influences, and they do a superb job.

However, part of the reason that these men and women felt the need to speak up in defense of science is that postmodernism's influence on their profession was gaining ground at an alarming rate. Truth and objectivity were being supplanted with sociopolitical goals. When scientists, willingly or unwillingly, sacrifice the truth and objectivity for another purpose, they render their profession equal to that of a social evangelist, leaning on the public's trust in science as a means for pushing their agendas. Often their tone and actions take on an element of religious fervor and impotent activism.

Case in point: James Hansen has an impressive résumé; he is a professor of earth and environmental sciences at Columbia and is the former head of NASA's Goddard Institute. He was one of the first people to raise the global warming alarm flag when he testified before Congress in 1988. However, recently he has turned to full-time activism to prevent further CO_2 emissions and subsequently has raised some concerns among professionals regarding his actions on political and economic issues, even being arrested (with much fanfare) at global warming protests. *New York Times* columnist Joe Nocera lamented, "What people hear from Hansen today is not so much his science but his broad, unscientific views on, say, the evils of oil companies. In 2008, he wrote a paper the thesis of which was that runaway climate change would occur when carbon in the atmosphere reached 350 parts per million—a point it had already exceeded—unless it were quickly reduced. There are many climate change experts who disagree with this judgment—who believe that the 350 number is arbitrary and even meaningless. Yet an entire movement, 350.org has been built around Hansen's line in the sand."[3]

One of the great thinkers of the twentieth century, Freeman Dyson, a highly influential theoretical physicist and mathematician who has never bothered to earn those three big letters *PhD*, also offered a critique both of Hansen's tactics and of the global warming movement in general. His criticism earned him derision in the media and blogosphere. "Al Gore's just an opportunist," he told one writer. "The person who is really responsible for this overestimate of global warming is Jim Hansen. He consistently exaggerates all the dangers. . . . . If what he says were obviously wrong, he wouldn't have achieved what he has. But Hansen has turned his science into ideology. He's a very persuasive fellow and has the air of knowing everything. He has all the credentials. I have none. I don't have a Ph.D. He's published hundreds of papers on climate. I haven't. By the public standard he's qualified to talk and I'm not. But I do because I think I'm right. I think I have a broad view of the subject, which Hansen does not. I think it's true my career doesn't depend on it, whereas his does. I never claim to be an expert on climate. I think it's more a matter of judgment than knowledge."[4]

Yet Hansen and other global warming alarmists remain in the spotlight and retain the status of prophets by public activist movements that seize on their words and works as a means of objectifying the rationality of their goals. It is a strange postmodern movement, one that rejects traditional Western logic and rationalism and then seeks to bolster its arguments with the fruits of those very tools by enlisting classically trained scientists and seizing upon studies that validate their viewpoints. But Hansen has crossed over; he has taken the step from rationalism rooted in reality to irrationalism rooted in faith, namely, faith that the world is drastically warming and the impending apocalypse is upon us. Anyone who critiques this argument is in for scalding retribution (please, God, don't let it be me).

Hansen has, in effect, committed himself to a cause and has refashioned his life according to that cause. Hence, the matter takes on a cultlike quality. The greatest danger this poses is that a cultish mind-set cannot easily, if ever, be changed. New information contrary to the cult's goals is rejected out of hand or dismissed as being corrupted by larger, conspiratorial interests. Dyson said, "According to the global-warming people, I say what I say because I'm paid by the oil industry. Of course I'm not, but that's part of their rhetoric. If you doubt it, you're a bad person, a tool of the oil or coal industry."[5]

Even those who are sympathetic to the cult's cause are chastised if they are not committed enough, or, more important, not committed to the right solution to the problem. Bjorn Lomborg is a Danish professor and environmentalist with a PhD in political science who argued against Al Gore before Congress regarding Gore's prescriptions for averting disaster. "In his prepared testimony, Lomborg argued that 'statements about the strong, ominous and immediate consequences of global warming are often wildly exaggerated.' 'Climate change is not the only issue on the global agenda,' he added, 'and actually one of the issues where we can do the least good first.'"[6] Lomborg had already come under fire for dissenting from the ideological line when he published "The Skeptical Environmentalist" in a Danish newspaper. He was brought before the Danish Committee on Scientific Dishonesty, which concluded that Lomborg's work was scientifically fraudulent. Lomborg retaliated by appealing to the DCSD's oversight organization, the Danish Ministry of Science, Technology and Innovation; they overturned the DCSD's ruling. Though Lomborg claims to believe that the earth is indeed warming, his main transgression is his belief that the proposed solutions to global warming would ultimately cost too much and cause too much economic damage. Instead, he offers ideas for adaptation and funding for eliminating problems of poverty and hunger.

All this leads one to suspect that perhaps the underlying issue is not the environment or global warming, per se, but rather, the economic implications of the proposed solutions, which, more than anything else, seek to put restrictions on the industrial capacity of the developed Western nations through carbon tax credits, cap-and-trade legislation, the carbon exchange program, and the imposition of emission goals that would place great strain on automobile manufacturers. This becomes, in essence, an attempt to level economic playing fields between nations, something with deeply Marxist undertones—the same undertones that have been evident in the postmodernist movement since the 1970s. The main focus of Marxist environmentalism is a "return to nature," so to speak—a breaking down of civilization and a return to living at one with the earth. This, of course, cannot happen without tearing down the capitalist economic system and forcing people to start foraging for their own food rather than going to their local grocery to buy genetically modified produce bred and raised by corporate devils.

"If, shall we say, incontrovertible evidence were to appear tomorrow that current and projected levels of atmospheric CO_2 pose no danger of disastrous climate change, thousands of eco radicals would ignore it or, if unable to do so, be devastated," Gross and Levitt contend. "They would undeniably find a hundred specious reasons for rejecting the good news. They have stripped the last layers of caution and qualification from the warnings of scientists and converted them to articles of faith, upon which mere empiricism has never had any purchase."[7] This is because the goals of the movement are not necessarily environmental, but rather, social "justice" through the deconstruction of Western society and its economic superiority to the rest of the developing world.

This leads us back to James Hansen. What are his true motivations? Can they even be known? Why would he leave scientific rationalism behind and take up rhetoric and invective that ignore dissenting opinions and studies, but still rely on his reputation as a scientist? Hansen's story is reminiscent of Eric Hoffer's analysis of people who join mass movements: "The slipping author, artist, scientist—slipping because of a drying-up of the creative flow within—drifts sooner or later into camps of ardent patriots, race mongers, up-lift promoters and champions of holy causes. Perhaps the sexually impotent are subject to the same impulses."[8] There certainly seems to be some kind of soul-searching in people like Hansen who give up everything, including their rational discernment, for the sake of a cause that is both apocalyptic in rhetoric and rather mild in effect. Global warming, like many other postmodern "holy causes" (Hoffer's words), takes on a sacred passion, something that was evident in the late '90s when Gross and Levitt were writing *Higher Superstition*: "As we see it, radical environmentalism wrongheadedness is rooted in three interlinked attitudes. First of all, it is intensely moralistic. . . . Unchanging casts of devils completely exclude the careful, unemotional weighing of costs and benefits, of relative risks and relative certainties that is a necessary part of making pragmatic judgments." They go on to critique the attitude of rejecting any idea that doesn't call for sweeping and immediate change and dismissal of any news contrary to holy causes. "The worse things get, the closer the moment of rapture and overthrow, when the world's population will realize the folly of industrialism, of the comforts of The Way Things Are, and the sooner a return to the wisdom of its Paleolithic (or Neolithic, or hunter-gatherer, or smallholder) ancestors."[9]

Second, it is often quite easy to spot a movement fueled by experts based on whether or not their theory is falsifiable. Falsifiability comes from philosopher Karl Popper, who asserted that any legitimate scientific theory must contain the key to its own undoing. According to retired chemistry professor Dr. James Barrante, "The point about the research on both sides of the argument is that neither side has proven scientifically that anything is true. That requires careful experimentation subject to the rules of the scientific method. Moreover, it is impossible to prove that a theory is true. One can only prove scientifically that it is false. In science, there are only two absolute conditions: a theory is either definitely false or it is possibly true (who knows)."[10] Albert Einstein was ready to discard his entire theory of special relativity if it did not pass a series of empirical tests.[11] However, no such tests exist for global warming, which is probably one of the reasons its advocates changed the original term from "global warming" to "climate change." the climate can get warmer or colder and either will confirm their theory. It is annoyingly evident in the media, as nearly every weather event is somehow linked to climate change; if it's hot, it's climate change;

cold, climate change; wet, dry, mild, sunny, or cloudy, lots of hurricanes or no hurricanes at all, every instance somehow confirms their theory. During periods of intense and extended cold (like the winter of 2014) the public is told two things: first, the extreme cold is an effect of global warming/climate change because the Arctic has warmed and thus allowed the "polar vortex" to expand into the United States, and second, that weather cannot be used to judge whether or not the entire climate is changing. And here we run into a logical fallacy so typical of postmodern thought; we are told that it is cold because of global warming, but simultaneously, we are told that the cold weather is not an indication of global warming.

The same idea of non-falsifiability can be used for religious theories about God and intelligent design. It is impossible to prove that God does not exist, and everything can be attributed to God as a root cause. Hence, God used evolution to create the world as it is, or, even more frustrating for scientists, you cannot actually prove that the world wasn't created six thousand years ago as depicted in the biblical story of creation.

Where did the fossils come from? The devil put them there to confuse us. We cannot prove he didn't. These are matters of faith. Thus, any questioning of one's faith is met with righteous indignation and fire-and-brimstone vitriol.

Nicholas Dawidoff wrote in *New York Times Magazine:*

> What may trouble Dyson most about climate change are the experts. Experts, he thinks, are too often crippled by the conventional wisdom they create, leading to the belief that "they know it all." The men he most admires tend to be what he calls "amateurs," inventive spirits of un-credentialed brilliance like Bernhard Schmidt, an eccentric one-armed alcoholic telescope-lens designer, or Milton Humason, a janitor at Mount Wilson Observatory in California whose native scientific aptitude was such that he was promoted to staff astronomer, and especially Darwin, who, Dyson says, "was really an amateur and beat the professionals at their own game."[12]

the influence of science

Since the Enlightenment, science has, rightly or wrongly, replaced organized religion as the means to determine how we are to live our lives and
structure society. This is why, not only do postmodernists attack science,
they also seize any scientist or scientific theory, study, or paper in order
to bolster their ideas for social or moral change. Thus, it is not an environmental activist being interviewed on television, but rather, someone
with scientific or expert credentials. It is not an overt moral argument
they are making, but one disguised as science. The reason is simple: men
and women determine their morality and their values based on their
individual beliefs. However, most are not in a position to argue against
the proclamations of a scientist to whom society ascribes a level of intelligence, objectivity, and verification. Thus, when an astrophysicist tells
us that an asteroid is on a collision course with Earth, we don't whip
out our calculators and start trying to verify his or her figures; instead,
we start digging a fallout shelter. It is precisely society's attribution of
intelligence and objectivity to science that grants it such enormous
influence, and by rights, science can be accomplished and understood
only through intelligence and objectivity. It is postmodernism's ability
to cast a shadow of doubt on science and objectivity through imbuing
science with politics and ideology that is so damaging.

Science and technology affect our lives a great deal, and their influence is not limited merely to scientific and technological realms. They
extend to the arts, social structure, government, and religion. Before the
Enlightenment, the great artists largely devoted their works to depictions
of religious or historical events and to faith. After the Enlightenment,
however, artists began to steer their work more toward science and
mechanics, occasionally veering into religion in order to mock it. Hence,
we have "modern" art. It is also no coincidence that the scientific revolution of the Enlightenment coincided with the birth of democracy and
the revolutions in France and America to gain equality for all people,
politically, economically, and socially. Science had destroyed the belief
in a monarchy of men and women who were granted power by God

and been given heritage to rule over others; thus, the revolutions to guarantee individuals the right to determine their own governments and to choose their own leaders began. "Historically, the 18th century Enlightenment had associated the rise of modern science with the rise of modern democratic ideology and politics," wrote political theorist Yaron Ezrahi. "As Louis Dumont argued, perhaps the most important political implication of the rise of modern individualism was anti-hierarchical sensibility, which led to the idea that the only legitimate political order is that which is built from the bottom up rather than from the top down."[13]

Albert Einstein remains, to this day, the quintessential image of the genius. He is celebrated in pop culture, and his work continues to inspire and inform scientists the world over. He is also quoted ad nauseam on almost every possible subject from politics to religion and science. Generally, in pop culture, if you can find an Albert Einstein quote to support your position, you've earned yourself a trump card. While Isaac Newton and Galileo ushered in the democratic political movement and the modern world, what effect has Einstein had? According to Ezrahi, it lies in the separation of science from commonsense, experience-based knowledge. Everyone is familiar with the myth of Isaac Newton being struck by a falling apple and conceiving of gravity based on this common, everyday experience. "Traditionally, science appeared to guarantee the possibility and the value of the distinction between facts and fictions just as the gold standard guaranteed the value of paper currency."[14] Einstein's work, however, did not have its basis in common sense and everyday experience; in fact, it called into question some of the previously held science. For all intents and purposes, Newton's physics is at work in the world each and every day; but relativity and quantum mechanics are at work behind the scenes and at speeds and lengths nearly inconceivable to the imagination, and this new science called into question our fundamental assumptions about the universe. If the Enlightenment and Newton were the fires that started revolutions in politics, then what are we to make of relativity and quantum mechanics—the basic building blocks of this universe—to which Newton's physics do not apply?

Often, however, the root cause of the problem is that the science is not correctly understood or not understood in its proper context or is inappropriately applied to human affairs. Does the theory of relativity mean that there is no truth? No. Einstein certainly didn't think so. Does Heisenberg's "uncertainty principle" mean that if we jump off the roof often enough, we may actually fly? No, again. "The argument, roughly but accurately paraphrased (and all too familiar from New Age tracts, among other things), is that since physics has discovered the uncertainty principle, it can no longer provide reliable information about the physical world, has lost its claim to objectivity," wrote Gross and Levitt. "Once obscurantism is stripped away, we recognize that the uncertainty principle is a tenet of physics, a predictive law about the behavior of concrete phenomena that can be tested and confirmed like other physical principles. . . . In other words, when viewed as a law of physics, the uncertainty principle is a very certain item indeed. It is an objective truth about the world."[15]

Gross and Levitt attribute the popularity of the uncertainty principle in postmodernism to its provocative name. Postmodernism, in attempting to use such theories as relativity and the uncertainty principle to restructure society or politics, is actually misunderstanding those theories and imbuing them with their own convoluted morals and values. They are used as a Trojan horse to sneak in ideology and tear down the existing city.

For his part, Ezrahi has now come to believe that twentieth-century physics had less to do with the postmodern onslaught and more to do with the camera, television, and mass media. For the most part, in terms of the past fifty years, I would agree with him; I do not believe that the two are entirely separate. Twentieth-century physics gave the mass media movement a scientific leg to stand on and, eventually, to run with. Mass media may be the end result, but it was not the beginning of the postmodern cesspool.

The great influence that science has had over society would seem to be a good thing; what could possibly be wrong with holding science as the basis for constructing society? The problem is that science is rational while humans are irrational. Humanity is driven by faith. It is not a character flaw, but actually a product of our rationality and consciousness. Thus, science can inform a society, but it cannot construct it and ultimately guide its changes and developments. Science built the atomic bomb but could not inform us as to whether or not to use it. That was a decision that had to be made based on faith, ethics, and values. Experts and the media want us to believe that science can tell us how to construct the good society, a philosophical problem that has existed since Socrates, and they believe that our current mastery of the sciences allows us the greatest opportunity at creating Utopia. But science cannot tell us or show us what is good and what is right and what is fair; it can only give us facts about the world—not human truths for creating and maintaining what is good. Our consciousness separates us from nature.

The concern that postmodernism has infected science is both true and untrue. (How's that for some relativism!) Part of the problem rests in how scientists convince the public to pay attention to the possibilities that their findings present. The earth's getting warmer could have effects that range across the spectrum from nothing happening at all to the apocalypse; unfortunately, the only thing that is going to get people to sit up and pay attention is the apocalypse. "In fairness, this does not amount to their throwing scientific caution to the winds. Rather it is a matter of emphasis and tone, of rhetoric and persuasive technique, of creating a public voice for oneself that differs quite consciously from one's 'scientific' voice,'" wrote Gross and Levitt.[16] They go on to excuse Paul Ehrlich for his *Population Bomb* theory, saying that it may actually have done some good in the long run by raising awareness. However, it did not merely raise awareness; it added fuel to a mass movement that resulted in people and countries being harmed. It was also completely wrong and reductionist, and, amazingly, Ehrlich continues to think he was or is right. Though I understand their sympathy for him, Ehrlich is exactly the type of scientist that Gross and Levitt are opposed to in their book. However, as we discussed in chapter 3, scientists have become the new high priests in a world where God is dead. Certainly some of them realize the power they wield, but it appears many do not. In essence, it is as if we never left the Dark Ages of faith; we only changed our gods. When the priest says we must change our ways to avoid damnation, the faithful sit up in the pew, pay attention, and take action. Scientists should believe in the intelligence of men and women and should not let their rhetoric lapse into fuel for those who would like to see the world burn.

be published or perish

Another element of the issue is the way science, as an industry, is conducted, particularly in the realm of higher education. In effect, one must produce results in order to stay employed and receive further funding from academia, government, and corporations. The old adage of "publish or perish," is doubly true for the hard sciences because they cannot deal in critical theory, like many other disciplines, but must show that work is being conducted and yielding helpful results. Part of this subculture is the "peer-reviewed" journal. Today, for a publication to be considered legitimate, it should appear in a peer-reviewed journal. When papers are submitted for inclusion in these journals, they are sent to individuals considered to be experts in the respective field of inquiry for their review. These men and women, usually three of them who are referred to as referees, decide whether or not the paper is of sound logic and consistent with current knowledge. However, this poses a problem precisely because the truly great scientific revolutions that changed our world were spawned by theories that contradicted the prevailing scientific thought.

These submissions are also at a disadvantage because those without scholarly degrees may be dismissed out of hand. Such a process would have eliminated Albert Einstein in the early twentieth century; he was a mere patent clerk with mediocre education who worked on problems of physics in his spare time.

Mathematical physicist Frank J. Tipler has argued that the peer review process is fundamentally flawed and does not allow for work that is outside the current thought process. "Today Einstein's papers would be sent to some total nonentity at Podunk U., who, completely incapable of understanding important new ideas, would reject the papers for publication. 'Peer' review is very unlikely to be peer review for the Einsteins of the world. We have a scientific social system in which intellectual pygmies stand in judgment of giants."[17] The point is that the truly revolutionary ideas in the sciences have often come from outside sources; Newton was not an established scientist, but rather, an eccentric who only published his work at the urging of a friend and spent much of his life pursuing alchemy. He was also a very religious man. Likewise, Einstein was not a degreed professor at a distinguished university, but rather, a menial wage laborer who worked his equations in the evening at home. Tipler states that the physics journals of Einstein's time would "publish any paper submitted by any member of the German Physical Society. It published quite a few worthless papers, but it also published quite a few great papers, among them Heisenberg's first paper on the Uncertainty Principle, a central idea in quantum mechanics."[18]

The problem is that such rigorous control of what qualifies as "legitimate science" causes a feedback loop in that the only work accepted for publication is that which enforces the current theories and beliefs in the scientific community. In essence, scientific knowledge becomes a more elite version of *Wikipedia*. Robert C. Post noted in *Democracy, Expertise, and Academic Freedom* that inclusion in *Wikipedia* is based on verifiability, not truth.[19] The problem with knowledge through consensus is that the consensus can be wrong. Peer review was originally enacted to keep crackpot papers from being published in journals, but eventually it became an impediment on any new ideas from original thinkers. Let's think about this using our global warming example. If a scientific, peer-reviewed journal about climate change were to receive a paper from a professor or scientist asserting that global warming was not that big of a deal, would it be accepted or rejected by that journal when reviewed by men and women who are considered experts in the field of global warming and climate change? If the reigning thought is that man-made global warming is going to be catastrophic, then which peers would favorably review a work that says otherwise?

A second problem is the way science is presented to the public: often not from the researchers themselves but through self-proclaimed experts in the media. Science is frequently filtered through media sources such as newspapers, websites, writers, or politicians. We discussed Chris Mooney earlier; Chris is an English major from Yale who is now a writer about science and culture. There is also Bill McKibben, a graduate of Harvard who majored in journalism and is now one of the most vociferous of global warming activists. "So: the paths we have tried to tackle global warming have so far produced only gradual, halting shifts. A rapid, transformative change would require building a movement, and movements require enemies. . . . And enemies are what climate change has lacked," he wrote. "But what all these climate numbers make painfully, usefully clear is that the planet does indeed have an enemy—one far more committed to action than governments or individuals. Given this hard math, we need to view the fossil fuel industry in a new light. It has become a rogue industry, reckless like no other force on Earth. It is Public Enemy Number One to the survival of our planetary civilization."[20] In other words, evil corporations are conspiring to kill all of humanity . . . including their customers.

We can also look to Graham Readfearn, who regularly writes for the *Guardian* about global warming. He also blogs at *DeSmogBlog*, which is dedicated to "Clearing the PR Pollution that Clouds Climate Science." There, he describes himself as an "independent journalist based in Queensland, Australia, with fifteen years' experience as a reporter and writer on newspapers, magazines, radio and online."[21] However, he does not list any educational or scientific background, nor does he have a history of compelling thought. Rather he seems to jump from one holy cause to another. These "journalists," dedicated to their holy causes, cannot objectively report or investigate any issue involving those causes.

They see themselves as heroes on a mission, not journalists whose calling is to objectively report information to the public. Their holy cause holds sway, and their work is subject to it.

With no devotion to objectivity and even less to reasoned inquiry, writers who are supposed to convey information to the public on the sciences make massive overstatements and even miss fairly obvious points of contention in their reporting. For instance, Readfearn quotes Professor Matt England of New South Wales Climate Change Research Centre: "Global warming has not stopped. People should understand that the planet is a closed system. As we increase our emissions of greenhouse gases, the fundamental thermal dynamics tells us we have added heat into the system. Once it's trapped, it can go to a myriad of places—land surface, oceans, ice shelves, ice sheets, glaciers for example."[22] Unfortunately for Readfearn (and England), he misses a major mistake in Professor England's assertion, namely, that the earth is NOT a closed system, because it gains energy and heat from the sun and loses heat and energy to space.* It is this very fact that makes our world possible.[23] It doesn't really matter whether or not this one mistake would affect England's warning on global warming, but the fact remains that he was taken at his word by a "journalist" who should have been skeptical by nature of his profession.

Science, filtered through a media that is made up of English majors and political science graduates, is molded to fit purposes that are anything but objective. Indeed, as stated previously, in postmodern philosophy, objectivity is considered a sin of white male European imperialism. Reporting on issues objectively means that sometimes you come across information that you don't like, but you are still obligated to report. Not doing so turns journalism into cheerleading for an ideology.

---

* Funny enough, the laws of thermodynamics are often brought up in intelligent design and creation-based arguments regarding evolution. If the earth were a closed system, creationists and intelligent design theorists would have a much stronger argument, which, ironically enough, would probably make Readfearn and Professor England very upset.

the tower of babble

In the biblical story of the Tower of Babel (Genesis 11), the people try to build a tower tall enough to reach heaven and therefore be like gods themselves. God, however, punishes them for their arrogance and corrupts their language so they can no longer understand one another, and the building ceases. Could the same thing be happening here?

By posing this question, I am not asserting that God is imposing some kind of biblical retribution upon science for going too far, but rather, that postmodernism has resulted in people's inability to communicate with each other, particularly with regard to building our shining tower in the sky—the great society. It is a clash of the rational with the irrational, of Aristotle and Nietzsche, and ultimately any ability to debate based on the same idea of rationality is halted, thus resulting in essentially two different languages. Scientists are confused by activist experts, professors, and students who proclaim that their work is the work of imperialism and that logic is useless; the impotent activists turn to a faith-based mentality, anger, Balkanization, and invective.

To give a superficial example of the confusing of languages, in *Fashionable Nonsense* Sokal and Bricmont spend a good deal of time analyzing the way postmodern academics use confusing language to give the appearance of science while all along selling . . . well . . . nonsense. "However, on closer examination, one sees that there is a great concentration of scientific terms, employed out of context and without any apparent logic, at least if one attributes to these terms the usual scientific meanings. . . . But what philosophical function can be fulfilled by this avalanche of ill-digested scientific (and pseudo-scientific) jargon? In our opinion, the most plausible explanation is that these authors possess a vast but very superficial erudition, which they put on display in their writings." This practice of using jargon is, according to the authors, "to give an appearance of profundity to trite observations about sociology or history."[24] In essence, the postmodern philosophers and science critics are confusing scientific language and spitting it back in the form of nonsense, which scientists can barely understand themselves. This is common practice among experts; if you put enough "isms" in a sentence and use scientific-sounding vocabulary, you can give the impression of knowledge so vast, complex, and deep as to make other readers marvel at your knowledge while having no way to judge it for themselves. It gives the impression of knowledge that is intimidating in its complexity and therefore in need of expert judgment, when, in fact, it is superficial, confusing, and rather ordinary.

A true professional, one who truly understands his work in the sciences, desires that knowledge be understood by the masses. Thus, he avoids the jargon and imposing equations that must sometimes accompany his professional work in order to present that information to the public in clear, concise, understandable language. That way, those without similar training can understand the merits or problems of a scientific issue. Above all else, truth must take precedence over ideology; otherwise, science is useless.

On a deeper and more troubling level is the disparity in the way logic and rationality themselves have been subverted for political and ideological causes. Philosopher Alasdair MacIntyre demonstrated in his work *Whose Justice, Which Rationality?* that rationality itself changes over the course of history based on a civilization's worldview. MacIntyre posits that one of the great achievements of the Enlightenment was to provide a standard of rationality by which to judge the merit of an argument. It made it possible for all men and women to make a judgment on the legitimacy of an argument.[25]

Our current form of logic and rationality is considered the ultimate form of thought because it is derived from empirical, objective science born out of the Enlightenment. It is formed around the function of science as opposed to, say, a religious worldview. What appears to be taking place currently is a revolt in language, logic, and rationality. Case in point: the *Atlantic* recently published an article by Jessica Carew Kraft titled "Hacking Traditional College Debate's White-Privilege Problem." The article highlighted a massive divide that has beset the college debate circuit, in which the normal rules for debating a subject, such as U.S.

military intervention in Iraq, are ignored by the participants, who change the subject to something reflective of their personal experience and angst. Kraft reported:

> On March 24, 2014, at the Cross Examination Debate Association (CEDA) Championships at Indiana University, two Towson University students, Ameena Ruffin and Korey Johnson, became the first African-American women to win a national college debate tournament, for which the resolution asked whether the U.S. president's war powers should be restricted. Rather than address the resolution straight on, Ruffin and Johnson, along with other teams of African-Americans, attacked its premise. The more pressing issue, they argued, is how the U.S. government is at war with poor black communities.
>
> In the final round, Ruffin and Johnson squared off against Rashid Campbell and George Lee from the University of Oklahoma, two highly accomplished African-American debaters with distinctive dreadlocks and dashikis. Over four hours, the two teams engaged in a heated discussion of concepts like "nigga authenticity" and performed hip-hop and spoken-word poetry in the traditional timed format. At one point during Lee's rebuttal, the clock ran out but he refused to yield the floor. "F--k the time!" he yelled."[26]

When colleges tried to form a new debate league in order to maintain traditional debate rules, they were accused of racism, and the new league subsequently never got off the ground. The ideological lines are largely being drawn along the multicultural, critical, race-theory line, with supportive professors arguing that the traditional debate rules of logic, objectivity, rationality, and civility unfairly favor white students; however, I believe that the divide may be even deeper than race. It reflects a dismissal of the classical, liberal rationality that was born out of the Enlightenment. And what is more troubling, it has not waned but has, in fact, gained power in culture, politics, higher education, and ultimately in how the sciences are conducted. Even Arthur Schlesinger Jr. wrote of the destruction this kind of divide could cause the nation in his work *The Disuniting of America: Reflections on a Multicultural Society*: "The ethnic upsurge (it can hardly be called a revival because it was unprecedented) began as a gesture of protest against the Anglocentric culture. It became a cult, and today it threatens to become a counter-revolution against the original theory of America as 'one people,' a common culture, a single nation."[27] Those words from a prominent intellectual of the political left were written more than twenty years ago.

All this does not bode well for the sciences, but let me repeat: science, the laws and functions of the natural world, does not change, but science as an industry has unfortunately been corrupted by this new (ir)rationality and has resulted in a modern-day Tower of Babel. Different groups are speaking different languages, and nothing more can be built of the good society.

Paul R. Gross and his colleague Norman Levitt wrote *Higher Superstition* nearly two decades ago. Professor Levitt is no longer with us, but Professor Gross was able to reflect on the past twenty years of progress:

> The 1980–90s relativist games played by social scientists with natural science failed. The natural sciences have gone on during the last two decades exactly as they did in the prior two (only faster), and that applies just as strongly to theory-making, theory justifying, and theory-discarding as it does to experimentation and observation. Scientists have *ignored* postmodernism, overwhelmingly, except, in rare instances, for making fun of its linguistic quirks. There are small but clever word-processing programs around that will write a postmodern essay for you with just a few prompts of subject and keywords. They are meaningless. I wish the same could be said about the plain, un-academic, media-supported *politicization* of science and science education. There the story is sadly different. The sharp and urgent polarization of political life in the West, especially during the last quarter-century, has leaked into the natural sciences. Thus we have—just for example—a string-theorist physicist (and popular science commentator) calling all scientists who doubt the adequacy of the proffered evidence for catastrophic, anthropogenic global warming,

now hedged as "climate change," incompetents or ideologists or fakers. Meanwhile one of the most distinguished mathematical physicists in the world insists that the current supercomputer circulation models, using fluid mechanics, are at least to date incapable of supporting the official claims, e.g., from the UN and most leading politicians. And those models are the key argument of the "warmist" position. Insults fly in all directions! The drivers are often (not, thankfully, always) political and ideological or power-group enthusiasms, not science. This is happening worldwide and it threatens to do for science—in the public mind—exactly what the postmodern critique failed to do![28]

Retired chemical physicist and columnist Dr. James Barrante had, perhaps, even more haunting words regarding the postmodern influence on the sciences:

Any type of research that relies on outside funding is going to be politicized. The sad part of science research today, which was unheard of 50 years ago when I started in the business, is that there are a number of dishonest "scientists" who apparently have no problem adjusting the outcomes of their research to suit their agenda. Moreover, if you look at the names of so-called skeptics like myself, we are mostly retired physicists and chemists. It is well known that scientists who are still trying to make a name for themselves or get promoted have to be very careful about what they publish. Many won't take the chance and bury their research. The U.S.A. now resembles Germany in the early 1930s in more ways than one. [29]

Germany of the 1930s was overtaken by a wave of irrationality born out of Nietzsche and World War I. However, this is not to accuse individuals of being Nazis, but rather to show that a "spirit of the times" can overtake even the most scientific and modernized of nations when the right conditions are in place. In the beginning of this work I drew a comparison between the United States and Vienna at the dawn of World War I, and now we find comparisons between the modern United States and Germany of the thirties. Both were times of transition, a changing of the guards on the world stage, and both were marked by a fundamental change in rationality and thought; traditions were discarded in favor of revolution, and objectivity and decency were exchanged for spirit and irrationalism. Communication between people was scrambled. Institutions and religious traditions broke down and any notion of moral adherence to truth was left behind. A society that has embraced a new rationality that is not based on truth and logic will crumble, and the experts are one of the drivers of that decline.

My grandfather was never educated past the eighth grade. He fought in World War II and, at one point, was a mere forty miles from Berlin. When he came home, he married my grandmother, became a carpenter, and began building houses in Ohio. He was born into the Amish community, but converted to the Mennonite faith in his early twenties. In the midst of remodeling a home for resale, a real estate agent, eager to get his house on the market, asked when the place would be ready. My grandfather pointed out that he had found some additional problems that needed to be repaired, so it wouldn't be as early as he had originally anticipated. The real estate agent balked and told him the repair really wasn't necessary since no one would see it. My grandfather simply looked up and said, "I don't work for you. I work for the Lord, and He sees everything."

This is the central issue that scientists and experts must face: who do you work for? Because if you do not work for something greater than yourself or politics, then you are subject to the whims and passions and corruption of petty and corrupt humans. But if you work for an ideal, if you work for Truth, then you subject your personal preferences to that ideal. Only in that way can a society actually move forward with a solid base of knowledge that can be trusted by the people, and only in that way can we stop speaking in confused languages, causing strife and misunderstanding and ultimately decline.

6

experts, complexity, and chaos

Since discourse on moral matters even in their universal aspects is subject to uncertainty and variation, it is all the more uncertain if one wishes to descend to bringing doctrine to bear on individual cases in specific detail, for this cannot be dealt with by either art or precedent, because the factors in individual cases are indeterminately variable. Therefore judgment concerning individual cases must be left to the prudentia of each person.

—st. thomas aquinas, *commentary on the ethics II*

Chaos isn't a pit. Chaos is a ladder. Many who try to climb it fail and never get to try again. The fall breaks them. And some are given a chance to climb. They refuse, they cling to the realm or the gods or love. Illusions. Only the ladder is real. The climb is all there is.

—littlefinger, *game of thrones* (season 3, episode 8)

Throughout the history of the modern world, self-proclaimed experts have claimed to have found the key to history—the equation to humanity—the final answer as to why we are here and how we should act. Karl Marx thought he had found the key to history in the study of economics, Charles Darwin in biology, and Sigmund Freud in sexuality, among many, many others. These men and women throughout history have discovered or recognized a piece of a larger, incomprehensible whole of life, and their insights deserve both praise and scrutiny. Unfortunately, their imaginary key to explaining life becomes a cult of belief by educated followers who are either unable or unwilling to admit ignorance in the face of a vast and chaotic universe or submit to traditional avenues of faith. Thus, our inability to predict weather patterns past ten days in the future does not faze those who proclaim to know the weather one hundred years in the future.

Arnold J. Toynbee was a famous historian during the 1940s and '50s and was even featured on the cover of *Time* magazine, which is about as famous as a historian can get. He served in British government in the Political Intelligence Department. His most famous work, however, was his twelve-volume *A Study of History*, in which he examined the rise and fall of twenty-eight civilizations throughout world history. It was a massive work that spanned more than a decade and became not only a best-selling popular phenomenon, but also one of the most revered historical works in academia. The sheer size of the undertaking was breathtaking. Throughout his work, though, Toynbee implied that he had found a key to understanding the rise and fall of civilizations, and that key rested on the moral and spiritual underpinnings of those societies. However, this "key" came under dispute, and the entirety of his work was eventually relegated to the forgotten past. If such a massive and studied undertaking could not find the key to history, the key to understanding humanity in a scientific way, then who or what possibly could? Whether or not you agree with Toynbee or any of the others comes down to a matter of faith rather than any notion of enlightened knowledge.

The problem is that the self-proclaimed experts seize onto a theory or idea and try to form a worldview around it; when life refuses to conform to that view, they feel it must be foisted upon the masses. Thus, the proletariat around the world has not risen up in revolution, and the population increase has not caused mass starvation. When the initial predictions of catastrophic global warming did not materialize and the public became skeptical, politicians and experts declared that the "debate is over" and proclaimed themselves the victors. In the modern world, arrogance and pride in man's abilities have resulted in a mass culture of people unwilling and unable to utter the two wisest phrases in the human lexicon: *I don't know* and *I was wrong.*

There are two perfectly natural reasons that we have not and cannot find the equation, the science that reveals the pattern of history, and the vision of things to come, namely complexity and chaos.

Complexity theory and *chaos theory* are two terms that have enjoyed great usage in postmodern science literature, but what do they mean and to what do they refer? A system that is complex, such as the economy, has many, many different people and things interacting that are interdependent on one another. What one does affects many others which then affect many others, and so on. Therefore, one person or thing—an agent—can affect a vast number of other agents. Apple releasing the iPhone drastically changed the way the entire business economy worked as well as the manufacture and sales of phones. However, an agent does not need to be as large as Apple; we could whittle it down to only Steve Jobs. Complexity is the reason so many expert predictions fail. In essence, Paul Ehrlich's *Population Bomb* prediction was a form of population determinism. Superficially it seemed to make perfect sense; we only have so much food, and if there are too many people, we won't be able to feed them all. However, it did not take into account human adaptability and ingenuity—namely, the interaction of six billion different individuals who inhabit the earth and have the ability to change their living conditions. This is why predictions so rarely materialize. A human being cannot know all the different agents acting simultaneously, and even if he or she could, that individual would still be unable to measure the outcome.

Chaos, on the other hand, does not require many individual interacting agents. Rather, the system—for example, the orbit of a planet in our solar system—is extremely sensitive to minute conditions and fluctuations that existed at its beginning. Since we cannot know for certain the placement and influence of every single atom at the initial start of a system, such as a planetary orbit, we cannot be sure that our calculations are accurate for the rest of time. Following Newton's discovery of the laws of physics, it was believed that with enough information, scientists (more likely a computer) could determine how everything in the universe came to be where it currently is and where it will go in the future. This is known as *determinism*. Such a theory is highly speculative, but it shows itself in other manifestations such as *economic determinism*, which posits that the economy marches along according to preset laws. Astrophysicist John Gribbin wrote in *Deep Simplicity*, "This means that a computer with an infinite memory is required to specify the state of a single particle. No computer can be bigger than the entire Universe, and if you define the Universe as 'everything there is,' this means that the only system that can replicate the behavior of the Universe in every detail—is the Universe itself."[1] Basically, this means that with nearly all of life there is the essence of chaos at its base. Jogging may help you live longer, but if you go jogging and suddenly get hit by a bus when the bus driver sneezes due to the high-pollen count of a late summer brought about by the effects of a solar flare a decade ago, your determination of the benefits of jogging has been rendered false. In essence, as Karl Popper said of science, things cannot be known to be absolutely true . . . but they can be proven to be false, sometimes fatally so. The popular notion of the butterfly effect is a product of chaos theory. The saying is that a butterfly flaps its wings in Brazil, and there is a typhoon in the Philippines (or some iteration of that saying). The point is not that small things necessarily effect big changes, but rather that we have no way of knowing whether or not a butterfly flapped its wings in such a way as to produce a typhoon. There are simply too many factors involved.

So what are we to make of this in relation to experts? Well, for the most part experts are not trying to predict the future of every individual on earth (though sometimes it seems that way). They are, however, trying to predict the futures of large, complex systems such as the climate and societies. Systems can be ordered in four different ways that are fairly self-explanatory: *stable, period, chaotic,* and *complex*. Experts tend to treat complex systems as being stable, like Paul Ehrlich's population-bomb prediction or the peak-oil predictions in the 1970s. Scott E. Page is a professor of complex systems, political science, and economics at the University of Michigan and uses oil prices as an example of a system that can be both stable and complex: "The production and sale of oil take place within a system capable of producing complexity. If you look at oil prices, they are complex. They're not random, but they are definitely not stable. If you look at oil production, it's on a pretty stable growth path. Not perfectly stable, but it's close. Therefore the same system produces class 4 (complexity) and class 1 (stable) or 2 (period) depending on how one classifies a stable growth path."[2] So we could look at a system over a selection of years in the same way that many experts were looking at oil production and sales during the '70s, believing it to be on a stable course to disaster and making their prediction as such. However, the system can and does change—sometimes quite dramatically. Now, for instance, with the development of fracking, the United States could be supplying most of its own energy, driving down oil prices worldwide. Once again, people are able to adapt and use technology to develop solutions that were previously unknown and unpredictable.

Oil production and prices are not chaotic, but they are complex. To a degree, we can make reasonable estimates as to how complex systems may play out in the future, but those estimates are far from the "science" that experts claim as reasons to assert power and influence. However, when dealing with a chaotic system, a system such as the weather, our ability to make predictions becomes vastly less accurate. To date, even using supercomputers, we can predict the weather in a given area only up to ten days in the future, and even those estimates are highly speculative, which leads to countless jokes about faulty weather forecasters. But it's really not their fault; it's the best humanity has to offer.

The weather, however, is different from the climate. The climate takes into account the total effects of the atmospheric conditions and is a vastly *complex* system. Based on ice core samples, we have been able to find a general pattern in the fluctuations of climate temperature over the last 400,000 years. During that time, "the globe has spent about 300,000 or so years at temperatures that would be very un-hospitable for North Americans. It appears that these low temperatures are, in fact, 'normal' temperatures of the globe, while present day temperature periods are short lived, lasting for only twenty to thirty thousand years, an extremely short period of time on a global scale."[3] So, based on the limited history of time that we have, there appears to be a pattern of climate changes and temperatures. However, as many climate change proponents will point out, this does not factor in mankind pumping the atmosphere with CO_2.

Climatologist Gavin Schmidt gives a fantastic account of the climate's complexity in his brief TED (Technology, Entertainment, Design) talk titled "The Emergent Pattern of Climate Change." Schmidt somewhat defeats his own argument at the onset by demonstrating the vastly limited understanding we have of the complexity of climate and by limiting his models to only the past century. He also makes the assumption that the climate is stable but uses only a tiny fraction of time—one hundred years—to demonstrate this stability, thus assuming that present temperatures are the "correct" temperatures for the globe. However, his graphics and his demonstration show just how amazingly complex such a system is. Schmidt ponders what happens when the complex climate system gets "kicked" and a new element is introduced. An example of a kick would be a volcano that spews tons and tons of dust, debris, and smoke into the atmosphere. It is something that was unforeseen.* So the CO_2 that we are introducing to the system is considered a kick. What this brings into question is how robust the complex system of the climate is, or how adaptable it is to the introduction of new factors. The earth itself has survived cataclysmic events in the past, including the asteroid that most likely killed off all the dinosaurs. But today's climate may not be quite as resilient, and a kick could potentially alter the climate.

However, Schmidt ignores another vastly complex factor—namely, humanity; thus he makes the same mistake that Paul Ehrlich made in the 1970s. Human beings are the most adaptable species on the planet. They occupy nearly every temperature clime, terrain, and ecosystem.

---

* It should be noted that volcanic activity, while often unpredictable, is natural to the planet's functioning; therefore, the kick is only unexpected to us, but this is an argument for another time.

Not only have they survived, but they have thrived. They have been able to adapt to different temperatures and to changes in climate. Human beings were present during the Ice Ages of the past, and indeed, it was during those times that they dispersed (or "scattered," as in Genesis 11:9) throughout the world, coming into North America via the Alaskan land bridge. A colleague recently remarked to me that Americans would be okay and able to adapt to a warmer climate and the challenges that it may present, but "what about the people in Bangladesh?" Yet, it is the Bangladeshis who are the true survivors; they live, work, and thrive in an environment that would probably cripple the average Westerner. The economic strength and comfort of the West do not translate into survivability in harsh or difficult environments. This "strength" has more to do with political environment rather than any innate ability to adapt to change and hardship. As Jared Diamond wrote in *Guns, Germs, and Steel*, "I reflected that the Aborigines who had made [the rock] paintings [in the desert near Menindee, New South Wales, Australia] had somehow spent their entire lives in that desert without air-conditioned retreats, managing to find food as well as water." Not only had the Aborigines survived, but they had survived much better than the Europeans on their expeditions to primitive Australia. Several times the Aborigines had to rescue the Europeans from starving to death despite the Europeans' obvious advantage of guns and formal education.[4] If you are concerned about the Bangladeshis, perhaps it would be better to offer economic help to them now, rather than by trying to alter the entire climate in the hopes that their situation will remain the same.

Climate models showing an increase in CO_2 in the atmosphere and a rise in temperatures also fail to take into consideration risk—another facet of complexity. For instance, there is a risk that the earth will be hit with a meteor tomorrow—but it's not a very high risk. Likewise, we are not given information on the probability of the doomsday scenarios that are often flashed across our television screens. Some even believe that a rise in temperature and CO_2 emissions would be a good thing for much of the planet, allowing more plant fertility and opening previously closed waterways.

The truth of the matter is that even if Schmidt and his fellow believers were 100 percent accurate in their predictions, the climate change debate would still come down to a matter of values and morals. Is it better to limit people's ability to survive in the present by causing price increases and supply shortages in order to help them survive in the future? One does not necessarily lead to the other. Making it more difficult for me to afford gas to get to work and support my family now does not ensure my survival in the future, nor that of my children. Only time—apparently an immense amount of it—will tell; but, so far, the climate experts' predictions have not panned out. This could more likely be an example of hubris—believing that we have a larger impact on the earth and the universe than is actually the case.

Similarly, economics is a vastly complex system, which frustrates some of the best minds when they make prophetic proclamations or claim to have a "solution" to economic instability and change. The problem with economics is that it directly affects large numbers of people in ways that can be more damaging than weather or the climate, so concerted efforts are made to control the economies of the world. Thus, certain economic systems develop, allowing more or less government control of and influence on the markets. Keynesian economics, for example, made the argument that the private sector, or free market, left to its own devices, would cause unstable conditions and inequalities that were unacceptable by Western nations and, therefore, warranted government intervention. Ultimately, these economists have judged that it is "wrong" for the free market to have absolute freedom, and "right" for government to manipulate the economy to its satisfaction— a moral argument. *The Concise Encyclopedia of Economics* tells us that "Keynesians' belief in aggressive government action to stabilize the economy is based on value judgments and on the beliefs that (a) macroeconomic fluctuations significantly reduce economic well-being and (b) the government is knowledgeable and capable enough to improve on the free market."[5] Several arguments over values can be made from this proposition, but the argument for Keynesian economics cannot be made from a strictly scientific or economic standpoint. This economic viewpoint was brought up many times during the debate as to how to best pull the country out of the recession following the 2008 financial collapse. It appears that the Keynesian argument won out, with a nearly $1 trillion stimulus package passed through Congress. The results of that stimulus, for whatever reason, were less than hoped for—if measurable at all. Once again, the immense complexity of so many factors that feed into the American economy thwarted the predictions of our best and brightest. Free market capitalism has been shown in the past to produce massive wealth, the United States being a prime example, while socialism and communism have historically been shown to lead to stagnation and, sometimes, collapse. However, the moral shortcomings of each system need to be judged. That is surely a debate to be had, but not under the guise of proven theories and settled economic debates.

So the future is unwritten. This we know. But what about the past? Experts often look to the past as a means of predicting the future or for the key or equation to humanity. As we discussed previously, Karl Marx and Arnold J. Toynbee both believed they had solved the mystery of history, but they have been shown (or at least judged) to be incorrect. As Dr. Barrante has written, "It's like watching a tree grow. We cannot see it happening. We only know that it has happened by observing that the tree is taller at some later date."[6] That the tree has grown, we are sure. Why the tree has grown, we still speculate. So how do we deal with the key to history in a world so complex as to seem chaotic?

Dr. Page wrote, "If I look at the path of history I see a system capable of producing all four phenomena (stable, period, chaotic, complex)."[7] History, as an accumulation of everything that has happened since the Big Bang, is certainly bigger than any one mind and bigger than any computer model. As John Gribbin said, it would take a computer the size of the universe to compute the course of history and of things to come. But what about the known history of humanity? Can we legitimately look at it and find patterns similar to those of the climate throughout millennia? If we do find patterns, what does that tell us about the future? Let us take a look at our tendency to see history in the light of our own minimal brain capacities.

The old saying is that those who don't learn from history are doomed to repeat it. However, it would seem that some who learn an immense amount of history are doomed to deify it. Historic determinism believes that the course of history—and thus the future—can be divined as a set, unalterable pattern. However, once this pattern is discovered, the historian then believes it to be his or her moral obligation to either forestall the inevitable change through dire warnings or, as in the case of Marx, to usher the future along through revolution. Conversely, historians such as Spengler and Toynbee, who see moral or spiritual decline as the cause of the collapse of societies, are often used as rallying cries for returns to cultural roots and practices. It seems that once the historian or philosopher discovers the key to history, he then takes it upon himself to try to move that history along. Marx, for example, believed that economic factors would cause a revolution against the upper classes. When this didn't happen quickly enough, he and his followers attempted to help it along by forming the revolution that was supposed to be born out of capitalism of its own accord, thus rendering his idea of economic determinism moot, opting instead for change by strong will.

Unfortunately, the idea that finding the key to history can somehow infer the future is just as mistaken as those that posit to know the future based on present situations. Albert Camus referred to this as "historical deification" and pointed out that trying to determine the future by studying the past is impossible. "Pure determinism is absurd in itself," he wrote. "If it were not, then one single affirmation would suffice to lead, from consequence to consequence, to the entire truth. If this is not so, then either we have never made a single true affirmation—not even the one stated by determinism—or we could simply happen occasionally to say the truth, but without any consequences, and determinism is then false."[8] The latter statement probably comes closest to the truth in that there is no one key to history that guides the course of the world, but rather an infinite interplay of different forces—economic, material, moral, and others that interact to form historical events. As Barrante indicated, we cannot see all of this taking place, nor can we predict how it will occur. We can only look back and see that it has, in fact, occurred.

History is the story of a vastly complex system that is still interacting with its past. For instance, Marx's theory of economic determinism and his prediction of revolution actually changed the course of history and thus disrupted his own deterministic theory through his *recognition* of history and his action. Thus, the communist revolutions were not born naturally out of a lack of goods, but rather with the recognition of exploitation and lack of goods through Marx's work, which caused people to act and thus influenced the history of the world. Likewise, Hitler's conception and myth of Germany's past influenced his ascendancy to leadership. The present is always interacting with the past, thereby influencing and changing the future. This results in an increasingly complex system, which, as Professor Page indicates, exhibits all the variables of different systems. In essence, it goes back to what Gribbin told us: it would take a computer the size of the universe itself to chart the history and future of one particle. So finding the key to history ultimately changes the locks, so to speak.

There also exists the problem of assuming expected patterns in historical events. For instance, if I believe that the fall of the Roman Empire was due to a failure of morality among the population, then I will be inclined to see that in other societies, eventually believing it to be a pattern. Complexity is capable of producing patterns, but they are not set in stone. And the emergence of patterns is not applicable to the complexity of human consciousness. A human is self-aware, knowingly interacting with his or her environment, and is not subject to the same unconscious forces that are inherent in nonhuman complex systems. Who could have foreseen World War I or Hitler? They were each born out of irrational reactions to political environments that spiraled out of control. The emergence of such historical events and figures then ultimately changes the course of the future. History is, in effect, a self-reference engine spinning like a planet in the solar system. While we often talk of progress and think of time and history as moving forward, it really has no direction; it only changes in perceived patterns that result from the present's interaction with the past.

But all is not lost. As Littlefinger said in the quote at the beginning of this chapter, "chaos is a ladder." It is in the chaos and complexity of the interactions of billions of people and systems, laws and forces of nature, that mankind is enabled to adapt, to persevere, and to build. As Musil wrote in *The Man Without Qualities*, all the physical exertion used by common men and women going about their daily routines adds up to more than the greatest athlete could ever lift. Likewise, the decisions and interactions of everyday individuals add up to a level of complexity that is incomprehensible to any expert. It is through the complexity of life, not in spite of it, that we are able achieve greater and greater rewards.

However, it is often the experts who see chaos and complexity as "the pit" and themselves as the proud knights come to the rescue. In their efforts to find the key to humanity, to throw a blanket over the peaks and valleys of infinite change, they give us a theory meant to maintain the status quo. Complexity and change, because they are unknowns, often present as frightening prospects, and experts use our fear of the unknown to drum up support for their theories. Thus, the climate change initiative is meant to preserve the current temperature; economic and social theories are meant to level inequalities by creating a static system rather than a dynamic one. People fear complexity, and chaos has a negative connotation, so both are used to generate fear among the population—a fear that their individual lives will be forever unbearably altered if the experts' warnings are not heeded. Catastrophic collapse and calamity are preached, whether due to climate, war, economics, or technology. It would appear at every turn that Armageddon is imminent for our species because those who claim to have found the key to history, the answer to humanity, believe that they and they alone wield the knowledge and power to coerce mankind to repent and change its ways. But they have been proven wrong time and time again.

I would be remiss if I didn't add that we, as human beings, desire this kind of "knowledge." It can be comforting to believe that we know "what is going on," even if it appears catastrophic. There is a certain feeling of comfort when we place our faith and fate in the hands of someone who proclaims to have the answer and is willing to share that answer with us. It is a simplification of that vast complexity of life. Perhaps its most visible and demonstrable manifestation is in conspiracy theorists, such as those who claim that the world is secretly run by the CIA or the Illuminati. It takes faith to believe that a single organization or cause could manipulate history. But that organization or cause need not be as ridiculous as aliens controlling world leaders. As Saint Thomas Aquinas said, allowing a blanket rule or ideology to sweep over the variations of life is a mistake. To see everything through only one lens is to limit our ability, not only to think critically, but also to see the richness and vast complexity of life. This does not mean that we shrug off warnings about man's effect on the climate or the social implications of income inequality; however, we should not take at their word those who espouse such warnings. We should look at the underlying moral and value judgments inherent in their remedies and, most of all, give heed to those who offer alternative ideas, solutions, or viewpoints.

Professor Page authored a book titled *The Difference* in which he posits that diversity is one of the greatest tools for problem solving—not necessarily racial diversity, but diversity of thought. He notes that racial and ethnic diversity does not necessarily mean diversity of thought, and that racial or ethnic homogeneity does not necessarily mean homogeneity of thought.[9] All peoples and groups are capable of groupthink; it is not limited to one group or another, and when a group has a lens through which they see history or the world—whether it is a lens built out of ideology, religion, or experience—they will automatically fail to see some of the other subtle shadings of life's complexity. Page explains this in terms of "heuristics," which are basically the tools we use to problem solve. A historian who uses economics as the tool by which to interpret the rise and fall of nations throughout history and then creates a "law" by which to view the future is using a heuristic. The only problem, as Page explains, is that one tool is *never* able to solve every complex problem.[10] For example, economic determinism may be right in some cases, but it will never be right in all cases. Marx tried it. Toynbee tried it. And both were found wanting.

I personally believe that finding the key to humanity is impossible. Why? It goes back to the idea of men and women being, at their core, irrational beings. The world may function by rational laws and principles that can be discovered in science, but mankind functions on belief, emotion, and reaction. This is why attempts at creating law, rules, or heuristics by which to explain and predict humanity will always fall short. Even in looking back on history we find that our own consciousness interferes with the ability to make pure sense and reason out of things that have already happened, let alone things that will happen in the future.

In 2014 a study funded in part by NASA was released to the world. It claimed that a team of researchers had developed an equation, based on the history of civilizations over the past five thousand years, showing, in essence, that income inequality was responsible for the collapse of societies and that the only recourse to save our nations would be to become more socialistic. "In sum, the results of our experiments . . . indicate that either one of the two features apparent in historical societal collapses—overexploitation of natural resources and strong economic stratification—can independently result in a complete collapse," the authors wrote. "Given economic stratification, collapse is very difficult to avoid and requires major policy changes, including major reductions in inequality and population growth rates. Even in the absence of economic stratification, collapse can still occur if depletion per capita is too high. However, collapse can be avoided and population can reach equilibrium if the per capita rate of depletion of nature is reduced to a sustainable level, and if resources are distributed in a reasonably equitable fashion."[11]

However, not everyone was convinced, including statistician and Cornell professor William Briggs. "The math is fine," he said, "it's the interpretation that's on top of it. There's nothing empirical that went into these equations. . . . There's no observations that went into [them]. . . . They just developed a set of equations and then said, 'This is the way reality should look.' And of course, reality doesn't look anything like that, as I tried to point out."[12] In essence, the researchers had tried to condense the key to history into mathematical equations, but as we have been discussing throughout this book, history and humanity are not so easily defined. Theoretical science and mathematics may show trends and pieces of large puzzles, but they cannot impart full understanding to life. Toynbee thought that the key to history could be found in the moral and spiritual underpinnings of civilizations. I wonder what he would think of this study that finds, in essence, the opposite—a history mired in material determinism. Perhaps the truth is somewhere in the middle. Unfortunately, the true middle is not a fixed point, but rather, an idea.

7

the culture of death

This is the way of things. This is the lot you have given them, because they are part of things which do not all exist at the same time, but by passing away and succeeding each other they all make up the universe, of which they are all parts. For example, our speech is accomplished by sounds which signify meanings, but a meaning is not complete unless one word passes away, when it has sounded its part, so that the next may follow it.

—augustine, *confessions*

If he's so smart, how come he's dead?

—homer simpson, *the simpsons* (season 11, episode 3)

O ne of my favorite headlines of all time comes from a Yahoo! News article in 2008 titled, "Test Predicts Chances of Dying." The "test" was performed at home and consisted of asinine things such as seeing how far you could push a couch across the room. Of course, the irony was the "chances of dying" part. Everyone's chance of dying is 100 percent. This is the ultimate truth of human life, the one that creates the human condition. We are the only living creature that is conscious of our impending doom and can reflect on it, fear it, and develop religions as a means of coping with it. Christianity, Buddhism, Hinduism, and Islam—all are methods of rationalizing, justifying, and offering comfort for our coming demise. It remains "the problem" of humanity, the thing in the back of our minds that causes a constant anxiety and, in fact, compels us to look to experts in order to delay or even prevent this finality. Our efforts to avoid death are understandable and probably unavoidable. Those of right mind do not want to die, but those of sound mind accept that death is inevitable. Buddhism teaches that nothing is permanent and everything is in flux. Desire for permanence is what creates misery because it is impossible on Earth. It also explains why the goal of religions is to reach heaven as a state of permanence. Recently, however, American obsession with death has reached somewhat unhealthy proportions. The Baby Boomer generation, in particular, appears to believe that, through some combination of health and science, they need not die. This may sound like science fiction, but it is not. Rather than seeking eternal life through religion, we now seek it through science, and the experts are our high priests.

In *Death, American Style*, Lawrence R. Samuel wrote:

> Baby boomers, hurtling through their fifties and sixties, continue to be youth oriented, ignoring or fighting off the effects of aging and physical decline. We should expect no less from the eternally young generation, of course, but this has serious implications. Boomers are taking few if any steps to prepare themselves for their own deaths or that of their siblings or friends, and this is not boding well for their individual and collective future. The huge wave of death that is fast approaching will be emotionally devastating, I believe, our society is simply not ready for the historically high numbers of people who will be dying. The immortality and "radical life extension" movement is only compounding the problem, giving people false hope that they may live forever or considerably beyond the average age of eighty years.[1]

The specter of death hovering over our collective conscience induces all manner of superstitions, beliefs, and practices meant to avoid death. Take a look in the science section of your local newspaper or at many of the studies cited in online news articles. On the surface they seem to offer bits of advice on "scientific" links between certain behaviors, health practices, herbs, medicines, foods, and chemicals meant to promote health and longevity. The surface story is living healthy; the subtext is keeping death at bay and living as long as possible. Everything from cell phones to coffee has been accused of causing cancer, with tenuous "links" in studies that are often retracted or disputed in follow-up studies that never receive the same amount of press. A cell phone giving you cancer is a huge story. Conversely, a cell phone not giving you cancer isn't a story at all. If you're a largely ignored science writer or struggling in a new medium, you lead with what bleeds—or in this case—with what is malignant. Take this headline from *The Nation*, for instance: "Cell Phones and Brain Cancer—Time to Protect Ourselves." Written by Dr. Gerard LaLande, the article states, "Taking account of the tobacco experience, it is not wise waiting for an official announcement to start protecting ourselves and others from the harmful effects of cell phone emissions."[2] Despite differing conclusions from the four different studies he cited, LaLande himself concluded that, obviously, cell phones cause brain tumors the same way smoking causes lung cancer. It took many years for scientists to conclude that smoking does, in fact, cause lung cancer, he says. There are many reasons why it took so long, one of which is that it takes years of heavy usage to produce the cancer and even then it is not a sure thing. Some people smoke all their lives and do not die of lung cancer. Therefore, finding a solid cause-and-effect link can be a difficult task, and science is constantly being revised, overturned, or outdated. The human body is a complex mechanism that interacts with the outside world in millions of ways and is subject to the use and abuse of a conscious creature that often pursues its own demise with practiced rigor and a dose of stupidity.

However, LaLande is making an unequivocal statement that the need for testing—the need to seek the truth—has come to an end; it is now time to instill fear and do something. The University of California in Berkeley has begun pressing for legislation to have cell phones require cancer warnings.[3] LaLande cites the case of tobacco to bolster his argument. However, what would happen if we were to take other cancer-causing claims as seriously as he does cell phone use? Numerous other things have been accused of causing cancer throughout the years, including coffee, power lines, GMO vegetables, and alien abduction. To date, none of these has been proven, and people continue to live longer and healthier lives. People often find claims of cancer-causing conditions or products convincing because, on the surface, it just seems to make sense. Holding an electronic device to your ear that sends and receives signals must cause cancer, right? But then, our bodies are bombarded by countless signals and radio waves every second of the day.

The point is not health, per se, but the fear of death. The media deals in fear. As mentioned before, something not killing you is not news; something that is secretly killing you is big news.

And writing news stories about things that may kill you is also big business. Most news websites and papers have specific sections dedicated to health news, which can garner much readership. The two most often read health articles of 2013 both involved the threat of cancer. One was with regard to a study that showed a link between the artificial sweetener Sucralose and leukemia in mice ("How Safe is Splenda?"), and the other was taken from Hollywood pop culture examining a link between oral sex and throat cancer ("Can Oral Sex Cause Throat Cancer?").[4]

So should we ignore these oft-repeated but seldom confirmed warnings? No, but neither should we tremble in fear. The modus operandi of the media is to instill concern and fear in its audience as a means to gain viewers and readers. The media also tends to emulate itself. One organization may find a story reported by a rival website or news outlet and then report it themselves. Soon, it appears that this dire warning of a link between aspartame and cancer, or jogging and heart failure, is an imminent threat. The reporting itself implants doubt and concern in a reader's mind that now exists regardless of the eventual truth attained by science. The latent anxiety of cancer lurking just around the corner, secreted in the ingredients of modern life, helps create an atmosphere of fear in which we must rely on the media and their bevy of experts to help us avoid death.

The underlying assumption is that the human body could, if given the opportunity, continue indefinitely and that death is just another disease to be conquered. This is why the experts are so venerated and influential in our lives, particularly in the realm of human health. The belief that if we take these experts' advice, we can keep death at bay for a few more years or, ideally, millennia, has become ingrained in human consciousness ever since science replaced religion as the primary worldview.

In 1969 Alan Harrington authored the book *The Immortalist: An Approach to the Engineering of Man's Divinity*. Harrington stated in his opening lines, "Death is an imposition on the human race, and no longer acceptable. Man has all but lost his ability to accommodate himself to personal extinction; he must now proceed physically to overcome it. In short, to kill death: to put an end to his own mortality as a certain consequence of being born."[5] A lofty goal, to be sure, but not one without precedence or without today's believers. Ever since Ponce de Leon searched for the fountain of youth, man has tried to overcome the prospect of his own mortality. Before the Enlightenment such mortal anxiety was quelled with religious belief in the eternal afterlife or perhaps magical thinking, as in the case of the fountain of youth, but the post-Enlightenment world sees death as primarily a scientific problem.

And, indeed, it would seem that humanity, as a whole, has made massive strides toward overcoming this essential problem. Humans on average now live longer, healthier lives. Diseases that were once deadly have been eradicated or downgraded to minor nuisances rather than to death sentences. The bubonic plague wiped out half of Europe in the 1300s but is now nearly extinct, with individual cases only occasionally popping up around the world. Influenza claimed millions of lives worldwide in the early 1900s; we now have vaccinations that lower the instances of death to a mere a fraction of its previous numbers. While no cure exists for the various types of cancer that form in the human body, treatments are now often successful, and science is making inroads and finding new treatments. HIV can be successfully treated to ensure long-term survival rates with a "cocktail" of medications and lifestyle changes. All in all, it would appear that humanity is slowly but surely engineering its own divinity, extending our average life span toward the triple digits.

But life doesn't give us such an easy solution to death as curing a couple of diseases. The complexity of life interferes with our cures, producing new diseases or new incarnations of diseases previously thought curable. Every year, influenza is slightly different from the previous year, requiring that the vaccine be changed or adjusted. New diseases pop up: bird flu, swine flu, flesh-eating bacteria, and exotic diseases transferred from other, impoverished nations. Even as I write this, Ebola is spreading at an alarming rate, capturing headlines around the world and stoking fears here in America that it could occur in this country as well. Nature is constantly changing, rearranging, mutating, and pushing forward; therefore, the science must continually adjust, and the experts must stay relevant.

It is not just nature doing the damage, however. Humanity itself seems bent on preserving death as the ultimate balance to life. Setting aside death caused by direct human interaction, such as war, murder, accidents, suicide, and intentional risk-taking, we also have to navigate the maze of human ingenuity, such as asbestos and radiation, which can sometimes have deadly side effects that we only learn about after the fact. We even get to participate in the death process ourselves by engaging in any number of risky activities and leisure practices, such as smoking, drinking, recreational drug use, fast food, and the occasional cliff dive gone wrong. All in all, it appears that if nature fails to do the job, men and women step in to help usher themselves into the light.

We also tend to be rather discerning as to what we voluntarily allow to kill us. Your newly legalized Denver pothead will tell of the dangers of cigarettes while inhaling from a five-foot bong, or the survivalist will talk of only eating what he grows or hunts and then ask you to hold his beer while he cleans his gun. We seem to do a pretty good job of ensuring death without the aid of disease, famine, hurricanes, earthquakes, and shark attacks.

At the heart of the modern death dilemma lies a paradox: we fear that the technology and innovations of the modern world are somehow killing us—cell phones, electric lines, GMO foods, diet soda, office jobs—but believe the very same science, technology, and innovation to be our savior. It plays both God and devil, and the experts can be our saints or sinners, depending on their affiliations. In this sense we imbue science, technology, and the experts with a morality, demonizing those we perceive to encourage death while applauding those who seem determined to save the world. It forms a narrative in our collective conscience, an archetype through which we absorb and process new claims, fears, and information. Perhaps unknowingly we fit new information into that archetypal narrative, and that narrative has a face—the cigarette industry.

As early as the 1920s, tobacco use had been discussed among researchers as a possible cause of the dramatic increase in lung cancer that was being witnessed. But at that point, tobacco was not a major consideration. Researchers were more focused on the possibilities of air pollution, the asphalting of roads, influenza, and gasoline use. However, through the '30s and '40s, researchers' suspicions began to grow, and by 1969, cigarette use was given wide consideration in the *Springer Handbook of Special Pathology*. These findings were based on aggregated human experience and a narrowing of possibilities down to the most likely cause. It took a long time, and surely the health of many people was negatively affected during that period of research and study, despite warnings as early as 1929 from German researcher Franz Lickint.[6]

The tobacco/lung cancer link finally culminated with lawsuits against the tobacco companies, increased taxation on tobacco products, strict government regulation, warnings on the packages, and activist advertising on television, in magazines, and on radio. These days the general public is well aware of the dangers of smoking, but many continue to smoke in spite of the warnings.

However, during the lead-up to this final culmination of research and death, researchers disputed over whether or not cigarettes actually were responsible for the increase in lung cancer, most notably those researchers whose studies were funded by the tobacco companies, which would often challenge the independent research. As indicated before, establishment of a direct link between an activity such as smoking and a disease such as cancer can be a long and drawn-out process, but even by the 1950s tobacco companies recognized that their product was indeed causing lung cancer. Thus, they set out to dispute those findings and maintain public doubt about their validity to ensure that their product remained in high demand. "Scientists were the perfect foil for the tobacco industry's public relations response to allegations that cigarette smoking was injurious to health," reads an article from a peer-reviewed medical journal. "Scientists could be counted on to call for more research, giving the impression that there was controversy. In addition, by supporting scientific research, the industry would be seen as doing something positive to address the serious allegations that smoking was harmful. . . . In summary, the internal industry documents show how tobacco companies deliberately confused the public debate about smoking and health by creating and supporting research organizations that were never really interested in discovering the truth about whether smoking was a cause of disease."[7]

This narrative of corporate-influenced scientific studies is readily accepted these days, thanks to a large public awareness campaign and the success of both state and federal lawsuits against the tobacco companies. Putting aside the obvious human damage caused by this manufactured controversy, there was also damage inflicted upon the public perception of science, scientific research, and scientists themselves. Because the tobacco companies had used science and scientific research as a way to mislead the public on the conclusiveness of the tobacco-lung cancer studies, the notion of "science for sale" found a permanent place in the public consciousness. Science and experts were thus imbued with a morality based on their willingness to be bought and sold by corporate interests. This became the archetypal narrative by which the media presented new stories regarding the threat of cancer-causing products and the companies that sold them, and the way in which the public perceived them. They were divided into "good guys" working for the general welfare of the public and the "bad guys," who were supporting greedy corporate interests. Today, this good expert/bad expert argument is used frequently and with powerful effect in nearly all areas of research where the public good somehow clashes with business interests. Cell phones, fast food, carbonated beverages, and global warming are all now viewed through this prism of "science for sale," in which researchers are willing to skew their results to satisfy the desires of whoever or whatever is funding them.

However, merely constructing narratives from the preexisting roles of companies, products, and scientists where there are heroes and villains ignores the deadly point of this double-edged sword. Namely, if science is indeed for sale, as our narrative asserts, it is for sale everywhere and for all things. The idea of dividing science and experts into heroes and villains is a fiction whereby whoever validates our preconceived notions is the hero and whoever disputes them is the villain. It is not enough to say that one group of researchers is corrupt and not allow for the possibility that the other group is just as corrupt. The implication that scientists can be bought and sold with rewards of publication, career advancement, and so on, does not only extend to the corporate world but also to government and independent research. The point is that scientists and experts are human and, therefore, subject to the same corruption as anyone else.

In the realm of physics, mathematics, biology, and astronomy, scientific results are largely testable and verifiable. The implications of those findings can be disputed, but generally the findings themselves are either accepted or rejected by others. However, this testing and verification does not work as well in highly complex fields, such as health, medicine, and environmental studies, where there are many interdependent and changing factors. We are left with "links" and "relationships" that can easily be questioned and disputed by someone who interprets the data differently. We end up relying on a sometimes-small preponderance of evidence or computer models that cannot possibly compute all the factors involved because the factors are unknown. The idea that scientific findings are empirically verifiable and able to be tested does not extend to certain areas of research. Thus, in fields such as health and environmental sciences, we are left with the experts, who either confirm or deny our fears and preconceptions—heroes and villains—and naturally we place them in our narrative.

Dr. LaLande did precisely that when he pointed out in his article on cell phone use and cancer that "in 2011, a large Danish study included 10,729 brain tumour cases and concluded that there were no increased risks of brain tumours with mobile phone use, consequently supporting the 'lack of evidence' finding. However, this study, which was sponsored by phone companies, had massive flaws, not least a grossly inaccurate usage rate among users and non-users. Many scientists stated that the outcome was totally unreliable and the trial must be disregarded."[8] LaLande established the researchers in this study as obviously in the employ of corporate interests, and therefore, their research was skewed to support their corporate sponsors. The average individual is in no position to evaluate the merits of the study itself and is reliant on the presenter—in this case LaLande—to make the judgment as to whether or not the research and evidence are accurate.

However, when I consult the American Cancer Society, I find a much more nuanced and lengthy examination of the evidence, without the alarmism. While the ACS does not deign to draw any solid conclusions, the overall message is that studies have not found any plausible link between cell phone use and brain tumors and, pending any further development, it would appear that cell phones are generally safe. The ACS also lists various agencies and their current recommendations and conclusions, which range from "possibly carcinogenic to humans" (the International Agency for Research on Cancer) to "There is no scientific evidence that proves that wireless phone usage can lead to cancer or a variety of other problems, including headaches, dizziness or memory loss" (Federal Communications Commission).[9]

LaLande himself is the director of CEO-Health, which describes its mission as follows: "To develop and implement a customized program, which combines a high-end medical check-up and the possibility of a life-enriching wellness experience in partnered hotels and resorts."[10] The company's focus is on wellness and preventative medicine. It caters to "medical tourists" [11] —those who seek health services in other countries for the purposes of saving money or having procedures that are not allowed in their home country (CEO-Health is based in Thailand). CEO-Health also provides "Health Retreats," at some very nice resorts and spas, where an individual is treated to a "3-night Wellness Retreat Relaxation package."[12]

While this in no way discredits Dr. LaLande, it does appear that he has some of his work invested in health and wellness retreats where someone avoids the pressures and ill effects of the modern world, such as cell phones.

LaLande, however, has established his belief narrative, as evidenced by his articles concerning cell phone use and cancer; he has also established his villains (cell phone companies) and his heroes (himself and others who have found an existent link). Thus, the conclusion is not based necessarily on the studies or preponderance of evidence, but on who reached a conclusion that fit into his narrative. When dealing in complex areas of study, belief becomes much more of a factor when choosing between sources, studies, and conclusions. For this work, our definition of experts means those who use science, or their status as scientists, as a means to mold and shape the public's beliefs. Thus, the largest disputes occur in the fields where there is the most complexity and the least number of verifiable and testable hypotheses.

This ultimately leads us to ask, what if a definitive link *were* established between cell phone use and cancer? Would we stop using them? Would we shy away from all the technology that has been spawned since the advent of cellular phones? Probably not, but you can be sure that there would be lawsuits and experts and politicians from every form of mass media twenty-four hours a day giving their opinions and spinning their wheels.

The introduction of the hero/villain, good/bad narrative into the sciences has resulted in the politicization of science and experts, particularly when it comes to health and the threat of death. Political rhetoric is constantly couched in terms of the threat of death and by salvation through science and experts. We hear the term "dying in the streets," as a call for health care reform. Global warming is presented as an existential threat to humanity that could result in the starvation and death of millions. Threats from foreign diseases and terrorists are used to push border security. All of it is supported by science and experts who agree with whatever position is being argued. The proliferation of expertise and information and the common threat of death serve the politics of fear, and the media couldn't be happier or more willing to participate.

In his work *Culture of Death*, Benjamin Noys examines the politics of death, asserting that death itself has now become political due in large part to the Holocaust and nuclear bombs in recent generations. "This new form of death produces an 'intolerable anxiety,' as we have to live with the knowledge that we are always exposed to mass anonymous death," he wrote. "This is not simply the anonymous death of the epidemic or war, but a deliberate and organized death, a kind of 'rational' or industrialized death at the hands of bureaucratic planners." The mass death seen in the twentieth century was not the work of nature but, by and large, the work of political entities for political goals.[13]

Politics has largely become about staving off death by means of bureaucratization of science and the oversight of experts, particularly with the aging of the Baby Boomer generation, who did not experience firsthand the mass loss of life that was World War II. Their belief in the abilities of their own genius, coupled with their belief that government is somehow supposed to seek an end to death, has become entrenched in the subtext of political speech. Fear of death at the hands of any number of boogeymen is largely the driving force behind political speech and media reporting.

But the phenomenon is also something more. "Politics is, more and more, a politics of the body and of life: biopolitics. The body forms the new basis for political identity and so bare life comes to stand at the centre of political life and our culture." The politics of health care, abortion, terrorist threats, assisted suicide, euthanasia, gender identity, and war all involve the political body's ability to interfere with the human body, and they are some of the most contentious issues of our day. In essence, the political body seeks to preserve life because it can retain no power over death. The political body has the power to cause death through force, is where its power ends. While alive, we are all subject to the political machinations of authority, but that all ends when we reach the End.[14] For instance, the Terri Schiavo controversy became a major political football game in both government and the media as lawyers, legislators, and experts debated whether or not Schiavo was "alive," or at least, "not dead." While Schiavo was still on machines that maintained her bodily functions, she remained a major cause for political wrangling, which objectified and bureaucratized her body. After she passed, however, her body was no longer a political cause and no longer subject to the state and the media. Our technology has allowed a blurring of the line between life and death. Artificial breathing machines, the ability to transplant organs, and the redefinition of death as "brain death" have all contributed to the belief that death can somehow be indefinitely postponed. The idea that our technology can deflect the inevitable and the latent desire for immortality has surreptitiously entered the political lexicon.

Death that is seen as political can also be seen as revolutionary. Society regularly makes martyrs out of those who have died, whether or not in the pursuit of politics. The shooting of Trayvon Martin in 2013 demonstrated how the death of a young man could be turned into a national political cause. More recently, another young man shot by police in Ferguson, Missouri, sparked a riot that has caused political leaders to descend on Missouri, and the media, on both the political right and left, to react with increasing vigor. Of course, the most disturbing and visible example of death as political revolution comes in the form of Islamic suicide bombers who kill themselves in an effort to attack political and religious enemies. Their disturbing sacrifice is then used as an example to be emulated by others who offer their deaths as a sacrifice for their revolution.

However, in our culture, death is seen as the ultimate object of fear, and it is this fear that causes the public to allow politicians and the government to claim greater and greater control in the name of staving off death. Noys correctly finds this in the modern culture of crisis in which fears and threats are presented as a cause for government action. "States of emergency are states when the normal operation of the law is suspended and new more extreme operations of power are permitted. If sovereign power has spread across our culture, then what has also spread is the state of emergency. No longer is this state exceptional but the exception has become permanent. Therefore we live in a state of permanent emergency."[15] This permanent state of emergency is one in which experts and the media fuel fear and impotent activism by "raising awareness." Facebook and Twitter "movements" result in no change to the actual reality of a situation; instead, they merely promote fear and the illusion of activism. It is, in effect, impotent. The media goes to the experts who, for reasons of self-aggrandizement or political and moral beliefs that supersede their dedication to objectivity and truth, fuel those fears and push for government intervention. The government, of course, will need the experts for the administration of the policies made to reduce the perceived threat, and politicians are happy to add to the fear of death and enact and promote policies as part of their immortal "legacy." We rely on a small troupe of Chicken Littles, each telling the world that the sky is falling, the earth is warming, markets are collapsing, diseases are spreading, and people are starving. They present the world of death as a great beast slouching toward your homes, when in reality, the beast is a kitten writ large by a media that functions like a funhouse mirror. The activists come out in droves attempting to give meaning to their lives under the specter of death. They call upon the government to intercede and take further control to alleviate the "crisis."

Thus, we are left with technology and experts as things to be both feared and venerated, criticized and celebrated as they feed into our fear of death and our longing for life. They present themselves as the ones in the position to both warn and save, to remind us of death's approach and to help us live indefinitely. They can be the cause of or the solution to the problem of death. And in a society that largely thinks of itself as capable of anything, solving the death dilemma is a horizon we are ever trying to reach. This brings us back to the *Immortalist* dilemma; if we discard our cell phones and cigarettes, our GMO foods and diet sodas, if we avoid the sun and eschew the dangers of travel, if we transplant our organs as they grow old and quit, can we prolong life or, perhaps, even cheat death? Can we use our technology and our knowledge to become gods?

Genius and computer pioneer Ray Kurzweil thinks we can, and he's not the only one. Kurzweil's life and work can largely be seen as an integration of technology with human consciousness, something known as *transhumanism*. His first introduction to the public was at age sixteen, when he revealed a computer he had designed that composed its own symphony, thereby transferring art to the realm of technology. His later companies and technologies included a device that read text, a synthesizer that perfectly mimicked a grand piano and other instruments, and an artificially intelligent financial analyst. In these and many other of his inventions, he has sought to use technology to enhance or even replace the work of the individual human conscience. Kurzweil believes in the Singularity, a coming time when the pace of technological development will exceed even human capability and machines will, for all intents and purposes, take over production and creation of new technologies. He also believes in a merger between humans and technology that will result in a man-machine synthesis. "What makes Kurzweil an outrage to some and an inspiration to others is that he is relentlessly and fiercely optimistic about these futures," wrote Joel Garreau in *Radical Evolution*. "He uses some charts and graphs to systematically portray a near future that to some seems indistinguishable from the Christian version of paradise. On top of everything else, he is convinced that medicine is moving sufficiently fast that any person who can stay healthy for the next 20 years may so benefit from the explosion in biological technology as to be immortal. He lays an extensive scientific, nonreligious, non–New Age case for personally planning to live for a thousand years."[16] Kurzweil also cofounded the Singularity University in California, which provides education and funding for various individuals and technologies that will help solve humanity's biggest problems.

Aubrey de Grey is the chief science officer of the Strategic Engineered Negligible Senescence (SENS) Research Foundation, a charity that is dedicated to funding and conducting research that will treat the diseases that cause aging. Aging is seen as the cumulative effect of mistakes in the functioning of our cells, which eventually ends in death. "Thinning skin, clouding eyes, muscles sapped of strength, heart disease, cognitive decline . . . all of the diseases and disabilities of aging flow from the inexorable degradation of the integrity of the cellular and molecular machinery that carries out the essential functions of our tissues," the website states. "And as this process continues, the body's increasingly desperate attempts to repair or compensate for the rising tide of damage become chronic and maladaptive, leading to self-perpetuating inflammation, oxidative stress, and other secondary metabolic aberrations that further impair our health."[17] Aging and death are not seen as inevitable to life, but rather as a by-product of a complex system interacting with both itself and the environment over an extended period of time. "Indeed, de Grey is confident that if we can figure out how to repair just seven bodily systems prone to breakdown—ranging from chromosomal mutations over time to protein junk accumulated from the cell disintegration that accompanies aging—there is no reason for any of us to die," wrote Charlotte Allen in the *Weekly Standard.*[18]

The desire for immortality is the subtext of much of our lives, whether through children and families, religion, fame and fortune, contributions to society, or the molding of society through politics (politicians constantly fretting over their "legacy"). In essence, it is the specter of death that drives much of our endeavor. Indeed, Ray Kurzweil and Aubrey de Grey, along with many others, have contributed vast amounts of information, money, research, and results to humanity through their quest for immortality. But society as a whole appears to be in denial of death. Perhaps the relatively easy life of developed Western democracies has so removed people from the everyday ordinariness of death that it comes to resemble something alien and wrong, whereas in underdeveloped and poverty-stricken nations, death remains a part of everyday life. We have tried to insulate ourselves from it while still knowing in the back of our collective mind that it awaits us all. In a sort of fetishization, we turn to experts, diets, herbs, pills, and lifestyles that are meant to postpone the end. And some have concluded that they will not even have to die. Our technology will save us, and we will become like gods.

In his response to *The Immortalist*, Ernest Becker's *The Denial of Death* analyzes the impact of the subconscious desire to live forever. Becker believes that Sigmund Freud got it wrong when he believed sexuality to be the underlying factor for our different neuroses. While Alan Harrington poses a paradise where many, if not all, of humanity's problems will be solved, Becker takes a different view. He poses that the idea of death strikes us as an absurdity because we know only life and cannot properly conceive of nonexistence. Human consciousness, by its very nature, creates the need for belief in a God or some kind of religious worldview. Those who seek to deny death also seek to deny the idea of life being transitory. The absurdity of death would be magnified one hundredfold if we could potentially live forever. Becker quotes Jacques Choron, author of *Death and Western Thought*, when he states, "The postponement of death is not a solution to the problem of the fear of death." Becker adds, "The smallest virus or the stupidest accident would deprive a man not of 90 years but of 900—and would be then 10 times more absurd. . . . If something is 10 times more absurd it is 10 times more threatening. In other words, death would be 'hyperfetishized' as a source of danger, and men in the utopia of longevity would be even less expansive and peaceful than they are today!"[19]

In other words, what would we be left with if we could live forever? We would be left with primitive belief systems meant to influence the workings of the world. Rather than end religious belief, it would multiply it a thousandfold. We would be afraid to move or act for fear that some accident might befall us and end our eternity. Just because we could live forever does not mean that we would. Death will always remain an antecedent to life, even "eternal life." Harrington acknowledged this possibility when he wrote, "Even when we no longer age and die, the need to worship some sort of mystery will undoubtedly remain. What symbols then will represent the Essential Mystery? This is impossible to forecast, but the children of eternity may worship variations of Luck, or That Which Cannot Be Controlled. There will be no point in worshipping anything else, since they will have everything else. . . . But Luck will be different: the only thing that can kill them, and for this reason they may go down on their knees before it."[20]

But this process has already begun; it began in the Enlightenment, and as knowledge and technology grow, so does the power of the experts. We worship them; we live their recommended lives and put faith in those who tell us that we can avoid the inevitable just a little bit longer. But, as Augustine pointed out in his *Confessions*, a life is like a spoken word; if it does not end, it has no meaning. It will never be relegated to the past as something completed—something that can be admired or despised, emulated or ridiculed. In essence, the very prospect of being immortal ensures that we will never live on in memory or influence; our immortality would be a denial of that very same immortality.

Ray Kurzweil, genius and master of technology, fears death. His father died at age fifty-one of diabetes, so Kurzweil, in his quest to live forever, goes to extraordinary lengths to ensure his longevity. He reportedly takes 250 pills a day to thwart death, many of them herbs and roots that have not been scientifically shown to have the effects advertised.[21] He has managed to subdue his own type 2 diabetes through his diet, exercise, and lifestyle changes, in essence seeking immortality through herbal talismans and potions. Even so, during the filming of the documentary *Transcendent Man*, which profiled Kurzweil among many other leading technologists, he had to be hospitalized due to a heart condition.

Kurzweil survived and continues his work, but his hospitalization was a heavy-handed reminder of the specter that hangs over us all, even over the most brilliant and optimistic among us. If experts believe they can solve the problems of the universe, they still remain subject to it and to the inevitable ebb and flow of life and death. The death of God and religion and their replacement by science and experts have not really changed latent human needs that are inherently part of the human condition; they only substituted new names for old ideas. Horror writer and literary cult figure Thomas Ligotti wrote, "Transhumanism is a secular retelling of the Christian rapture, and some of its true believers foresee it happening within the lifetime of many who are alive today, just as the early Christians believed in an impending Judgment Day."[22]

"When we are young," wrote Becker in the closing pages of his *Denial of Death*,

> we are often puzzled by the fact that each person we admire seems to have a different version of what life ought to be, what a good man is, how to live, and so on. If we are especially sensitive it seems more than puzzling, it is disheartening. What most people usually do is to follow one person's ideas and then another's depending on who it is that looms largest on one's horizon at the time. The one with the deepest voice, the strongest appearance, the most authority and success, is usually the one who gets our allegiance; and we try to pattern our ideals after him. . . . Each person thinks that he has the formula for triumphing over life's limitations and knows with authority what it means to be a man, and he usually tries to win a following for that particular patent. Today we know that people try so hard to win converts for their point of view because it is more than merely an outlook on life: it is an immortality formula.[23]

The experts speak with authority based on science, and we listen. They divulge secrets of longevity, health, healing, and immortality, and we can't help but hope that they may have the secret "fountain of youth" in their grasp. We have conquered things that appeared as major limitations in the past—space travel, splitting the atom, decoding the genome—so why should death be any different? Our lack of acceptance, however, comes at a price. And as the Baby Boomer generation approaches that end time, the effects of that repression may make itself more visible as we turn to the experts, to technology, and to modern talismans for the gift of eternal life.

8

media manipulation

No individual can obtain for himself the information needed for the intelligent discharge of his political responsibilities. . . . By enabling the public to assert meaningful control over the political process, the press performs a crucial function in effecting the societal purpose of the First Amendment . . . a cantankerous press, an obstinate press, a ubiquitous press must be suffered by those in authority in order to preserve the even greater values of freedom of expression and the right of the people to know.

—supreme court justice lewis f. powell

Ron Burgundy will read anything that is put on that teleprompter. And when I say anything, I mean anything.

—anchorman: the legend of ron burgundy

many of us are familiar with the old humorous image of the news anchorman dressed in shirt, tie, and sport coat but no pants. The camera focuses only on the upper half of his body to present a dapper, cool professional, while leaving out the fact that he has either forgotten his pants or simply refuses to wear them. It's a well-worn trope but one with an element of truth at its core: what's missing in television news is the full picture. This, of course, is unavoidable when working through a medium. The camera can capture only so much; it cannot beam the entire reality of any given situation straight into our living rooms. Similarly, when we look out the windows of our homes, we can see only a piece of the outdoors, not all of the outdoors that surrounds us. Some is necessarily hidden. However, in our current age of the twenty-four-hour media cycle, which copies itself continually through repetition, we are not given a window to the world, but rather a funhouse mirror. In their quest to be the first with a story, news outlets often neglect particular facts, get them completely wrong, knowingly manipulate stories in order to reinforce political opinions, or leave out inconvenient truths that may undermine their story. Media outlets copy one another, repeating the same stories gleaned from other news sources. Thus, one rather minor story can suddenly appear to be a major story. The media's playbook of preying on people's fears and anxieties in the modern world only serves to push their narrative toward alarmism, and their presentations of particular narratives spur public outrage that is sometimes unwarranted.

But the greatest effect the television media has over people is a kind of deification of both the presenters and the people they turn to for guidance. The face on the screen commands an audience of sometimes millions, so we infer that he or she must have some quality—some attribute that makes that individual worthy of attention, money, and influence. Similarly, we assign an amount of trust and authority to such a television personality because he or she is *somebody*; fame can cause a loss of critical analysis. Likewise, the experts presented in the news media are given similar deference: "This guy must know what he's talking about because he is being interviewed by this newspaper" (or news program or website).

Tossed into this cultural mix is the rise of Internet reporting and the continuing decline of print newspapers. In essence, the field of news coverage is virtually limitless, and our ability to pick and choose our stories based on preconceived ideas is ensured. Believe that the CIA planned 9/11? There's a news website for that. Believe that the United States is becoming a tyrannical oligarchy? There's a news website for that too. The democratization of information has both positive and negative effects. It acts as a check on the powers and influence of large media organizations, which is a good thing. However, on the flip side, the Internet also allows for truth to be supplanted by hoax, lies, and rumors. In the illusory world of the net, sometimes satirical news sites, such as the Onion, can be taken seriously by both viewers and fellow news media.

Believe it or not, this is not the first time in our nation's history when the news media has been fractured into a kaleidoscope of multiple versions of distorted reality. At the inception of our country, the establishment of freedom of expression meant that outlets could publish virtually anything they wanted. "Most newspapers were then violently partisan, and they resented attempts to induce them to publish materials favorable to, or slanted in the direction of, the opposition party," wrote the late Frederick Siebert, author of *Freedom of the Press in England*. This partisanship and fractured truth-telling led newspapers and reporters to regulate themselves in an attempt to garner readers. Rather than just appealing to a small group of readers with the same political affiliations, newspapers could appeal to the masses by reporting objectively and relegating their opinions to the editorial pages.[1] Thus, the idea of objective reporting was thought to be the best way to give the citizen a window to the world.

However, as time passed and the world changed, merely objective reporting began to change; reporters, journalists and news outlets felt they had a responsibility to the public to inform them, thus enabling them to make knowledgeable choices with regard to public life. "Chiefly of their own volition, publishers began to link responsibility with freedom," wrote author and professor Theodore Peterson. "They formulated codes of ethical behavior, and they operated their media with some concern for the public good—the public good as they regarded it, at least."[2] Thus, in deciding what was "good" for the public, the press began to make moral judgments about the information they presented and the manner in which they presented it. Today we have cable news outlets that are considered liberal, such as MSNBC, and those considered conservative, such as Fox News. These ideological distinctions are made, not by the news company themselves, but rather by what information they choose to distribute to their audiences and the range of opinions they offer in the form of commentary. Often, commentary and reporting overlap. The advent of the Internet and its various blogs and websites means that one can subscribe to a view of the world that is not predicated on truth and objective reality, but rather on a moral position and fixed ideology.

This is not necessarily new. Certainly the addition of the web has increased the fracturing and creation of news based on moral and ideological goals, but the idea that the public was being sold a false bill of goods, particularly in the area of mass media, developed quite quickly during the 1950s with the creation of mediums such as radio and television that were able to reach millions of people simultaneously.

Gabriel Marcel, writing in France following the German occupation in World War II, wrote about the effect of propaganda and opinion making on the public: "It is . . . broadly noteworthy that even the sense of truth cannot fail gradually and unconsciously to be destroyed in those who assume the task of manipulating opinion."[3] In discussing the influence of radio, he made it clear that he considered this a "technique of degradation." Marcel believed he was witnessing the disappearance of the individual and the emergence of mass society. "Do we not find, both on the world scale and at the level of national existence, that the development of communications entails a growing uniformity imposed on our customs and habits?"[4]

The manipulation of information through mass communication and the development of mass society during the '50s led Daniel J. Boorstin to write the book *The Image: A Guide to Pseudo-Events in America* in 1961. Boorstin believed that the media culture was being dominated by inauthentic events designed to create drama where there was none in order to reach and hold viewers in suspense. Political events, press releases, and world news were presented in a concerted effort to be more intelligible, and thus more reassuring; they could be repeated again and again and have vested, moneyed interests. Men and women could stand at the office water cooler talking about pseudo-events that had been manufactured to be newsworthy but that were not authentic glimpses of reality, only bits of political theater. Thus the pseudo-events created a "common discourse" based on false representation that led to further pseudo-events.[5] "Pseudo-events thus lead to emphasis on pseudo-qualifications," said Boorstin. "Again the self-fulfilling prophecy. If we test presidential candidates by their talents on TV quiz performances, we will, of course, choose presidents for precisely these qualifications. In a democracy, reality tends to conform to the pseudo-event. Nature imitates art."[6] Christopher Hedges, nearly fifty years later, wrote, "A public that can no longer distinguish between truth and fiction is left to interpret reality through illusion. Random facts or obscure bits of data and trivia are used either to bolster illusion and give it credibility or to discard them if they interfere with the message. . . . When opinions cannot be distinguished from facts, when there is not a universal standard to determine truth in law, in science, in scholarship, or in reporting the events of the day, when the most valued skill is the ability to entertain, the world becomes a place where lies become true, where people can believe what they want to believe."[7] To that brilliantly worded paragraph, I would add that people can believe what they want to believe and find an information source on television or on the Internet to reinforce that belief. In the postmodern world, discarding the belief in truth, logic, and rationality in favor of irrationality and relativism has resulted in an "anything goes" intellectual culture—which is, essentially, not an intellectual culture at all.

In essence, we have moved backward, not forward. The progress of history has only the illusion of moving forward; humanity, however, can fall in and out of primitive states.

The influence of illusion and mass media comes under attack from both the right and left of the political spectrum. Conservative writers regularly lash out at the liberal media, and leftists such as Noam Chomsky attack the media as offering nothing more than propaganda approved by moneyed interests. In Chomsky's view, nothing becomes news or makes headlines unless the powers that be want it to be news.

The most extreme version of the illusion in mass media comes from philosopher Jean Baudrillard, who wrote that the world has become a simulated version of reality—all of nature imitating art, everything filtered through so much opinion and interpretation that it no longer has any objective truth. "Is any given bombing in Italy the work of leftist extremists, or extreme-right provocation," he asks, to prove his point, "or a centrist mise-en-scene to discredit all extreme terrorists and to shore up its own failing power, or again, is it a police-inspired scenario and a form of blackmail to public-security? All of this is simultaneously true, and the search for proof, indeed the objectivity of the facts does not put an end to this vertigo of interpretation. That is, we are in a logic of simulation, which no longer has anything to do with a logic of facts and an order of reason."[8]

Quite similarly, everything reported in our postmodern mass society is subject to interpretation and fantasy. Following the mass murder of twenty-six schoolchildren and teachers at the Sandy Hook Elementary school, conspiracy theories began to pop up that the media was covering something up or that the tragedy was staged to push an antigun agenda. Many of the conspiratorial ideas were born out of the way the media covered the tragedy; there were mistakes and numerous guesses that proved to be wrong in the long run. In truth, it was just a voracious and overeager media that felt the need to fill time through speculation based on few available facts while trying to give the illusion of knowledgeable commentary. They reported erroneously on the types of weapons used, the number of shooters involved, the number of dead and injured, and then named the perpetrator's brother as the shooter, among many other departures from the truth.[9] It was clumsy and in poor taste, but it has become a regular feature of news reporting—reporting on rumor and speculation. While journalism may say it seeks the truth, such a feat is nearly impossible when a twenty-four-hour news cycle has news agencies clambering over each other to be the first to report anything, regardless of its truth. As Marcel, Boorstin, Hedges, and Baudrillard have said, the truth becomes impossible to ascertain when everything is clouded in rumor, superstition, and ideology.

Of course, there have been conspiracy mongers in American life since the Kennedy assassination, but in the postmodern Internet age, such ideas have been pushed into hyperdrive and infect all aspects of news coverage. In all this, one thing remains certain: no one trusts the media to actually give them the true story.

So what does this have to do with experts? The media, be it television, newspaper, magazine, radio, or the Internet, is the vehicle through which experts express their opinions and supposedly give us facts and science by which we are to run our lives. Therefore, the same illusion, the same funhouse-mirror effect, goes into making the expert as goes into the news presenters. In fact, this is even truer of the experts who are brought in to provide knowledge that is unavailable even to the news presenter. The experts are imbued with an authority granted them by virtue of their credentials, their employment, or various studies they may have conducted or panels on which they may have served. However, their greatest authority comes by virtue of the medium through which they are presented to the public. The fact that they are on television or sought out by journalists gives weight to their opinion as opposed to that of any other person who may be just as qualified. The expert has, in effect, been chosen by those who offer a window to the world, to bequeath to the public his knowledge. By choosing one particular expert over another, the media has, in essence, chosen one voice to rise above the others, which effectively gives that expert more authority, more credibility, and more deference than would otherwise be due.

"Within the last century, and especially since about 1900, we seem to have discovered the processes by which fame is manufactured. Now, at least in the United States, a man's name can become a household word overnight. The Graphic Revolution suddenly gave us, among other things, the means of fabricating well-knowness," Boorstin wrote. "Discovering that we . . . can so quickly and so effectively give a man 'fame,' we have willingly been misled into believing that fame—well-knowness—is still a hallmark of greatness."[10]

The selection of this one voice for fame and recognition can often tell us more about the position of those presenting the news than any real glimpse of reality. Edward Herman and Noam Chomsky wrote that experts are brought on to reinforce the official positions, which they call a form of "propaganda": "The propaganda model also incorporates other closely related factors such as the ability to complain about the media's treatment of the news . . . to provide 'experts' to confirm the official slant on the news, and to fix the basic principles and ideologies that are taken for granted by media personnel and the elite, but are often resisted by the general population."[11] Case in point: Following the revelation that a man in the United States had been diagnosed with Ebola after he flew into the country on a flight from West Africa, the media was suddenly deluged with people wondering why the United States was still permitting flights and individuals from Ebola-stricken nations to enter the country. This was after the public had been repeatedly assured that the United States was not in danger of an Ebola outbreak. In trying to stem public outrage and increase public confidence, experts working for various federal and global government organizations were quoted ad nauseam in the press and cited by the president and his administration as to why certain seemingly simple precautions would not actually help, but somehow make things worse. The basic argument coming from World Health Organization and CDC officials was that a travel ban would make the outbreak worse because it would limit the help that could be supplied to the Ebola-ravaged countries. Of course, this official reason for not enforcing a travel ban ignored the fact that we were not helping in any official capacity to stop the outbreak and that most of the doctors working to stop the disease were missionary volunteers. It also ignored the fact that imposing a travel ban on the public was not the equivalent of banning military and medical aid from reaching those countries and assisting them in trying to control the epidemic.[12]

During the media coverage there were dissenting opinions from doctors who accused the CDC and WHO of making too little out of the potential for Ebola infection, but since these were not "official" sources and "official" experts, the basic narrative that played out was that a travel ban was unnecessary and even harmful. Perhaps one of the most outrageous reasons for not banning travel was that the United States' medical infrastructure was prepared to handle and control Ebola; outrageous because our ability to control it still meant that some people would be infected, and they would probably not be comforted much by the idea that it wouldn't spread much further.

Voices from professionals who dissent from the official government narrative are given short shrift precisely *because* they are not being used for the official government narrative. Furthermore, the government can co-opt those dissenting voices and draw them into the fold, at which point they become the officials to whom the media turns to obtain the official position. "The dominance of official sources is weakened by the existence of highly respectable unofficial sources that give dissident views with great authority," wrote Herman and Chomsky. "This problem is alleviated by 'co-opting the experts'—i.e., putting them on the payroll as consultants, funding their research, and organizing think tanks that will hire them directly, and help disseminate their messages. In this way bias may be structured, and the supply of experts may be skewed in the direction desired by the government and 'the market.'"

These authors also cited Henry Kissinger, who once stated that experts are "those who have a vested interest in commonly held opinions; elaborating and defining its consensus at a high level has, after all, made him an expert."[13] Likewise, Hofstadter wrote that the expert becomes subject to power when he or she becomes a part of it. "The characteristic failure of the expert who advises the powerful is an unwillingness to bring his capacity for independent thought to bear as a source of criticism. He may lose his capacity for detachment from power by becoming absorbed in its point of view."[14] Fame, power, and influence can be a temptation to even our best and brightest. These factors, combined with a belief that they are the most informed and intelligent (a status bestowed upon them by virtue of the government and media co-opting them for work and commentary), can make for an arrogance and unwillingness on the part of the experts to either speak their true minds or admit that they are wrong or do not have the answers.

Kissinger's remark about the expert simply reinforcing the reigning opinion is similar to Frank J. Tipler's criticism of the peer-review process for scientific papers, which is, of course, how an expert makes a name for him- or herself. The problem with all of this is a reliance on consensus and the idea that the more people agree with an idea, the more right it is. Essentially, this is the political idea of democracy, but one that does not translate well to the realm of the sciences or problem solving.

In an effort to give the official narrative, which is often the most easily accessible because the officials gladly make themselves available to journalists and reporters, the media is complicit in whatever political machinations are at play in the government. They choose whom to make famous and influential and whom to label a crank or a crackpot, and generally, these selections follow the official government narrative. Implicit in this kowtowing is the belief that the United States government is, in every way, the most knowledgeable, best prepared, and best able to handle a situation. Indeed, in some cases, it is the only entity with the power to handle particular crises, but that doesn't mean they are handled intelligently or with the public's goals in mind. The government's various elected representatives and bureaucrats have an intrinsic need to maintain their status of power, and thus every act is tinged with politics, deceptions, and inherent self-interest.

The use of the government's official experts in the making and reporting of news sets the terms by which the media discusses the issues at hand. While there will always be moderate fluctuations, the official line is the measure by which media outlets and the public determine the validity of other reports. The public often has a limited capacity for determining the true nature of a situation such as, say, the Ebola outbreak. The average Joe or Jane isn't going on a fact-finding mission to Africa to determine the true nature of the disease, so instead, they absorb the media reports, which use as their baseline the official government stance based on a variety of political considerations. So, if the public sees the report of a doctor, virologist, or reporter claiming that the

CDC and WHO are lying, exaggerating, or minimizing the danger of the Ebola virus, it can be quickly dismissed. "[T]he 'societal purpose' of the media is to inculcate and defend the economic, social, and political agenda of privileged groups that dominate the domestic society and the state. The media serve this purpose in many ways: though selection of topics, distribution of concerns, framing of issues, filtering of information, emphasis and tone, and by keeping debate within the bounds of acceptable premises."[15]

In essence, the media is a carnival house of mirrors, showing images in seemingly infinite regression, and an echo chamber, where the terms and lines and talking points are repeated back to each other again and again. The twenty-four-hour media machine has become less a window to reality than a distortion designed to create real-life drama. And as this drama unfolds, we can find two subtexts of fearmongering and the echoing of officialdom; the public has much to fear, and the only way we can rest assured of our safety is through the increase in government control and influence.

In the previous chapter, we examined how our fear of death influences our reliance on experts. We seek the experts because they appear to have answers to life's innumerable anxieties and problems. To properly implement their ideas and controls, we must turn to government, the only entity capable of providing the funds and expertise necessary to stave off these dangers. The media acts as the echo chamber; its trade depends on frightening news in order to attract viewers. They then choose experts either to emphasize the danger posed to the citizens, offer solutions through government action, or offer calming words of assurance that the government has everything under control. Herman and Chomsky's assertion that the media benefits those in control rings true in every case; the ultimate goal is expanded control. Rarely (if ever) will you hear an expert in the media say that there actually is no problem, there is no solution—government or otherwise—or that it is a matter of individual responsibility. Instead we are urged to impotent activism, "awareness," fear, and a search for government intervention.

While Chomsky himself is a rather notorious leftist, his assertions have found expression in the conservative and political right. While he may decry the effects of capitalism on the media and assert that corporate entities are in control, manipulating government and media, conservative writers such as Mark Steyn have similar assertions with the idea that what is needed is less government and more capitalism. Both writers assert that the true nature of the problem is much more deeply ingrained in the political system and human nature in the form of groupthink.

Fostering groupthink, a spirit of the times or zeitgeist, is the goal of propaganda. The effect of groupthink is to foster conformity and consensus and reject the individual—the different. Beginning in the '50s with the rise of radio and television, the idea of "mass society" began to take hold, spurring the work of writers such as Boorstin, Hofstader, and Marcel. Mass society, effected through technology, has increasingly led toward the gathering of consensus and the degradation of the individual. And in a media that is an echo chamber for government and corporate interests, the very philosophy upon which the United States was founded is affected. Marcel wrote, "But we get a much more dangerous situation when propaganda moves out of its original orbit; when it ceases to be exercised on behalf of a number of competing movements and parties within the State, and instead is taken over by the State itself; when the State, in short, begins to behave as if it were itself a movement or a party."[16] Marcel may have been writing in the wake of the Nazi Party and World War II, but the lessons learned need not be limited to murderous political movements. The idea is that when government and the medium through which it reaches the public begin to propagandize for their own sakes, they become the means by which they grow themselves rather than growing by any true desire of the people they represent. It is a usurpation of the democracy.

The media fosters fear and offers experts with solutions that only government can enact through its own growth. The technological progress which has enabled television and the Internet has not had the effect of creating an informed citizenry as much as it has created mass movements and groupthink. Marcel wrote about the effects of radio; one cannot help but think of how these effects must be multiplied in this time of mass communication technology. "A Hitler or a Mussolini, speaking into the microphone, could really seem invested with the divine privilege of being everywhere at once," he said. "In theory, of course, it is conceivable that this privilege of ubiquity, if it were at the service of a genuinely universal mode of thinking, could confer on that mode of thinking a wonderful and almost providential range of impact . . . our most recent and most wretched experience shows us that the principles on which official propagandists put most emphasis are, in the vast majority of cases, a pitiful camouflage for their concealed purposes, which are marked by the most cynical imperialism."[17]

Marcel warned about the fast-paced march of technology without mankind's concurrent spiritual development: "Every kind of outward technical progress ought to be balanced in man by an effort at inner conquest, directed towards an ever greater self-mastery. Unhappily, what we still have to ask is whether for an individual who every day takes more and more advantage of the facilities which technical progress has put at his disposal, such an effort at self-mastery does not become more and more difficult."[18] There are few places where such an imbalance between technology and self-mastery is on display as in both news and social media. The development of such interconnectedness and instant access as we have on Facebook and Twitter, combined with the anonymity of the Internet, has allowed the worst of humanity to be paraded before our eyes. We may all be able to interact instantaneously, but that does not mean that we have the self-control to be able to handle such instantaneous interaction. On Facebook, Twitter, blogs, and the reader comment sections of online news media, the very worst that mankind has to offer is on display. A man or woman (or worse, an adolescent) can, at the slightest irritation, single out an individual online and issue abuse and insults, get others to play along, and ultimately threaten and berate someone with whom he or she may never have come in contact in real life. In extreme instances, this has led to suicide, the end of marriages due to infidelity, and the termination of careers through thoughtless tweets or posts online. Worse, social media can be used to fuel rumor and outrage, whereas in the past it would have taken a much more Herculean effort, one incorporating genuine sentiment, to get such results. The anonymity of the online community and the intercon-nectedness result in a kind of spirit—a groupthink—which can have disastrous effects. While in theory such interconnectedness of mankind could foster feelings of oneness and togetherness, it has instead brought division and turmoil and the ability of such turmoil to reach a massive audience. ISIS beheads people and broadcasts it via online video, which has the capacity to reach the world with their evil, and people begin joining the movement, even from countries and cultures that ISIS has targeted. The technology of the Internet allows for not only the spread of humanity but also for the spread of insanity through ideology, rumor, and dissolution of truth.

Arnold J. Toynbee, in his *Study of History*, argues that technological advancement is not the sign of a progressing society, but rather some-thing that can make cultural and psychological issues in that society more acute. He uses the metaphor of a road "thronged with primi-tive wheeled vehicles: wheel-barrows and rickshaws and ox-carts and dog-carts, with a stage coach . . . and a foot propelled bicycle here and there as a portent of things to come." Toynbee points out that on this crowded road of primitive vehicles, collisions do occur; but due to the nature of the vehicles involved, no one is very badly injured. However, fast-forward a few centuries to the age of motorized travel: "On this road the problems of speed and haulage have been solved, as is testified by the motor-lorry with its train of trucks that comes lumbering along with more momentum than a charging element and by the sports car that goes whizzing past with the swiftness of a bee or bullet. . . . Hence on this latter-day road the problem is no longer technological but psychological. The old challenge of physical distance has been trans-muted into a new challenge of human relations between drivers who, having learned how to annihilate space, have thereby put themselves in constant danger of annihilating one another."[19] The speed, interconnectedness, and omnipresence of modern media have shined a light on the psychological and cultural problems that we face as a nation. Our problems do not lie in the technology but in ourselves and our ability to use restraint and principled reason when anonymity and fame, power and groupthink are at our fingertips.

Politicians, news media organizations, publishers, and corporations can now immediately reach the public with whatever happens to pop into their heads and push whatever agenda they want. While the idea of such ability seems as if it would make our window on the world clearer, it has had the exact opposite effect. Our view of the world has become even more clouded with competing versions of reality.

Who doesn't desire safety? It is one of the principle motivators of civilization—to come together in an effort to protect against the elements and predators and to continue the propagation of the species. We build houses and have families, send our children to schools, and listen to the best and brightest minds tell us how to remain safe in the modern world. Who would dare to speak out against following the ideas of a learned man or woman of science who is advising us on ways to keep our children safe, prolong our lives, preserve our oceanfront houses from the effects of climate change, and increase our stock portfolios? In this question there is a morality, the violation of which often earns ridicule and consternation, if not just a casual ignoring by the interconnected masses. To question the validity of the media's experts, to question how they achieve their ultimate goal of relinquishing individual and personal responsibility to the control of government and the opinion of the group, becomes a violation of the group's (or individual's) morality that cannot be tolerated. In essence, to challenge these assumptions—this morality—is viewed as speaking out against safety and in support of death, destruction, and chaos, and mass society does not tolerate it well, even if it is in defense of individuality and democracy.

In the wake of the first U.S. citizen diagnosed with the Ebola virus, there appeared a column in the *Washington Post* by RoseAnn DeMoro, executive director of National Nurses United, the largest nursing labor union in the country. DeMoro wrote, "We know what works: a federal agency with the authority to ensure local, state and national coordination in response to outbreaks. In such an empowered public health system, local health officials are assured of having the resources to identify the source of an outbreak, isolate and treat the sick, and follow up with those who have had close contact with the sick. Only greater integration and the authority of a public health system with national, uniform standards can protect Americans."[20] Thus, the media provides both the problem and the solution with ever-expanding governmental powers to combat the threat of Ebola. The same can be said of terrorism, school shootings, poverty, hunger . . . take your pick. The solution is meant to encourage a single-mindedness—a national, if not international, cohesion of togetherness under the blanket of security provided by the only corporation able to do so—government. It is not something that needs to be forced upon society. Rather, stoked by media fear, rumor, superstition, and a dissolution of truth, the public will ask for this comfort, this security of knowing that the official story is what *is* and all there *is*. They are given a sense of truth, but it is only an illusion. The future is not Orwell's *1984*, but rather Huxley's *Brave New World*. The modern media world is not for the individual, but rather for the group. It encourages the public to think with one mind, and any effort to speak against the consensus is met with moral outrage in the form of political correctness or deferring to the expert opinion in order to quiet the individuals, the primitives, the backwards of society, who will be left on the "wrong side of history."

Not knowing what is true or what to think, we turn to the experts, believing that the most educated, informed, and objective among us will be able to offer a glimpse of truth in the turmoil of competing stories. Is global warming man-made or not? Are we in danger of an Ebola outbreak? Is the economy actually getting better? Will this cell phone give me a tumor? In our media-induced anxiety of the ever-present threat of death lurking around the corner and our need to believe that we *know* what is going on, we turn to the exalted experts streamed to us via television, Internet, or print media. But as we turn to them for answers, we begin to realize that they are as handicapped by their humanity as the rest of us, and that for all their knowledge and technology, life offers more than can be competently computed. Our error comes in marveling at mankind's intellectual prowess but failing to understand its limitations. Technological and mechanical abilities do not translate to a greater understanding of the human condition, nor do they provide answers to the great mysteries of life. Our ability in the past to answer questions through science such as, "Where does lightning come from?" leads us to believe that such questions as, "Why are we here?" "What does the future hold?" or "How can we stop killing each other?" can also be answered through this same science and technology. But they are not, and this truth is becoming more and more evident as time and technology march forward.

9

pseudo-reality prevails! now what?

At times, Diotima would try to blame a materialistic age that had turned the world into an evil, purposeless game in which atheism, socialism, and positivism left no freedom for a person with a rich inner life to rise to true being; but even this was not often of much use.

—the man without qualities

This was my wretched attempt to understand our blankness in the face of God's enormity. This is what I respected about God. He keeps his secret. And I tried to approach God through his secret, his unknowability. Maybe we can know God through love or prayer or through visions or through LSD but we can't know him through the intellect.

—don delillo, underworld

large section of the novel *The Man Without Qualities* is titled "Pseudo-Reality Prevails!" and, considering the ideas and examples we have examined in this book, I believe it would be safe to say that this is the case in our current society. The warnings from writers such as Musil, Boorstin, and Marcel were noted but unheeded in society's inexorable drift toward the technology age. In this new era of mass society, mass media, and mass communication, our world has suddenly been made much larger, and instantaneous information that encompasses the entire globe has to be organized, analyzed, and distributed to the public. With this development we've seen the rise of the media's experts, men and women who are in the know and, despite all evidence to the contrary, in control. With our best and brightest in positions of power, the public can rest assured that they are safe and secure, can know how to stave off the newly realized dangers of the technological age, and can empower the experts and the media to keep us informed of various dangers and keep us safe through the implementation of their ideas. Unfortunately, however, this tendency toward groupthink based on expert opinion has led us down a road that has caused this media illusion to flicker and fade, occasionally laying bare for the world the chaotic possibilities and mysteries of life. The all-too-human limitations of the experts began to be recognized by the public. Our only recourse to "deal with" these limitations (we believed) was better technology, more education, more expertise, and more media coverage of the events in real time. In the words of George Ball, onetime advisor to President Kennedy, who forewarned of intervention in Vietnam, "It was like taking a drink. The effect wears off and you take another."[1]

There is an inherent, human need to feel that we know what is going on and what to expect from the future, but any profession of such knowing is an illusion. This illusion is conferred upon us by our experts who, with the backing of the higher education system and the fame and recognition bestowed upon them by the media for being, well, famous and recognized, impart to the public their knowledge so that everyone can have the benefit of seeing things the same way. It is an effort toward one national mind and a melding between the people and the government that represents them. But this tendency toward groupthink can be costly, resulting in unnecessary panic in some cases and an ill-informed public action in others. More insidious, however, is the general feeling of unease that rests like a fog on our national conscience—the constant worry about our health and safety, with a governmental security blanket offered as reassurance.

As indicated at the beginning of this work, there are undoubtedly people in science and politics and world affairs who have access to a vast amount of information that is not available to the public—but information does not equal wisdom. Sometimes a person mired in information will fail to take in the larger picture in favor of bits of information sewn together into whatever design best fits his or her personal beliefs and biases. It is when these men and women of science reach outside their professions and move into the realm of morals and values that they become one of us, because the understanding of right and wrong, moral and immoral, and the values we revere are things that are accessible to all citizens regardless of education or expertise. In violating the boundaries of their professions, experts have tried to become philosopher kings in the style of Plato's *Republic* without realizing that Plato's vision was one of a brutal totalitarian regime which even he knew could never be realized.

So we are confronted with men and women who, in their own minds, have such a rational grasp on the complexities and chaos of the world that they can direct the masses to move in accordance with their wishes as a conductor directs an orchestra. However, when their numbers, statistics, and ideas don't pan out as they would like, many are compelled to make minor changes—tweak the numbers a bit—with full knowledge that few, if any, in the public realm will be equipped to analyze or dispute their findings. The only people who can accurately dispute an expert's figures are other experts, and we are then left with a conundrum; who do we listen to? As we have seen, political lines have been drawn in the sciences, so it is no longer merely a question of who is right, but rather a question of politics and ideology that is assigned to the experts themselves. In essence, as we said earlier, we make one a "good guy" and the other a "bad guy." If one expert says that global warming is a coming catastrophe and the other says that it is not a big deal, then good and bad lines have been drawn. One expert is trying to save the world while the other is content to let people drown in the second iteration of Noah's flood.

History and evidence show that experts can, in fact, be bought by special interests, but these special interests need not be limited to greedy corporations. Once we have confirmed that science is for sale, then we can conclude that it is for sale to everyone, including the government. Implicit in the corporate-experts-versus-government-experts dichotomy is the idea that one is good and the other bad. This black-and-white thinking ignores the complexity of life and the interests that move people and entities to act. Governments desire more control, more popularity, and more power. Corporations desire more sales, more money, and less competition. Each desires more groupthink. Wading through the implications of experts' analyses and recommendations can be a full-time job, and most people have neither the time nor the interest. We are more concerned with the major fundamentals of life— right and wrong, good and bad, in essence, how to live our lives; and when it comes to these basic questions, experts are of little help. They may have information, but even if the information is genuine and not subjected to their personal ideology or their sponsor's goals, they still cannot tell us whether the implications of the use of that information are right or wrong. As we discussed in chapter 3, the discovery of natural selection as the means by which nature evolved does not mean that we, as a civilization, should start acting in accordance with nature, preserving the lives of only the fittest and allowing the weak and sick to die off in droves in order to foster the rise of a great race. Hitler had his own natural selection ideas. The application of pure, logical science to the human realm without human values and morals results is an evil that mankind cannot abide. When discussing how we should live our lives and form our society, experts and science have a limited role. Science tells us what has been and what is, not what should be. That is a question of morals and values and one that is answerable only by the individuals of that society. Any attempt to corrupt or coerce that dialogue through "expertise," "facts," and "science" is a violation of the boundaries of those very ideas and, in and of itself, misleading.

Albert Camus wrote that to be human, we must give up acting like gods. Indeed, the belief in our own godlike abilities has been the dominant factor in the rise of the expert since the Enlightenment of the eighteenth century. Science has afforded us much technology and growth, better medicine, more comfortable lives, and the ability to interact on a global scale, but it would not appear that our technological prowess has been matched by any spiritual mastery, as Gabriel Marcel lamented in his work. Similarly, historian Arnold J. Toynbee, in his review of the history of all civilization, wrote, "In an ever-increasing number of Western minds, as physical science has extended the frontiers of its intellectual empire over one field of existence after another—until at last, in our own day, when science is laying claim to the whole of the spiritual as well as the material universe, we see God the Mathematician fading right out into God the Vacuum."[2] In this vacuum where God once was, we have placed our scientific and technological abilities.

A colleague of mine, when discussing this work, made the point that the world was just as big and bloody a mess before the Enlightenment, when religion was at the center of society, as it is now that science and technology are at the center of our society. This is true, but it is no excuse for pretending that "progress" has been made. Humanity supplanted one God with another and continued on the same trajectory; we have changed very little and are still searching for the answers to questions once asked of the clergy, hoping that science will give us better answers. But to attribute godlike status to science or technology is folly. Men and women of science remain just that—men and women—prone to the same temptations, ideologies, follies, and limitations as you or me. Their ability to speak in technological terms or professional lingo, their degrees and letters after their names, do not exclude them from their imperfect humanity.

Of all the qualities that may be lacking in experts, the greatest of these is humility. Indeed, this lack of humility is not limited to scientists and experts but is something that has infected all of society. In this Google generation, where information that accords with your ideology is accessible with a few swipes of your thumb on a smartphone, the idea of saying, "I don't know," or "There is no answer," has gone out of vogue. Even more out of vogue is the idea of offering personal choice and responsibility as a possible answer to some of these questions. In this day and age of information access, we believe that we can find reasons for everything—that we can find the physics of society and humanity through studies, theories, and social "laws." But no such laws exist. Many have tried to find them and all have failed. In the face of such immense complexity as that offered to us by society, the human mind reaches its limits. Some believe these limitations can be overcome through technology—supercomputers and whatnot—but our technology is only as good as the man or woman wielding it.

With this in mind, there are certain precautions we can take when trying to digest the deluge of information, studies, and experts that assails us every day. First and foremost is learning to separate the moral argument from the scientific. Science explains what is and what has been, but when the argument moves into the realm of what should be, it ventures into the realm of morals and values, and no amount of data can make a moral argument the correct one. This is a judgment that is available to all men and women and one that is not accessible to the realm of science. Human beings, at their core, are faith-based creatures, and faith is ultimately irrational. It is not fully explainable; it is not subject to equations and psychology. Indeed, we often cannot explain the roots of our beliefs ourselves much less have someone else purport to explain them for us. One example that often comes to mind is the question of whether or not the United States should have used the atom bomb on Japan to end the Second World War. Science was able to give us the bomb, break open the atom, and deliver it in such a way as to create the desired amount of destruction. But science could not tell us whether or not it was right to use it. The answer to that question is based on individual beliefs that cannot be narrowed down to a scientifically defensible position. Rather, we base our personal answer to this question on an irrational core of belief, emotion, and faith. Weighing the complexities of such a question, men and women place greater or lesser value on a number of different considerations that ultimately cannot be calculated and are specific to each individual.

In separating the scientific argument from the moral argument, we must recognize that there exists a duality in people that must be maintained in balance. Men and women are not fully rational; they do not act in accord with set laws and principles the way that, say, gravity functions. Nor should they give themselves over to complete irrationality, following only their feelings and beliefs to the point of acting only on those considerations. To do so is insanity. To assert that one's beliefs are absolutely true is to replace faith with the illusion of knowledge and fact. Faith is the ability to say, "I believe this is true, but I do not know this is true." Those who treat their faith as fact can easily succumb to insane actions, such as flying jetliners into buildings. Likewise, those who believe that the rationality of science is wholly applicable to people venture into insanity, ignoring the implications and moral shortcomings of their actions.

This is a difficult line to tread in a complex world, but the ability to admit *I don't know* and to practice humility in the face of technological prowess is a step toward a more practiced and cautious consideration of ideas, science, facts, and technology.

The second precaution is to better understand how science works. Science is often a dialogue in which men and women offer hypotheses and evidence, conduct studies, and reach conclusions, only to be debated by peers and colleagues who offer criticism, research that refutes the previous study, and so on. Therefore, a study reported in the news is not the end of the story but, rather, a line of dialogue in an ongoing conversation in search of the truth, which is rarely attainable, particularly in dealing with extremely complex systems such as human interaction, society, and health. Thus, sudden activist campaigns in these realms are often premature, leading to public frustration and distrust in science itself. For instance, in my own lifetime eggs have gone from being bad for your health to good twice over. These dramatic reversals make all of science look questionable, but this is not the fault of the public. Rather, it is the fault of impotent activists in both the scientific community and the government sphere who attempt to create a latent anxiety in the public—to perform social "good" through instilling fear and offering "education." When their claims blow up in their faces, they simply move on to the next cause or deny that they were ever wrong in the first place.

Understanding that science is a dialogue, not only between scientists but between scientists and life, is a good step toward acknowledging that studies and their findings do not necessarily constitute conclusive evidence for one position or another and that their conclusions are subject to dramatic change. Professionals readily admit this fact, while experts and media figures often do not.

Part of that dialogue is listening to those who dissent with the prevailing opinion. As indicated before, often those who turn out to be correct in the end are the voices that were overlooked by the "consensus" of experts. A good rule of thumb is that if everyone is looking in one direction, it would be prescient for someone to turn around and at least glance in the opposite direction to gain a more complete grasp of questions, possibilities, and potential answers.

A third precaution is to recognize and respect the boundaries between theoretical and practical knowledge. Many experts make their proclamations based on theories and ideas that have not been proved in real life, or they expand on limited study data in order to "verify" their theories. In essence, experts should really have to prove that their recommendations have merit in practical life before the public is expected to listen. Trust must be earned and expertise must be demonstrable when making sweeping proclamations on how society should be or how we should live our lives. One of the biggest questions we can ask when presented with studies and expert theories is, so what? Many of these studies are completely inapplicable to the average American's daily life or merely conclude what most people already regard as common sense based on experience.

One of the theorists' biggest arguments is that often science is not based on what would appear to be common sense or experience. This is an argument stemming from Einstein's relativity and quantum mechanics, in which the scientific facts bear little resemblance to experience. Thus, experts conclude that those who look for science to be based in some actual human experience are merely not acknowledging the true nature of the universe as proved by Einstein and Bohr. Consequently, the experts are the only ones with the education and information to make or assess their theories and conclusions. But this ignores a major caveat: relativity and quantum mechanics, which seemingly defy our experiential knowledge, are applicable only at speeds approaching light speed and at the very smallest of atomic scales. Yes, at such speeds and distances and sizes our experiential knowledge of the world goes out the window, but these are extreme cases. The world, as we interact with it, continues to function much as it always has, which is why practical knowledge that we can apply to real-life situations is still the most productive and helpful knowledge for our lives.

There is also a major difference between finding new ways of looking at reality and actually acting within that reality. This is where postmodernism often goes so far off the rails. Theorists believe that changing the way we view and interpret life and science and society will actually change reality. But their theories have never borne out, which is why science itself has largely remained immune to the proclamations of postmodern theorists. The politics of science and the culture of science have changed, but not the science itself. I do not deny that some postmodern ideas and theories are unique and can offer interesting glimpses into the way we conceive of both ourselves and our world, but it does virtually nothing that actually affects the world. Positing that biology has largely been based on male-centric verbiage and perceptions doesn't actually change the way biology works. There is no feminist science. Science works the same way whether viewed by a feminist or by a chauvinist. Rather, it is the moral implications that a feminist or chauvinist tries to draw out of the science that is changed based on his or her personal ideology. But once again, morality and values are not the purview of science, and the moral implications of science and its value to society are discernible by your average nonexpert. Theories may sound nice and may offer interesting new ways of interpreting the world, but not necessarily of acting within the world. Garnering new ideas based on critical theories may help us in our own spiritual quests for truth and understanding of life, but they are limited to the individual and cannot be forced upon the rest of the population regardless of how good they sound or how excited a professor is about his or her newfound philosophy. Trying to force life into the limits of an ideology through activism and coercion is the basis of a totalitarian urge toward groupthink and the elimination of the individual as the greatest arbiter of truth.

No one man or woman possesses the equation to life, the one truth, the universal answers. Instead, finding such truth is a personal quest and an individual task. That being said, there are pieces of truth everywhere, even in the minds of those with whom we disagree most. Often, those with whom we disagree can offer arguments and lines of thought that can ring true to us. By listening to dissenting opinions, we allow ourselves a larger view on the question before us. The greatest disservice to the public is the quieting of dissenting views on any number of topics. Such bullying tactics do not allow for an informed public; they only attempt to foster groupthink for personal, political, or professional gain. Truth comes in bits and pieces, which we, as individuals, are left to piece together into our own worldview.

For this very reason we need not confine ourselves to looking to experts for pieces of truth; indeed, glimpses of truth, moments of brilliance, practical wisdom, and surprising genius reside in the everyday, average Joe and Jane. It is not limited to or supplied by higher education, fame, recognition, or published studies. Some of our greatest minds have come from outside the accepted mainstream venues of expertise. Different ways of thinking and of viewing the world can result in new and innovative solutions to problems. As professor of complexity Scott E. Page wrote, "We might think about gathering together the best and brightest minds, but that's a flawed approach. We also need to pay attention to the diversity of those minds, all the more so if the old saying that 'great minds think alike' holds true."[3] Diversity in thought and the mental tools that each individual mind uses contribute to a greater understanding of problems and solutions and thus have a greater chance at uncovering those bits of truth that fuel our personal search.

Case in point: In 2014 a mechanic's assistant, Earl Morrison, built a new device for patients in the intensive care unit in response to a new initiative to get patients moving around more often in order to aid in recovery. Known to the biomedical engineering department as a guy who "takes cars apart," Earl used pieces and parts from his own workspace to fabricate the EARL (Early Ambulation Rehabilitates Lives), a modified walker and equipment carrier that is now in use at Connecticut's Hartford Hospital. His ability to recognize a problem and find a solution in the parts and pieces around him has contributed to the recovery of patients in the ICU, thus filling a gap in the medical equipment field that was not addressed by equipment manufacturers.[4]

In 2013 *Nature News* reported that a thirteen-year-old boy had discovered a way to revolutionize solar energy. By mimicking the Fibonacci sequence, a mathematical spiral common in nature (e.g., in the way leaves grow on trees), he was able to increase the energy gathered by solar cells from 20 to 50 percent at different times of the year. A different way of seeing the world from a young, curious mind produced big results.[5]

In 2011, researchers at the University of Washington were frustrated, trying to map the structure of a protein that caused AIDS in rhesus monkeys. Unable to complete the work with microscopes and imaging techniques, researchers turned to gamers in the University's Center for Game Science and Professor Seth Cooper, who had developed a game called Foldit, in which players competed against each other to "design the most accurately folded proteins." "[AIDS Researcher] Khatib decided that human intuition might succeed where high-powered computers and microscopes had failed. He gave the Foldit players a task: take the best available models of the mystery protein and see if you can actually figure out the structure correctly. They did it in 10 days."[6] Once again, diversity of thought, looking at things in new ways that may not have been considered by researchers directly in the field of study, found a solution where others had failed.

Human intelligence and ingenuity, cognitive diversity and hard work are not limited to a bevy of experts who are given their authority by the media. To limit these qualities to the experts would be to discount and ignore potential wisdom, solutions, and contributions from people outside the realm of expertise. With experts encouraging both fear and expansion of power in an effort to move toward the goal of monolithic groupthink, the concern is that the average Joe or Jane or the amateur thinker outside the realms of academia will stop trying or be dismissed out of hand. If not considered part of the phalanx of experts, an individual's ideas may be given short shrift rather than due consideration. Often, critics of climate change come from outside the world of professional climate studies, and this is used against them as a way to discount their warnings, criticisms, or ideas. But this is folly. It is precisely because of their outside perspective that they should be given a hearing and consideration.

In this trend toward mass media and groupthink, what is lost is the individual as the master of his or her own destiny, capable of independent and unique thought. Indeed, this was the main focus of Marcel's *Man against Mass Society*, the idea of trying to maintain one's individuality and autonomy of thought in a world that is increasingly interconnected. Part of this autonomy is realizing the limits of our knowledge and our technology. It is perhaps why some of our best ideas come from those who have been told that their ideas are not worthy of merit because they lack the requisite moniker of "expert." Those from the nonexpert class have a humility that is forced upon them through the fact that they are not experts, and thus, they are more willing to accept that they do not have all the answers. First Corinthians 1:20 says, "Where is the wise man? Where is the scribe? Where is the debater of this age? Has not God made foolish the wisdom of the world?" Religion does not have all the answers, but that is part of the point. The universe, God, life, the Great Mystery, or whatever you may choose to call it is too large and too great for our understanding, and those who purport to see the future or offer a solution to the Mystery are made to look like fools in the end.

Faith and belief are at the irrational heart of humanity, because we can never really know for sure. Remember, science cannot say if something is absolutely true; it can only prove that something is false.

The sun rising in the East tomorrow is a very strong possibility, but it is not set in eternal stone. Skepticism and critical thinking help aid us in understanding the limits of our knowledge and the small reach of our influence. In this, the mind of the individual is vastly important. It is easy to get caught up in a mass movement toward one particular way of thinking. The psychological effect of seeing everyone around you in agreement can lend itself to a kind of delusion in which any information that disputes the group consensus is not only at odds with a group of people but also at odds with life itself. But this is not the case.

The individual, in seeing him or herself as a lone, cognizant creature in a vast and complex universe not bolstered by a choir of concurring voices, cannot help but be humbled by the specter of insignificance. The great minds that have discovered the makings of our world, the Newtons and Einsteins, faced a humbling experience in unraveling some of the mysterious forces that guide the physical world. Mystics humble themselves before transcendence. Yet the best and brightest among us tend to view the world as conforming to their whims, not recognizing that they themselves have come under a spell of ideology and hubris. Those in our society who consider themselves to be completely rational are often blind to their own beliefs that form the core of their being. And such blind faith can lead to, in the words from 1 Corinthians, foolishness.

Faith is recognition that we do not have all the answers, and humility is recognition that some questions can never be fully answered except in personal, spiritual ways. In our rush to declare ourselves gods over life, we have traversed what previously appeared to be impossible bridges; we have deconstructed the basic building blocks of life—atoms, DNA, the forces of physics and quantum mechanics—but in so doing, humanity has not reached a more enlightened state. While we may have technological prowess, our mental, emotional, and spiritual states have remained very much unchanged. As we move forward, perhaps we will see the cult of expertise begin to unravel as prophecy after prophecy fails to materialize, and perhaps this will cause men and women—individuals—to examine their inner selves for answers to questions about life's mysteries. Similarly, perhaps individuals will recognize their ability to act within their own spheres of influence rather than rely on government or mass society to do it for them. If we know someone who is hungry, we can help feed him. If we know someone who is suffering, we can try to help her. Not "we" as a group, but "we" as individuals.

We should reject the idea that those who are in the know and in positions of governmental power are the only ones equipped to help. We should also reject the notion that all of life's problems are answerable through science, experts, and groupthink. We should instead accept our roles as limited beings and critically examine the moral implications of policies set by experts and the governments. In all things we should ask *Why?* and then search for the answers ourselves, with the recognition that we are faith-based individuals, incapable of perfection, and all too human.

notes

introduction: vienna and the gulf

1. Achenbach, *A Hole at the Bottom of the Sea*, 69.
2. Reuters, "Full Text of President Obama's BP Oil Spill Speech."
3. Achenbach, 96. Italics in original.
4. Ibid., 9–10.
5. Ibid., 95. Italics in original.
6. Ibid., 160–63.
7. Martosko, "Energy Sec. Chu Doesn't Own Car."
8. Achenbach, 92.
9. Musil, *The Man Without Qualities*, 13.
10. Rand, *Atlas Shrugged*, 132.
11. Morton, *Thunder at Twilight*, 1–2.
12. Ibid., 42.
13. LiveScience, "Suicide the No. 1 Cause of Injury-Related Death in U.S."
14. Morton, x.
15. Jonsson, "BP oil spill."
16. Jonsson, "Joe the Plumber (Not That One) Says He Helped Stop Gulf Oil Spill Leak."
17. Ibid.
18. Ibid.
19. See http://www.villagevoice.com/2008-08-27/columns/serrano-s-shit-show/full/.

chapter 1: who are the "experts"?

1. Sowell, *Intellectuals and Society*, 8.
2. Ibid., 4–5.
3. Hofstadter, *Anti-Intellectualism in American Life*, 5.
4. Seethaler, *Lies, Damned Lies, and Science*, xvii.
5. Carroll, "Running farther, faster and longer can kill you."
6. Wagner, "Confirmed."
7. Miller, "Marijuana Smoke Linked to Cancer."
8. American Association for Cancer Research, "Marijuana Cuts Lung Cancer Tumor Growth in Half."
9. Connor, "Warning."
10. Ganos, "The World Will Never Run Out of Oil."
11. Eilperin, "Climate Shift Tied to 150,000 Fatalities."
12. Allegre, et al, "No Need to Panic About Global Warming."

13. *Daily Mail*, "Unhappy Feet."
14. Stone, "Antarctic Sea Ice Hits Record . . . High?"
15. Goldacre, *Bad Science*, 210.
16. Ibid., 229.
17. Seethaler, 36–37.
18. San Diego State University, Experts Directory page.
19. AllExperts, "How to apply to be an expert."
20. Hedges, *Empire of Illusion* (2009), 146.
21. Steyn, *After America*, 63.
22. Hedges, 184.
23. Gould, *Rocks of Ages*, 4-5.
24. Goldberg, "Do Republicans Have Bad Brains?"
25. Mooney, "Diagnosing the Republican Brain."
26. Goldacre, 228.
27. Goldacre, 98.
28. Jefferson, "Born This Way."
29. Henley, "Paedophilia."
30. Jefferson, "Born This Way."
31. Marcel, *Man Against Mass Society*, 26.
32. Hedges, 91.
33. Grinnell, *Science and Society*, 4.
34. Marcel, 81.

chapter 2: experts and media: a call to impotent activism

1. Asimov, Foundation, 14.
2. Gutting, "On Experts and Global Warming."
3. Ibid.
4. Russell, A History of Western Philosophy, 105.
5. Ibid., 107.
6. Seib, "In Crisis, Opportunity for Obama."
7. Gardner, *Future Babble*, 11.
8. Tetlock, Expert Political Judgment, 20–21.
9. Jowlt, "Paul Ehrlich, a Prophet of Global Population Doom Who Is Gloomier than Ever."
10. Pearce, *The Coming Population Crash*, 62–63.
11. Pearce, 78–79.
12. Johnson, *Modern Times*, 276–77.
13. Freedman, *Wrong*, 43.
14. Ibid., 52.
15. Peterson, Maier, and Seligman, *Learned Helplessness*, 11.
16. Ibid., 309.
17. Goldacre, *Bad Science*, 20.
18. Pappas, "Duh!"
19. Goldacre, 21.
20. Gardner, 124.
21. Schofield, "Money We Spent."
22. de Jager, Managing Change & Technology. http:///www.technobility.com.
23. United States Department of Agriculture, "Overview."
24. Wunderlich and Norwood, *Food Insecurity in the United States*, 43.
25. Wood, "A Clown at the Table."

26. USDA, "Overview"; and http://healthyamericans.org/report/98/.
27. http://feedingamerica.org/how-we-fight-hunger/advocacy-public-policy.aspx.
28. Diamond, "Why The 'Real' Unemployment Rate Is Higher Than You Think."
29. Citro and Michael, *Measuring Poverty*, 1.
30. Vozick-Levinson, "Is Weed Really Bad for You?"
31. Gwynn, "Carl Hart." Interestingly enough, this article was published around the same time as the *Rolling Stone* article.
32. Frood, "Pot Smokers Might Not Turn into Dopes after All"; and Meier et al., "Persistent Cannabis Users Show Neuropsychological Decline from Childhood to Midlife."
33. Vozick-Levinson, "Is Weed Really Bad for You?"
34. Vozick-Levinson, "Debunking Myths about the Physiological Effects of Marijuana."
35. Haney, "Columbia Psychiatry: Ask the Experts."
36. Vozick-Levinson, "Is Weed Really Bad for You?"
37. Kershaw, "Marijuana Is Gateway Drug for Two Debates."
38. Vozick-Levinson, "Is Weed Really Bad for You?"
39. Freedman, 108.
40. Gardner, 36.
41. Tetlock, 146.

chapter 3: culture of crisis

1. Hibbert, *Days of the French Revolution*, 232–33.
2. Yeats, *The Collected Poems*, 187.
3. Johnson, *Modern Times*, 5.
4. Voegelin, *Crisis and the Apocalypse of Man*, 217.
5. Johnson, 1–2.
6. Tucker, Marx, and Engels, *The Marx–Engels Reader*, 413.
7. Ibid., 725.
8. Ibid., 700.
9. Pearce, *The Coming Population Crash*, 4.
10. Bannister, *Social Darwinism*, 3.
11. Ibid., 9.
12. Pearce, 20.
13. Sanger, "The Eugenic Value of Birth Control."
14. Bannister, 16.
15. Pearcey, *Darwin Meets the Berenstain Bears*, 56–57.
16. Bannister, 210.
17. Guignon and Pereboom, *Existentialism*, 17.
18. Ibid., 121.
19. Halberstam, *The Best and the Brightest*, 217.
20. Ibid., 215.
21. Ibid., 143.
22. Ibid., 144.
23. Ibid., 218.
24. Pearce, 49.
25. Guignon & Pereboom, 98.
26. Camus, *The Rebel*, 305–6.
27. Euronews, "FEMEN Crashes Christmas Service."

chapter 4: higher learning and the credentialed age

1. Kirn, *Lost in the Meritocracy*, 8.
2. Ibid., 119–21.
3. Bloom, *The Closing of the American Mind*, 201.
4. Ripley, "College Is Dead."
5. Bloom, 338–39.
6. Hedges, *Empire of Illusion*, 89.
7. Murray, "Education Blogger Fired"; see also Riley, "The Most Persuasive Case for Eliminating Black Studies?"
8. Gladwell, *Outliers*, 52.
9. Ibid., 42.
10. Ibid., 95, 113.
11. Arum and Roska, *Academically Adrift*, 36.
12. Roggenbuck, "Why I Dropped Out of My Poetry MFA Program."
13. Ibid., "I am like october when i am dead."
14. Arum and Roska, 37.
15. Hagen, interview with author.
16. Hicks, *Explaining Postmodernism*, 14.
17. National Organization for Women, "NOW Calls for Resignation of Harvard University's President."
18. Clawson, "Notorious Sexist."
19. Wolin, *The Seduction of Unreason*, 283–84.
20. Chiaramonte, "Oregon Professor Fired for Bizarre Tirade."
21. University of Minnesota Women's Center, "The Female Orgasm."
22. Hua, "Sex Weekend." See also Moran, "What the Yale?"
23. Gantert, "MSU English Professor Threatens Students."
24. Celock, "David Guth."
25. Walters, "Florida Atlantic University 'Jesus Stomping' Case."
26. MSN, "A Professor at Florida Atlantic University…".
27. Haggz51, "Mad College Professor Claims Nobody Murdered by Stalin," https://www.youtube.com/watch?v=PdajUraK0LM.
28. Horkheimer, *Eclipse of Reason*, 18–19.
29. Marcel, *Man Against Mass Society*, 8.
30. Post, *Democracy, Expertise, and Academic Freedom*, 63.
31. Mamet, *The Secret Knowledge*, 125. It should also be noted that Mamet was brought before a campus-wide town hall meeting to determine if he should be allowed back on campus due to his "racially derogatory comments."
32. Hamilton, "McGill Student Forced to Apologize."
33. Korn, "The Doctrine of Academic Freedom." Interestingly, Korn is a double major in history of science and studies of women, gender, and sexuality. One wonders what kind of "science" she will be promoting when she inevitably goes on to a career as a journalist at one of the major news organizations. After all, she's from Harvard.
34. Anonymous, "The Plan for Dartmouth's Freedom Budget."

chapter 5: quantum confusion: a postmodern science?

1. Sokal and Bricmont, *Fashionable Nonsense*, 1.
2. Gross and Levitt, *Higher Superstition*, 8.
3. Nocera, "A Scientist's Misguided Crusade."
4. Dawidoff, "The Civil Heretic."
5. Ibid.
6. MSNBC staff, "Gore Takes Warming Warning to Congress."

7. Gross and Levitt, 169.
8. Hoffer, *The True Believer*, 34.
9. Gross and Levitt, 160–61.
10. Barrante, e-mail interview.
11. Johnson, *Modern Times*, 3.
12. Dawidoff, "The Civil Heretic."
13. Ezrahi, *Einstein's Unintended Legacy*, 49.
14. Galison, Peter L., Gerald Holton, and Silvan S. Schweber, eds. *Einstein for the 21st Century: His Legacy in Science, Art, and Modern Culture*. Princeton: Princeton University Press, 2008, 50.
15. Gross and Levitt, 51–52.
16. Ibid., 167.
17. Tipler, "Refereed Journals," In *Uncommon Dissent: Intellectuals Who Find Darwinism Unconvincing*. Edited by William Demski, Washington, DC: ISI Books 2005, 121.
18. Ibid, 118.
19. Post, *Democracy, Expertise, and Academic Freedom*, 8.
20. McKibben, "Global Warming's Terrifying New Math."
21. http://www.desmogblog.com/bio/7036/graham-readfearn.
22. Readfearn, "The 'Pause' in Global Warming Is Not Even a Thing."
23. Siegel, "22 Messages of Hope (and Science) for Creationists."
24. Sokal and Bricmont, 153–55.
25. MacIntyre, *Whose Justice? Which Rationality?*, 5–6.
26. Kraft, "Hacking Traditional College Debate's White-Privilege Problem."
27. Schlesinger, *The Disuniting of America*, 49.
28. Gross, e-mail interview.
29. Barrante, e-mail interview.

chapter 6: experts, complexity, and chaos

1. Gribbin, *Deep Simplicity*, 72.
2. Page, interview with author, May 1, 2014.
3. Barrante, *Global Warming for Dim Wits*, 18.
4. Diamond, *Guns, Germs, and Steel*, 296.
5. Blinder, "Keynesian Economics."
6. Barrante, xi.
7. Page, interview.
8. Camus, *The Rebel*, 199.
9. Page, *The Difference*, 14.
10. Ibid., 60–61.
11. Motesharei, Rivas, and Kalnay, *Human and Nature Dynamics*.
12. Hollingsworth, "Ivy League Statistician."

chapter 7: the culture of death

1. Samuel, *Death, American Style*, xxi.
2. LaLande, "Cell Phones and Brain Cancer."
3. Jones, "Berkeley Pushes for Cancer Warning Stickers on Cell Phones."
4. Medical News Today, "Most Popular Health Articles of 2013."
5. Harrington, *The Immortalist*, 3.
6. Witschi, "A Short History of Lung Cancer."
7. Cummings, Brown, and O'Connor, "The Cigarette Controversy."

8. LeLande, "Cell Phones and Brain Cancer."
9. American Cancer Society, "Cellular Phones."
10. CEO-Health, "About Us."
11. Ibid., "CEO-Health: excellence in medical tourism."
12. Ibid., "CEO-HEALTH and luxury wellness experience."
13. Noys, *The Culture of Death*, 20.
14. Ibid., 54.
15. Ibid., 40–41.
16. Garreau, *Radical Evolution*, 89–91.
17. Sens, "Aging as We've Known It."
18. Allen, "So You Want to Live Forever."
19. Becker, *The Denial of Death*, 267.
20. Harrington, 288.
21. Allen, "So You Want to Live Forever."
22. Ligotti, *Conspiracy against the Human Race*, 127.
23. Becker, 255.

chapter 8: media manipulation

1. Siebert, "The Libertarian Theory," 60–61.
2. Peterson, "The Social Responsibility Theory," 77.
3. Marcel, *Man against Mass Society*, 37.
4. Ibid., 64.
5. Boorstin, *The Image*, 39–40.
6. Ibid., 43–44.
7. Hedges, *Empire of Illusion*, 51.
8. Baudrillard, *Simulacra and Simulation*, 16.
9. Kaczynski, "9 Things the Media Got Wrong."
10. Boorstin, 47.
11. Herman and Chomsky, *Manufacturing Consent*, xi.
12. Phillip, "Why Hasn't the U.S. Closed Its Airports?"
13. Herman and Chomsky, 23.
14. Hofstadter, *Anti-Intellectualism in American Life*, 429.
15. Herman and Chomsky, 298.
16. Marcel, 36–37.
17. Ibid., 39.
18. Ibid., 40–41.
19. Toynbee, *A Study of History*, 205–6.
20. DeMoro, "U.S. Hospitals Not Prepared for Ebola Threat."

chapter 9: pseudo-reality prevails! now what?

1. Halberstam, *The Best and the Brightest*, 175.
2. Toynbee, *A Study of History*, 497–98.
3. Page, *The Difference*, 17–18.
4. Maminta, "Mechanic Built Device for ICU Patients."
5. Devon, "13-year-old Inventor."
6. NPR, "When Scientists Fail, It's Time to Call in the Gamers."

bibliography

A Place at the Table. Directed by Kristi Jacobson and Lori Silverbush. Performed by Jeff Bridges. Participant Media, 2012. DVD.

Achenbach, Joel. *A Hole at the Bottom of the Sea: The Race to Kill the BP Oil Gusher*. New York: Simon & Schuster, 2011.

Allegre, Claude, J. Scott Armstrong, Jan Breslow, Roger Cohen, Edward David, William Happer, Michael Kelly, et al. "No Need to Panic About Global Warming." Editorial. *Wall Street Journal*, January 28, 2012.

Allen, Charlotte. "So You Want to Live Forever." *Weekly Standard*, May 12, 2014. Accessed March 18, 2015. http://www.weeklystandard.com/articles/so-you-want-live-forever_788982.html.

AllExperts. "How to apply to be an expert." http://www.allexperts.com/central/expert.htm.

American Association for Cancer Research. "Marijuana Cuts Lung Cancer Tumor Growth in Half, Study Shows." *Science Daily*. April 17, 2007.

American Cancer Society, "Cellular Phones." Cancer.org. Accessed November 18, 2014. http://www.cancer.org/cancer/cancercauses/othercarcinogens/athome/cellular-phones.

Anonymous. "The Plan for Dartmouth's Freedom Budget: Items for Transformative Justice at Dartmouth." *dnews*. February 24, 2014. Archived at Scribd. http://www.scribd.com/doc/208843285/The-Plan-for-Dartmouth's-Freedom-Budget-Items-for-Transformative-Justice-at-Dartmouth.http://www.sciencedaily.com/releases/2007/04/070417193338.htm.

Arum, Richard, and Josipa Roksa. *Academically Adrift: Limited Learning on College Campuses*. Chicago: University of Chicago Press, 2011.

Asimov, Isaac. *The Foundation Trilogy: Three Classics of Science Fiction*. Garden City, NY: Doubleday, 1982.

Bannister, Robert C. *Social Darwinism: Science and Myth in Anglo-American Social Thought*. Philadelphia: Temple University Press, 1979.

Barrante, James R. *Global Warming for Dim Wits: A Scientist's Perspective of Climate Change*. Boca Raton, FL: Universal-Publishers, 2010.

———. Interview with author. E-mail interview. August 3, 2013.

Baudrillard, Jean. *Simulacra and Simulation*. Illustrated ed. Translated by Sheila Faria Glaser. University of Michigan Press, 1994.

Becker, Ernest. *The Denial of Death*. New York: Free Press, 1973.

Blinder, Alan S. "Keynesian Economics." *The Concise Encyclopedia of Economics*. Econlib (Library of Economics and Liberty) website. Accessed May 2, 2014. http://www.econlib.org/library/Enc/KeynesianEconomics.html.

Bloom, Allan. *The Closing of the American Mind*. New York: Simon & Schuster, 2012.

Boorstin, Daniel J. *The Image: A Guide to Pseudo-Events in America*. New York: First Vintage Books, 1992.

Camus, Albert. *The Rebel*. New York: Vintage International, 1991.

Carroll, Linda. "Running Farther, Faster and Longer Can Kill You." *Today*. Health. December 3, 2012. http://todayhealth.today.com/_news/2012/12/03/15625246-running-farther-faster-and-longer-can-kill-you?lite.

Celock, John. "David Guth, Kansas Professor, on Leave after Controversial Tweet—But GOP Lawmakers Want Him Fired." *Huffington Post*. September 20, 2013. http://www.huffingtonpost.com/2013/09/20/david-guth-kansas-fired_n_3963351.html.

CEO-Health. "About Us." CEO-HEALTH. Accessed September 30, 2014. http://www.ceo-health.com/about-us.html.

———. "CEO-HEALTH: excellence in medical tourism in Thailand and in South-East-Asia." http://www.ceo-health.com/services-medical-tourists.html.

———. "CEO-HEALTH and luxury wellness experience at the Mandarin Oriental, Bangkok." http://www.ceo-health.com/retreat-oriental.html.

Chiaramonte, Perry. "Oregon Professor Fired for Bizarre Tirade, Allegedly Threatening Student Protesters." Fox News. March 18, 2013. http://www.foxnews.com/us/2013/03/18/university-oregon-teacher-fired-after-threatening-student-protesters-in-bizarre/.

Citro, Constance F., and Robert T. Michael. *Measuring Poverty: A New Approach*. 1995. On the website of National Academies Presse. Accessed August 14, 2013. http://www.nap.edu/openbook.php?record_id=4759&page=R1.

Clawson, Laura. "Notorious sexist with notoriously bad judgment is reportedly top candidate for Fed chair" *Daily Kos*. July 23, 2013. http://www.dailykos.com/story/2013/07/23/1226007/-Notorious-sexist-with-notoriously-bad-judgment-is-reportedly-top-candidate-for-Fed-chair.

Connor, Steve. "Warning: Oil supplies running out fast." *Independent* (UK), August 3, 2009. http://www.independent.co.uk/news/science/warning-oil-supplies-are-running-out-fast-1766585.html.

Cummings, K. Michael, Anthony Brown, and Richard O'Connor. "The Cigarette Controversy." *"CEBP Focus: Nicotine and Tobacco-Control Research"* 16 (June 2007): 1070. Accessed March 18, 2015. http://cebp.aacrjournals.org/content/16/6/1070.full.pdf+html.

Daily Mail Reporter. "Unhappy Feet: Global Warming and Melting Sea Ice Risk Wiping out Antarctic's Emperor Penguins, Scientists Warn." *Mail Online* (UK). June 20, 2012. http://www.dailymail.co.uk/sciencetech/article-2162074/Global-warming-melting-sea-ice-risk-wiping-Antarctics-Emperor-penguins.html.

Dawidoff, Nicholas. "The Civil Heretic." *New York Times Magazine*. March 25, 2009. http://www.nytimes.com/2009/03/29/magazine/29Dyson-t.html?pagewanted=4&_r=0&sq=Freeman%20Dyson.

de Jager, Peter. Managing Change & Technology. Accessed December 24, 2013. http://www.technobility.com/index.html.

"Debunking Myths about the Physiological Effects of Marijuana: 5 Questions for Neurobiologist Margaret Haney." *Encyclopedia Britannica Online*. October 25, 2010. Text available at http://www.britannica.com/blogs/category/special-features/proposition-19-forum/feed/.

DeLillo, Don. *Underworld*. New York: Scribner, 1997.

DeMoro, RoseAnne. "U.S. Hospitals Not Prepared for Ebola Threat." *Washington Post*. October 13, 2014. http://www.washingtonpost.com/opinions/roseann-demoro-us-hospitals-not-prepared-for-ebola-threat/2014/10/13/4351ffc2-52cf-11e4-892e-602188e70e9c_story.html.

Devon, L.J. "13-year-old Inventor Cracks the Secret of Trees to Revolutionize Solar Energy." *Natural News* (blog). December 29, 2013. http://www.naturalnews.com/043351_solar_energy_13-year-old_inventor_Fibonacci_sequence.html.

Diamond, Dana. "Why The 'Real' Unemployment Rate Is Higher Than You Think." *Forbes*. July 5, 2013. http://www.forbes.com/sites/dandiamond/2013/07/05/why-the-real-unemployment-rate-is-higher-than-you-think/.

Diamond, Jared M. *Guns, Germs, and Steel: The Fates of Human Societies*. New York: W. W. Norton, 1998.

Eilperin, Juliet. "Climate Shift Tied to 150,000 Fatalities." *Washington Post*. November 17, 2005. http://www.washingtonpost.com/wp-dyn/content/article/2005/11/16/AR2005111602197.html.

Euronews. "FEMEN Crashes Christmas Service, Nude Woman Plays Christ in Church." Euronews.com. December 26, 2013. http://www.euronews.com/2013/12/26/femen-crashes-christmas-service-nude-woman-plays-christ-in-church/.

Ezrahi, Yaron. "Einstein's Unintended Legacy: The Critique of Common-Sense Realism and Post-Modern Politics." In *Einstein for the 21st Century: His Legacy in Science, Art, and Modern Culture*. Edited by Peter L. Gallison, Gerard Holton, and Silvan S. Schweber. Princeton, NJ: Princeton University Press, 2008, 48–59.

Freedman, David H. *Wrong: Why Experts* Keep Failing Us—and How to Know When Not to Trust Them: *Scientists, Finance Wizards, Doctors, Relationship Gurus, Celebrity CEOs, High-Powered Consultants, Health Officials, and More*. New York: Little, Brown, 2010.

Frood, Aaron. "Pot smokers might not turn into dopes after all." *Nature*. January 14, 2013. http://www.nature.com/news/pot-smokers-might-not-turn-into-dopes-after-all-1.12207.

Ganos, Todd. "The World Will Never Run Out of Oil—Might Its Price Tank?" *Forbes*, August 23, 2011. http://www.forbes.com/sites/toddganos/2011/07/03/the-world-will-never-run-out-of-oil-might-its-price-tank/.

Gantert, Tom. "MSU English Professor Threatens Students in Anti-Republican Rant." CAPCON: Michigan Capitol Confidential. September 4, 2013. http://www.michigancapitolconfidential.com/19106.

Gardner, Dan. *Future Babble: Why Expert Predictions Are Next to Worthless, and You Can Do Better*. New York: Dutton, 2011.

Garreau, Joel. *Radical Evolution: The Promise and Peril of Enhancing Our Minds, Our Bodies—and What It Means to Be Human*. New York: Doubleday, 2005.

Gladwell, Malcolm. *Outliers: The Story of Success*. New York: Little, Brown, 2008.

Goldacre, Ben. *Bad Science: Quacks, Hacks, and Big Pharma Flacks*. New York: Faber & Faber, 2010.

Goldberg, Jonah. "Do Republicans Have Bad Brains?" Republican American, May 9, 2012.

Gould, Stephen Jay. *Rocks of Ages: Science and Religion in the Fullness of Life*. New York: Ballantine, 1999.

Gribbin, John. *Deep Simplicity: Bringing Order to Chaos and Complexity.* New York: Random House, 2004.

Grinnell, Richard W. *Science and Society.* New York: Pearson Longman, 2007.

Gross, Paul. Interview with author. E-mail interview. March 7, 2014.

Gross, Paul R., and Norman Levitt. *Higher Superstition: The Academic Left and Its Quarrels with Science.* Baltimore, MD: Johns Hopkins University Press, 1998.

Guignon, Charles B., and Derk Pereboom. *Existentialism: Basic Writings.* Indianapolis: Hackett, 1995.

Gutting, Gary. "On Experts and Global Warming." *The Opinionator* (blog). December 7, 2011. http://opinionator.blogs.nytimes.com/2011/07/12/on-experts-and-global-warming/?_php=true&_type=blogs&_r=0.

Gwynne, Kristen. "Carl Hart: Drugs Don't Turn People into Criminals." Salon. June 17, 2013. http://www.salon.com/2013/06/17/carl_hart_drugs_dont_turn_people_into_criminals_partner/.

Hagen, Edward. Interview with author. Personal interview. December 12, 2012.

Haggz51. "Mad College Professor Claims Nobody Murdered by Stalin." YouTube video, 3:41. October 26, 2012. http://www.youtube.com/watch?v=hRPTZF5zSLQ.

Halberstam, David. *The Best and the Brightest.* New York: Ballantine, 1993.

Hamilton, Graeme. "McGill Student Forced to Apologize for Racial 'microaggression' after Emailing Joke Obama Clip." *National Post.* February 18, 2014. http://news.nationalpost.com/2014/02/18/mcgill-student-forced-to-apologize-for-racial-microaggression-after-emailing-joke-obama-clip/.

Haney, Margaret. "Columbia Psychiatry: Ask the Experts." Columbia University Medical Center. Accessed December 30, 2013. http://asp.cumc.columbia.edu/psych/asktheexperts/ask_the_experts_inquiry.asp?SI=217.

Harrington, Alan. *The Immortalist: An Approach to the Engineering of Man's Divinity.* New York: Random House, 1969.

Hart, Carl. *High Price: A Neuroscientist's Journey of Self-Discovery That Challenges Everything You Know About Drugs and Society.* New York: Harper, 2013.

Hedges, Chris. *Empire of Illusion: The End of Literacy and the Triumph of Spectacle.* New York: Nation, 2009.

Henley, Jon. "Paedophilia: Bringing Dark Desires to Light." *Guardian* (UK), January 2, 2013. http://www.guardian.co.uk/society/2013/jan/03/paedophilia-bringing-dark-desires-light.

Herman, Edward S., and Noam Chomsky. *Manufacturing Consent: The Political Economy of the Mass Media.* New York: Pantheon, 1988.

Hibbert, Christopher. *The Days of the French Revolution.* New York: Harper Perennial, 2002.

Hicks, Stephen R. C. *Explaining Postmodernism: Skepticism and Socialism from Rousseau to Foucault.* Loves Park, IL: Ockham's Razor, 2011.

Hoffer, Eric. *The True Believer: Thoughts on the Nature of Mass Movements.* New York: HarperPerennial, 2010.

Hofstadter, Richard. *Anti-intellectualism in American Life.* New York: Vintage, 1991.

Hollingsworth, Barbara. "Ivy League Statistician Debunks NASA-Funded 'Socialism or Extinction' Study." CNSNew.com. March 28, 2014. http://www.cnsnews.com/news/article/barbara-hollingsworth/ivy-league-statistician-debunks-nasa-funded-socialism-or.

Horkheimer, Max. *Eclipse of Reason.* Reprint. London: Bloomsbury, 2004.

Hua, Cynthia. "Sex Weekend Examines Sexual Culture." *Yale Daily News*. March 4, 2013. http:// yaledailynews.com/blog/2013/03/04/sex-weekend-examines-sexual-culture/.

Hyatt, Michael S. *The Millennium Bug: How to Survive the Coming Chaos*. New York, Regnery, 1998.

Idiocracy. Directed by Mike Judge. Performed by Luke Wilson and Maya Rudolph. Milano: Twentieth Century Fox Home Entertainment, 2008.

"Issue Brief: Analysis of Obesity Rates by State." Trust for America's Health. August 2012. http:// healthyamericans.org/report/98/.

Jefferson, Cord. "Born This Way: Sympathy and Science for Those Who Want to Have Sex with Children." *Gawker*. September 7, 2012. http://gawker.com/5941037/born-this-way-sympathy-and-science-for-those-who--want-to-have-sex-with-children.

Johnson, Paul. *Modern Times: The World from the Twenties to the Nineties*. New York: HarperPerennial, 2001.

———. *Intellectuals: From Marx and Tolstoy to Sarte and Chomsky*. New York: HarperPerennial, 2007.

Jones, Carolyn. "Berkeley Pushes for Cancer Warning Stickers on Cell Phones." *SFGate*. July 15, 2014. http://www.sfgate.com/bayarea/article/Berkeley-pushes-for-cancer-stickers-on-cell-phones-5621382.php.

Jonsson, Patrik. "Joe the Plumber (not that one) says he helped stop Gulf oil spill leak." *Christian Science Monitor*, July 17, 2010. http://www.csmonitor.com/Environment/2010/0717/Joe-the-Plumber-not-that-one-says-he-helped-stop-Gulf-oil-spill-leak.

———. "BP oil spill: 'Mystery plumber' may be brains behind containment cap." *Christian Science Monitor*, July 15, 2010. http://www.csmonitor.com/Environment/2010/0715/BP-oil-spill-Mystery-plumber-may-be-brains-behind-containment-cap.

Jowlt, Juliette. "Paul Ehrlich, a Prophet of Global Population Doom Who Is Gloomier than Ever." *Guardian* (UK). October 23, 2011. http://www.guardian.co.uk/environment/2011/oct/23/paul-ehrlich-global-collapse-warning.

Kaczynski, Andrew. "9 Things the Media Got Wrong about the Sandy Hook Shooting." BuzzFeed News. December 17, 2012. http://www.buzzfeed.com/andrewkaczynski/9-things-the-media-got-wrong-about-the-sandy-hook#.anxlNWW9b.

Kershaw, Sarah. "Marijuana Is Gateway Drug for Two Debates." *New York Times*, July 7, 2009. http:// www.nytimes.com/2009/07/19/fashion/19pot.html?pagewanted=all&_r=1&.

Kirn, Walter. *Lost in the Meritocracy: The Undereducation of an Overachiever*. New York: Doubleday, 2009.

Korn, Sandra Y. L. "The Doctrine of Academic Freedom." *Harvard Crimson*. February 18, 2014. http:// www.thecrimson.com/column/the-red-line/article/2014/2/18/academic-freedom-justice/?page=1.

Kraft, Jessica Carew. "Hacking Traditional College Debate's White-Privilege Problem." *Atlantic*. April 16, 2014. http://www.theatlantic.com/education/archive/2014/04/does-traditional-college-debate-reinforce-white-privilege/360746/.

LaLande, Gerard. "Cell Phones and Brain Cancer: Time to Protect Ourselves." *The Nation*. July 1, 2014. http://www.nationmultimedia.com/life/Cell-phones-and-brain-cancer-time-to-protect-ourse-30237459.html.

Levitt, Steven D., and Stephen J. Dubner. *Freakonomics: A Rogue Economist Explores the Hidden Side of Everything*. New York: William Morrow, 2005.

Ligotti, Thomas. *The Conspiracy Against the Human Race: A Contrivance of Horror*. New York: Hippocampus Press, 2011.

LiveScience. "Suicide the No. 1 Cause of Injury-Related Death in U.S." Fox News. September 26, 2012. http://www.foxnews.com/health/2012/09/26/suicide-no-1-cause-injury-related-death-in-us/.

MacIntyre, Alasdair. *Whose Justice? Which Rationality?* Notre Dame, IN: University of Notre Dame Press, 1988.

Mamet, David. The Secret Knowledge: On the Dismantling of American Culture. New York: Sentinel, 2011.

Maminta, Jocelyn. "Mechanic Built Device for ICU Patients." WTNH. February 12, 2014. http://wtnh.com/2014/02/12/mechanic-built-device-for-icu-patients-2/.

Marcel, Gabriel. *Man against Mass Society.* South Bend, IN: St. Augustine's Press, 2008.

Martosko, David. "Energy Sec. Chu doesn't own car, but his wife drives BMW gas-guzzler." *Daily Caller*, September 3, 2012. http://dailycaller.com/2012/03/09/energy-sec-chu-doesnt-own-car-but-his-wife-drives-bmw-gas-guzzler/.

McKibben, Bill. "Global Warming's Terrifying New Math." *Rolling Stone*, July 19, 2012. http://www.rollingstone.com/politics/news/global-warmings-terrifying-new-math-20120719.

Medical News Today, "Most Popular Health Articles of 2013." MNT website. Accessed September 30, 2014. http://www.medicalnewstoday.com/popular/2013.

Meier, Madeline H., Avshalom Caspi, Antony Ambler, Honalee Harrington, Renate Houts, Richard S. E. Keefe, Key MacDonald, Aimee Ward, Richie Poulton, and Terrie E. Moffitt. "Persistent cannabis users show neuropsychological decline from childhood to midlife." *PNAS* 109, no. 40 (October 2, 2012).

Miller, Kelli. "Marijuana Smoke Linked to Cancer." Web MD. June 23, 2009. http://www.webmd.com/cancer/news/20090623/marijuana-smoke-linked-to-cancer.

Mooney, Chris. "Diagnosing the Republican Brain." *Mother Jones*. March 30, 2012. http://www.motherjones.com/politics/2012/03/chris-mooney-republican-brain-science-denial?page=3.

Moran, Lee. "What the Yale? Ivy league students admit to bestiality, desires about incest, during 'Sex Weekend' workshop," *Daily News*. March 6, 2013. http://www.nydailynews.com/news/national/yale-students-admit-beatiality-sex-workshop-article-1.1280746.

Morton, Frederic. *Thunder at Twilight: Vienna 1913–1914.* Cambridge: Da Capo, 2001.

Motesharrei, Safa, Jorge Rivas, and Eugenia Kalnay. *Human and Nature Dynamics (HANDY): Modeling Inequality and Use of Resources in the Collapse or Sustainability of Societies* (abstract). March 19, 2014. http://www.cnsnews.com/sites/default/files/documents/motesharrei-rivas-kalnay.pdf.

MSN. "A Professor at Florida Atlantic University Has Suggested That the Sandy Hook Elementary Massacre Was a Hoax." MSN News. January 10, 2013. http://news.msn.com/rumors/rumor-a-professor-suggests-sandy-hook-elementary-tragedy-was-a-hoax. No longer accessible.

msnbc.com staff and news service reports. "Gore Takes Warming Warning to Congress." NBCNews.com. Upd. March 22, 2007. http://www.nbcnews.com/id/17718399/ns/us_news-environment/t/gore-takes-warming-warning-congress/#.VGoL1fnF_To.

Murray, Rheana. "Education Blogger Fired for Calling Black Studies Dissertation Topics 'left Wing Victimization Claptrap.'" *Daily News*. May 9, 2012. Accessed January 21, 2013. www.nydailynews.com/news/national/education-blogger-fired-calling-black-studies-dissertation-topics-left-wing-victimizationclaptrap-article-1.1075392.

Musil, Robert. *The Man Without Qualities.* Translated by Sophie Wilkins. New York: Vintage International, 1995.

National Organization for Women. "NOW Calls for Resignation of Harvard University's President." News release. January 20, 2005. http://wiseli.engr.wisc.edu/archives/NOW.pdf.

Nocera, Joe. "A Scientist's Misguided Crusade." *New York Times*. March 4, 2013. http://www.nytimes.com/2013/03/05/opinion/nocera-a-scientists-misguided-crusade.html?ref=jamesehansen.

Noys, Benjamin. *The Culture of Death*. Oxford: Berg, 2005.

NPR Staff. "When Scientists Fail, It's Time to Call in the Gamers." NPR. October 2, 2011. http://www.npr.org/2011/10/02/140979241/when-scientists-fail-its-time-to-call-in-the-gamers.

Office Space. Directed by Mike Judge. Performed by Ron Livingston. Austin: Twentieth Century Fox Corporation, 1999. DVD.

Onion. "Nation Mostly Alarmed That Government's Top Programs Handled by 29-Year-Olds." *The Onion*, June 12, 2013. http://www.theonion.com/articles/nation-mostly-alarmed-that-governments-top-program,32792/.

Page, Scott E. *The Difference: How the Power of Diversity Creates Better Groups, Firms, Schools, and Societies*. Princeton: Princeton University Press, 2007.

Pappas, Stephanie. "Duh! The 13 Most Obvious Findings of 2013." Fox News. December 27, 2013. http://www.foxnews.com/science/2013/12/27/duh-13-most-obvious-findings-2013/.

Pearce, Fred. *The Coming Population Crash: And Our Planet's Surprising Future*. Boston: Beacon, 2011.

Pearcey, Nancy R. "Darwin Meets the Berenstain Bears: Evolution as a Total Worldview." In *Uncommon Dissent: Intellectuals Who Find Darwinism Unconvincing*, edited by William A. Dembski, 53–73. Wilmington, DE: ISI, 2004.

Peterson, Christopher, Steven F. Maier, and Martin E. P. Seligman. *Learned Helplessness: A Theory for the Age of Personal Control*. New York: Oxford University Press, 1993.

Peterson, Theodore. "The Social Responsibility Theory." In *Four Theories of the Press*, by Fred S. Siebert, Theodore Peterson, and Wilbur Schramm. Chicago: University of Illinois Press, 1963.

Phillip, Abby. "Why Hasn't the U.S. Closed Its Airports to Travelers from Ebola-Ravaged Countries?" *Washington Post*. October 4, 2014. http://www.washingtonpost.com/news/to-your-health/wp/2014/10/01/why-hasnt-the-u-s-closed-its-airports-to-travelers-from-ebola-ravaged-countries/.

Post, Robert. *Democracy, Expertise, and Academic Freedom: A First Amendment Jurisprudence for the Modern State*. New Haven, CT: Yale University Press, 2012.

Rand, Ayn. *Atlas Shrugged*. New York: Plume, 1999.

Readfearn, Graham. "The 'Pause' in Global Warming Is Not Even a Thing." *Guardian* (UK). February 11, 2014. http://www.theguardian.com/environment/planet-oz/2014/feb/12/global-warming-fake-pause-hiatus-climate-change.

Reuters. "Full Text of President Obama's BP Oil Spill Speech." Reuters, June 15, 2010. http://www.reuters.com/article/2010/06/16/us-oil-spill-obama-text-idUSTRE65F02C20100616.

Riley, Naomi Schaeffer. "The Most Persuasive Case for Eliminating Black Studies? Just Read the Dissertations." *Chronicle of Higher Education*. April 30, 2012. http://chronicle.com/blogs/brainstorm/the-most-persuasive-case-for-eliminating-black-studies-just-read-the-dissertations/46346.

Ripley, Amanda. "College Is Dead. Long Live College!" *Time*, October 29, 2012, 33–41.

Roggenbuck, Steve. "I am like october when i am dead." Accessed February 12, 2014. http://www. iamlikeoctoberwheniamdead.com/2010/10/i-dont-care-about-reading-poem-who-do.html.

———. "Why I Dropped Out of My Poetry MFA Program." *Live My Lief* (blog). February 11, 2014. http://livemylief.com/post/76388729646/in-september-2010-i-started-the-poetry-mfa-program.

Russell, Bertrand. *A History of Western Philosophy*. New York: Simon and Schuster, 1972. http:// newscenter.sdsu.edu/experts/directory.aspx.

Samuel, Lawrence R. *Death, American Style: A Cultural History of Dying in America*. Lanham, MD: Rowman & Littlefield, 2013.

San Diego State University. SDSU Experts Directory. Accessed September 15, 2014. https://newscenter. sdsu.edu/experts/directory/.aspx

Sanger, Margaret. "The Eugenic Value of Birth Control." The Public Writings and Speeches of Margaret Sanger. October 1921. http://www.nyu.edu/projects/sanger/webedition/app/documents/show. php?sangerDoc=238946.xml.

Schlesinger, Arthur M. *The Disuniting of America*. New York: Norton, 1992.

Schmidt, Gavin, "The Emergent Patterns of Climate Change." TED Talks. March 2014. https://www. ted.com/talks/gavin_schmidt_the_emergent_patterns_of_climate_change.

Schofield, Jack. "Money We Spent." *Guardian* (UK), January 5, 2000. http://www.theguardian.com/ technology/2000/jan/05/y2k.guardiananalysispage.

Seethaler, Sherry. *Lies, Damned Lies, and Science: How to Sort through the Noise around Global Warming, the Latest Health Claims, and Other Scientific Controversies*. Upper Saddle River, NJ: FT Press, 2009.

Seib, Gerald F. "In Crisis, Opportunity for Obama." *Wall Street Journal*. November 21, 2008. http:// online.wsj.com/article/SB122721278056345271.html.

SENS Research Foundation, "Aging as We've Known It." SRF website. Accessed September 30, 2014. http://www.sens.org/research/aging-as-weve-known-it.

Siebert, Fred S. "The Libertarian Theory." In *Four Theories of the Press*, by Fred S. Siebert, Theodore Peterson, and Wilbur Schramm. Chicago: University of Illinois Press, 1963.

Siegel, Ethan. "22 Messages of Hope (and Science) for Creationists." February 12, 2014. http://medium. com/p/8712e42fbb0d.

Simmons, Dan. *The Terror: A Novel*. New York: Little, Brown, 2007.

Sokal, Alan, and Jean Bricmont. *Fashionable Nonsense: Postmodern Intellectuals' Abuse of Science*. New York: Picador, 1998.

Sowell, Thomas. *Intellectuals and Society*. Rev. and enl. New York: Basic Books, 2011.

Steyn, Mark. *After America: Get Ready for Armageddon*. Washington, DC: Regnery, 2011.

Stone, Daniel. "Antarctic Sea Ice Hits Record . . . High?" *National Geographic*. October 13, 2012. http:// news.nationalgeographic.com/news/2012/10/121013-antarctica-sea-ice-record-high-science- global-warming/.

"Take Action Against Hunger." Feeding America. Accessed September 16, 2014. http://feedingamerica. org/how-we-fight-hunger/advocacy-public-policy.aspx.

Tetlock, Philip E. *Expert Political Judgment: How Good Is It? How Can We Know?* Princeton, NJ: Princeton University Press, 2005.

Tipler, Frank J. "Refereed Journals: Do They Enforce Quality or Orthodoxy?" In *Uncommon Dissent: Intellectuals Who Find Darwinism Unconvincing*, by William Dembski, 115–30. Wilmington, DE: ISI, 2005.

Toynbee, Arnold J. *A Study of History: Abridgement of Volumes I–IV*. Edited by D.C. Somervell. Oxford: Oxford University Press, 1946.

Tucker, Robert C., Karl Marx, and Friedrich Engels. *The Marx-Engels Reader*. 2nd ed. New York: Norton, 1978.

United States Department of Agriculture, "Overview: Measurement." Last updated September 3, 2014. http://www.ers.usda.gov/topics/food-nutrition-assistance/food-security-in-the-us/measurement. aspx#.VBhg3CjFSc4.

University of Minnesota Women's Center. "The Female Orgasm: A Program About Sexual Health and Women's Empowerment" (event description). University of Minnesota website. Accessed September 21, 2014. https://events.umn.edu/024614.

Voegelin, Eric. *Crisis and the Apocalypse of Man*. Vol. 8. *History of Political Ideas*. Columbia, MO: University of Missouri Press, 1999.

Vozick-Levinson, Simon. "Is Weed Really Bad for You?" *Rolling Stone*. June 20, 2013, http://www. rollingstone.com/culture/news/is-weed-really-bad-for-you-20130610.

Wagner, Neil. "Confirmed: He Who Sits Most Dies Soonest." *Atlantic*. April 19, 2012. http://www. theatlantic.com/health/archive/2012/04/confirmed-he-who-sits-the-most-dies-the-soonest/256101/.

Walters, Ashleigh. "Florida Atlantic University 'Jesus Stomping' Case: Student Ryan Rotelas Upset, Rick Scott Comments." News Channel 5 (West Palm Beach, FL). March 27, 2013. www.wptv.com/dpp/ news/region_s_palm_beach_county/boca_raton/florida-atlantic-university-jesus-stomping-case-gov-rick-scott-upset-over-deandre-poole-class.

Witschi, Hanspeter. "A Short History of Lung Cancer." *Toxicological Sciences* 64, no. 1 (2001): 4–6. http://toxsci.oxfordjournals.org/content/64/1/4.full.

Wolin, Richard. *The Seduction of Unreason: The Intellectual Romance with Fascism: From Nietzsche to Postmodernism*. Princeton, NJ: Princeton University Press, 2004.

Wood, Graeme. "A Clown at the Table." *National Review*, June 3, 2013, 33–36.

Wunderlich, Gooloo S., and Janet L. Norwood, eds. *Food Insecurity in the United States: An Assessment of the Measure*. Washington, DC: National Academies Press, 2006. Accessed July 29, 2013. http:// www.nap.edu/openbook.php?record_id=11578&page=R1.

Yeats, W. B., and Richard J. Finneran. *The Collected Poems of W. B. Yeats: A New Edition*. Basingstoke, UK: Macmillan, 1993.

index

A

Abdumutallab, Umar Farouk, 52
Abraham (patriarch), 69–70
Academically Adrift (Arum and Roska), 85, 87
"academic justice," 102
Achenbach, Joel, viii, ix, x, xi, xii, xvii
Adorno, Theodor W., 17
aging, 146, 156, 160
Allen, Charlotte, 160
Allexperts.com, 7
American Cancer Society, 154
American Revolution, 56–57
animal testing, scientific findings based on, 34–35
Anti-Intellectualism in American Life (Hofstadter), 3
"apocalypse of man," 59
Aristotle, 80, 122
Arum, Richard, 85
Asimov, Isaac, 21, 22, 54
Ask the Experts, 46
Atlantic, 123–24
Augustine, 145, 162
Authentic Happiness and Learned Optimism (Seligman), 34
average debt of college graduate, 81

B

Baby Boomer generation, 146, 156, 163
Bad Science: Quacks, Hacks, and Big Pharma Flacks (Goldacre), 5
Bailey, J. Michael, 14
Ball, George, 184
Bannister, Robert C., 66, 69
Barrante, James, 112, 126, 137, 139
Barthes, Roland, 79

Baudrillard, Jean, 169–70
Becker, Ernest, 161, 163
Behe, Michael J., 64
Bell, Sean, 44
Benjamin, Walter, 79
Bernal, J. D., 32
Best and the Brightest, The (Halberstam), 72
bestiality, 95
biopolitics, 155
birth control, 65, 67, 75
"black studies," 94
Bloom, Allan, 79–80, 82, 88, 94, 107
Bohr, Niels, 50, 88, 190
Boorstin, Daniel J., 168–69, 170, 171, 176, 183
Boston Marathon bombings, 51, 52
BP (British Petroleum) oil spill, viii–xii, xvi–xvii, 2, 59, 82
Bradbury, Ray, xvi
Brave New World (Huxley), 8, 180
Brea, Robert, xvi–xvii
Bricmont, Jean, 107, 108, 122
Bridges, Jeff, 39, 40
Briggs, William, 143
Bush, George H. W., 99
Bush, George W., 99
butterfly effect, 132

C

Caldart, Joe, xvi, xvii–xix, 2, 9, 25
Campbell, Rashid, 124
Camus, Albert, 59, 79, 138, 186
cancer, 5, 45, 47, 147–48, 149, 151–52, 154, 155
Capital (Marx), 62
capitalism, 31, 32, 37, 62, 63, 65, 92, 137, 138, 176
cap-and-trade legislation, 110

Carter, Jimmy, 37
CDC, 172, 175
cell phones, 102, 147, 150, 153, 154, 155, 159
CEO-Health, 154–55
Centers for Disease Control. *See* CDC
chaos, experts, complexity, and. *See ch. 6*
    (129–43)
chaos theory, 50, 131, 132
China, 30, 32, 51, 63
Chomsky, Noam, 169, 172, 173, 175–76
Choron, Jacques (*Death and Western Thought*),
    161
Christianity, 56, 57, 92, 145
Chronicle of Higher Education, 83, 86
Chu, Steven, x, xi, xii
CIA, 141, 166
cigarettes, 45, 46, 150, 151–52, 159
climate change, 13, 108, 110, 111, 112–13,
    119–20, 126, 134, 136, 140, 179, 194
Clinton, Bill, 40, 99
Closing of the American Mind, The (Bloom),
    79–80, 107
Cold War, 3, 31
college. *See in general ch. 4, "Higher Learning and
    the Credentialed Age"* (77–103)
    enrollment numbers, 81
    majors obtain by most politicians and media
        talking heads, 98
    tuition costs, 81
colonialism, 80, 90, 93
Columbia University, 43, 45, 47, 48, 86, 100,
    106, 108
Coming Population Collapse, The (Pearce), 30
communism, 8, 31, 32, 63, 91, 137
complexity. *See in general ch. 6, "Experts, Complex-
    ity, and Chaos"* (129–43)
complexity theory, 131
compulsory sterilization program (India), 30, 74
Concise Encyclopedia of Economics, 136–37
Cooper, Seth, 193
Copernicus, 24, 57, 88
corporations, viii, 6, 8, 26, 78, 94, 118, 120, 179,
    185–86
critical thinking, 10, 32, 85, 86, 100, 195
Cuba, 63
Cult of Reason, 56
culture of death. *See ch. 7, "The Culture of Death"*
    (145–64)
Culture of Death (Noys), 156

D

Daily Kos, 93
Danish Committee on Scientific Dishonesty
    (DCSD), 110
Dartmouth College, 102
Darwin, Charles, 57, 58–59, 60, 61, 64, 65, 67,
    68, 69, 113, 129
Darwinism, 66, 69
Davies, Joseph E., 31
Dawidoff, Nicholas, 113
Days of the French Revolution (Hibbert), 56
Death, American Style (Samuel), 146
death, the culture of. *See ch. 7, "The Culture of
    Death"* (145–64)
debt of average college graduate, 81
de-Christianization movement (France), 56
Declaration of Independence, 57, 90
Declaration of the Rights of Man and of the
    Citizen (French), 57
deconstruction, 90, 92, 106. *See* postmodernism
Deep Simplicity (Gribbin), 132
Deepwater Horizon oil spill, vii–xii, xvi–xvii, 2,
    59, 82
de Grey, Aubrey, 160
de Jager, Peter, 39
Delillo, Don, 77, 183
de Man, Paul, 91
Dembski, William A., 64
Democracy, Expertise and Academic Freedom (Post),
    99, 119
DeMoro, RoseAnn, 180
Denial of Death, The (Becker), 161, 163
Derrida, Jacques, 91
Descartes, René, 72
DeSmogBlog, 121
determinism, 131, 132, 138–39, 143
Diamond, Jared, 135
DiCaprio, Leonardo, 7
diet soda, 150, 159
Difference, The (Page), 141–42
difference, the politics of, 93
diseases, 149–50, 156, 158, 160
Disuniting of America (Schlesinger), 124–25
duality between man and nature, 96–97
Dubner, Stephen, 38
Dumont, Louis, 115
Dyson, Freeman, 109, 110, 113

E

Ebola, 150, 172–73, 174, 175, 179, 180
economic determinism, 132, 138, 139, 142
"economic equality," 42, 45
economics, xiii, 8, 16, 62, 65, 129, 132, 136–37, 140, 142
Ehrlich, Paul, 28–30, 49, 117–18, 131, 132, 134
Einstein, Albert, 24, 50, 53, 58, 88, 112, 115, 116, 118, 119, 190
Eisenhower, Dwight D., 3, 73–74
Emanuel, Rahm, 25
emissions, 108, 121, 135–36, 147
Empire of Illusion (Hedges), 7–8
Engels, Friedrich, 62, 63, 70
England, Matt, 121
Enlightenment, 56–57, 58, 59, 60, 65, 66, 70–71, 72, 88, 90–91, 92, 107, 114–15, 123, 124, 149, 162, 186, 187
environmentalism, 65, 111, 112. See also climate change; global warming
equality, 29, 31, 32, 47, 49, 57, 91, 93, 94, 98, 102, 114
ethics, 13, 16, 62, 63, 64, 75, 87, 94, 106, 117,
eugenics, 66–67
"evidence," 9, 11, 27, 64, 153, 189
evolution, 13, 27, 50, 60, 64–65, 66, 67, 68, 70, 113, 121n
Existentialism (Guignon and Pereboom),
expert, as used in media and pop culture, 3
Expert Political Judgment (Tetlock), 27
Experts Directory (SDSU), 7
"experts"
        and media, 21–54
        source of their legitimacy, 81
        two different classes of, per Tetlock, 27
        who they are, 1–19
Ezrahi, Yaron, 115, 116

F

Facebook, 158, 177
Fahrenheit 451 (Bradbury), xvi
faith, xii, 59, 66, 69–71, 75, 80, 81, 91, 94, 96–97, 109, 111, 113, 114, 117, 118, 130, 141, 188–89, 194, 195–96
fascism, 8, 23, 91
Fashionable Nonsense: Postmodern Intellectuals' Abuse of Science (Sokal and Bricmont), 107, 122
fast food, 150, 153

FBI, 51
fear of death, 148, 156, 158, 161, 175
Federal Communications Commission, 154
Feeding America (Feedingamerica.org), 39, 41
FEMEN, 76
"feminist science," 107, 191
Ferguson, Missouri, shooting, 157
Florida Atlantic University, 95–96
"food insecurity," 39–41
food stamps, 40, 41
forced sterilization, 30, 67, 74
Ford, Gerald, 99
Fort Hood shooting, 51, 52
fossils, 113
Foucault, Michel, 91
Foundation series (Asimov), 21–22, 54
Fox, Michael J., 7
"foxes" (as a class of "experts" per Tetlock), 27, 53
Fox News, 167
Franco, James, 43
Freakonomics (Levitt and Dubner), 38
Freedman, David H., 26, 28, 33, 34
French Revolution, 55–57, 59, 61, 63, 67, 76
Freud, Sigmund, 129, 161
Future Babble (Gardner), 26

G

Gadamer, Hans-Georg, 79
Galileo, 10–11, 24, 56, 57, 58, 88, 115
Galton, Francis, 67
Gardner, Dan, 26, 28, 37–38, 50
Garreau, Joel, 159
Garwin, Richard, xi
Gates, Bill, 84
Gawker, 14
Gay Science, The (Nietzsche), 57
Gandhi, Sanjay, 30
Germany, 18, 32, 67, 72n, 76, 97, 126, 139
Gladwell, Malcolm, 84–85
global warming, 4, 5, 11, 13, 23, 24, 25, 29, 108–10, 112–13, 119–21, 125, 130, 153, 156, 180, 185
GMO foods, 148, 150, 159
God
        "death"/elimination of, 57, 61, 64, 70–71, 163, 187
        humanity's revolt against, 59
        results of a world without, 60
Goddess of Reason, 56, 76
Goldacre, Ben, 5–6, 12, 16, 26, 36–37, 48

Goldberg, Jonah, 11
Gore, Al, 7, 109, 110
Gould, Stephen Jay, 10
Graham, Ramarley, 44
Great Depression, 31, 41
"Green Revolution," 29
Gribbin, John, 132, 137, 139
groupthink, 86, 94, 98, 141, 176, 177, 178, 179,
        184, 186, 192, 194, 196
Guardian (UK), 14–15, 29, 120
Guignon, Charles, 70
Guns, Germs, and Steel (Diamond), 135
Gutting, Gary, 22–23, 24–25

H

Hagan, Edward, 91–92
Halberstam, David, 72
Haney, Meg, 45–46, 47
Hansen, James, 108–9, 111
hard science(s), 9–10, 33, 36, 88, 89, 90, 92,
        105, 118
Harrington, Alan, 149, 161, 162
Hart, Carl, 43–45, 46–48, 106
Harvard Crimson, 102
Hasan, Nadal, 52
Hayward, Tony, viii
"hedgehogs" (as a class of "experts"), 27–28, 29,
        52–53
Hedges, Chris, 7–8, 17, 82, 88, 169, 170
hedonism, 94
"heuristics," 141–42
Heidegger, Martin, 80, 81, 98
Herman, Edward, 172, 173, 175
Hibbert, Christopher, 56
Hicks, Stephen R. C., 92
Higgs boson particle, 16, 89
higher education. *See in general ch. 4, "Higher
        Learning and the Credentialed Age"*
        (77–103). *See also* xviii, 8–9, 106, 116,
        124, 184, 192
*Higher Superstition: The Academic Left and Its
        Quarrels with Science* (Gross and
        Levitt), 107, 112, 125–26
High Price (Hart), 43
Hill, Jonah, 43
historicism, 90, 96. *See* postmodernism
Hitler, Adolf, 32, 63, 67, 87, 139, 177, 186
Hoffer, Eric, 85, 111, 112
Hofstadter, Richard, 23, 88, 173
Hole at the Bottom of the Sea (Achenbach), viii

homelessness sham, 38
Horkheimer, Max, 97
*House Built of Sand: Exposing Postmodernist Myths
        about Science*, 107
housing collapse of 2008, xv, 26
Humason, Milton, 113
"hunger" in America, 39–41
Hurricane Katrina, ix
Huxley, Aldous, 8, 68, 180
Hyatt, Michael S., 38

I

Illuminati, 139
Image, The (Boorstin), 168–69
Immortalist, The (Harrington), 149, 159, 161
incest, 95
income inequality, 141, 142
Intellectuals and Society (Sowell), 3
intelligent design, 13, 64, 113, 121n
International Agency for Research on Cancer, 154
Internet, xviii, 3, 4, 7, 51, 86, 166–67, 168, 169,
        171, 176–77, 178, 181
irrationalism, 63, 64, 67, 71, 72, 80, 94, 98, 101,
        105, 109, 127
irrationality, 69, 70, 71, 75, 97, 126, 169, 189
ISIS, 178
Islam, 91, 145, 157

J

Jefferson, Cord, 15
Jobs, Steve, 84, 131
jobs requiring college education (percent), 81
Johnson, Korey, 124
Johnson, Lyndon B., 73, 74
Johnson, Paul, 58
Judeo-Christian culture/tradition, 59, 92
"justice," 6, 57, 98, 102, 111

K

Kansas State University, 82, 95
Kennedy, John F., 72 73, 74, 171, 174
Keynesians, 136–37
Khatib, Firas, 193
Kierkegaard, Søren, 69–70
Kirn, Walter, 77–79, 80
Kissinger, Henry, 173, 174
Kimball, Roger, 107
knowledge, on recognizing the boundaries be-
        tween theoretical and practical, 190

Koh, Harold, 99
Korn, Sandra, 201n33
Kraft, Jessica Carew, 123–24
Kurzweil, Ray, 159–60, 162

L

LaLande, Gerard, 147, 154, 155
Langan, Christopher, 85
Lawrence Livermore National Laboratory, xii
"learned helplessness," 34–35, 36
Lee, George, 124
Leno, Jay, 102
Levitt, Norman, 107, 111, 112, 116, 117–18,
    125
Levitt, Steven, 38
Lickint, Franz, 151
Life Sciences Research Office (LSRO), 40
Ligotti, Thomas, 163
Locke, John, 57
logic, 11, 28, 64, 68, 97, 106, 107, 108, 109, 118,
    122, 123, 124, 127, 169, 170
logical fallacies of postmodernism, 93, 113
Lomborg, Bjorn, 110
Los Alamos National Laboratory, x
Lost in the Meritocracy (Kirn), 78

M

MacIntyre, Alasdair, 123
Maher, Bill, 43
Maier, Steve, 34
Mamet, David, 100–1, 103, 200n31
majors obtain by most politicians and media talk-
    ing heads, 98
Malthus, Thomas, 65, 67
man and nature, the duality between, 96–97
Mao Zedong, 30, 32
Man against Mass Society (Marcel), 194
Man Without Qualities, The (Musil), xiii–xiv, xv,
    140, 183
Marcel, Gabriel, 17, 18, 97, 98, 168, 170,
    176–77, 183, 187, 194
marijuana (aka "pot"; "weed"), 5, 42–46
Martin, Trayvon, 44, 157
Marx, Karl, 32, 57, 60, 61–64, 69, 70, 91, 129,
    137, 138, 139, 142
Marxism, 63, 94
mass society, 168, 170, 176, 179, 183, 196
McKibben, Bill, 120
McLachlan, Sarah, 39

McNamara, Robert, 72, 73, 74–75
Measuring Poverty (Citro and Michael), 42
media, viii, ix, xii–xiii, xiv, xvi, xviii, xix, 2, ,–4,
    6, 7–8, 9, 10, 13, 16, 17, 18, 81, 89,
    96, 98, 101, 102, 103, 109, 112, 116,
    116, 117, 120, 121, 152, 155–58,
    183–84, 193, 194
    experts and, 21–54
    manipulation. See ch. 8, "Media Manipula-
        tion" (165–81)
    modus operandi of the, 148
Meier, Madeleine, 45
"metaphysical rebellion," 59
Michigan State University, 82, 95
microaggression(s), 101, 102
Millennium Bug, The (Hyatt), 38
MMR vaccine controversy, 6
Modern Times (Johnson), 58
Montclair State University, 96
Mooney, Chris, 11–13, 120
moral argument, separating from the scientific,
    188
morality, xiv, 11, 16, 18, 35, 62, 63, 79, 87, 90,
    92, 100, 106, 114, 139, 151, 152,
    179, 191
morals, 16, 18, 59, 64, 75, 81, 87, 116, 136, 185,
    186, 188
Morrison, Earl, 192–93
Morton, Frederic, xiv–xv
Mother Jones, 11
MSNBC, 167
multiculturalism, 90, 93. See postmodernism
Musil, Robert, ix, xiii–xiv, 10, 55, 60, 140, 183
Mussolini, Benito, 32, 63, 177

N

NASA, 108, 142
National Academies Press, 40, 42
National Security Administration (NSA), 51, 52
Natural History of Rape, A (Thornhill and Palmer),
    68
natural selection, 64, 65, 66, 67, 68, 186
nature, duality between man and, 96–97
Nature News, 193
Nazis, 72n, 81, 91, 126
Nazism, 81, 97, 98
Nazi Party, 176
Newton, Isaac, 50, 56, 57, 59, 70, 88, 115–16,
    119, 131
New York Times Magazine, 113

Nietzsche, Friedrich, 57, 61, 69, 71–72, 75, 80, 81, 91, 98, 122, 126
1984 (Orwell), 180
Nocera, Joe, 108
no-fault divorce, 38
Non-Overlapping Magisteria (NOMA), 10–11, 17
Noys, Benjamin, 156, 158
NRA, 95
NSA (National Security Administration), 51, 52

O

Obama, Barack, ix–x, 93, 99, 102
Obama, Michelle, 39
obesity epidemic, 39, 42
one-child policy (China), 30
On Morality (Engels), 62
On the Origin of Species (Darwin), 64
Onion, 51, 167
Opinionator (blog), 22
"oppression," 102
"optics," xviii, 2
oral sex, 148
Orwell, George, 18, 180
Outliers (Gladwell), 84
overpopulation, 30, 65

P

Page, Scott E., 132–33, 137, 139, 141–42, 192
Palmer, Craig T, 68
Pearce, Fred, 30
Pearcey, Nancy, 68
pedophilia, 14–15
peer review, 119, 174
"peer-reviewed" journal/studies, 37, 115, 119, 152
percent of jobs requiring college education, 81
Pereboom, Derek, 70
Peterson, Theodore, 167
philosophy, xii, xiv, 3, 10, 16, 18, 58, 63, 72, 80, 81, 88, 89–90, 92, 98, 106, 176, 192. *See also* postmodernism; postmodern philosophy
Place at the Table, A (documentary), 39, 40
Planned Parenthood, 67
Plato, 19, 22–24, 25, 49, 80, 185
political correctness, 101–2, 180
politics, ix, xii, xiii, xviii, 3, 8, 10, 32–33, 49, 69, 93, 97, 101, 107, 114, 115, 116, 124, 127, 156–57, 160, 174, 184, 185, 191

pop culture, 3, 99, 115, 148
Popper, Karl, 112, 132
Population Bomb (Ehrlich), 28, 30, 117, 131, 132
Post, Robert C., 99, 119
postmodernism. *See in general ch. 5, "Quantum Confusion: A Postmodern Science?"* (105–27); *see also* 90–94, 101, 102, 191
    logical fallacies of, 93, 113
    most evident example of, in popular culture, 99
    most popular manifestations of, 91
    overarching theme of, 90
    where it has had its strongest effect, 106
postmodern philosophy, 92, 100, 121
post-structuralism, 90. *See* postmodernism
poverty, 42, 45, 47, 71, 80, 85, 110, 161, 180
power/electric lines (and cancer), 148, 150
precautions to take when trying to listen to experts, 188–90
Princeton University, 77–78
principles
    student lack of, 79, 87
    transcendental, 60, 75
private school four-year program costs, 81
propaganda, 17, 168, 169, 172, 176
pseudo-events, 168–69
pseudoscience, 12, 31. *See in general ch. 5, "Quantum Confusion: A Postmodern Science?"* (105–27)
psychology, 9, 11, 22, 36, 49, 70, 105, 188
public university program tuitions, 81
"publish or perish," 118–19

Q

quantum confusion. *See ch. 5, "Quantum Confusion: A Postmodern Science?"* (105–27)
quantum mechanics, 24, 50, 115, 116, 119, 190, 191, 195

R

racism, 34, 80, 90, 91, 124
Radical Evolution (Garreau), 159
Rand, Ayn, vii, ix, xiv
rationalism, 57, 71, 72, 80, 89, 98, 106, 107, 109, 111
rationality, 31, 61, 72, 73, 81, 92, 94, 96, 109, 117, 122, 123–24, 125, 127, 169, 189
Readfearn, Graham, 120–21

Reagan, Ronald, 65
reason, xiv, 56, 59, 70, 71, 72, 73, 75, 80, 87, 89,
    90, 92, 93, 94, 97, 98, 170, 179
Rebel, The (Camus), 75–76
Reign of Terror, 55–56, 57, 61, 67, 69
relativism, 16, 49, 90, 102, 107, 117, 169. *See
    also* postmodernism
Republic (Plato), 23, 25, 49, 185
Republican Brain, The (Mooney), 11
Ridgeway, Matthew, 73
Rocks of Ages (Gould), 10
Rogeberg, Ole, 45, 47
Roggenbuck, Steve, 86–87
Rolling Stone magazine, 42–43, 45, 46, 47, 48
Roska, Josipa, 85
Rosenthal, Richard N., 47
Ruffin, Ameena, 124
Russia, 31, 51, 62, 63
Russell, Bertrand, 23–24

S

Samuel, Lawrence R., 146
Sandia National Laboratories, x
San Diego State University, 7
Sandy Hook Elementary School shooting, 96,
    170
Sanger, Margaret, 67
Schiavo, Terri, 156
Schlesinger, Arthur, Jr., 124–25
science. *See in general ch. 4, "Higher Learning and
    the Credentialed Age"* (77–103); *and ch.
    5, "Quantum Confusion: A Postmodern
    Science?"* (105–27); *see also,* 147–50,
    155–56, 163, 171, 184–91. *See also*
    hard science(s); social sciences
    cannot say if something is absolutely true,
        132, 194
    cultural impact of, 59–63
    dilemma of, 70
    how science works, 189–90
    the influence of, 114–18
    inherent differences in various types of,
        49–50
    postmodern? *See ch. 5, "Quantum Confu-
        sion: A Postmodern Science?"*
        (105–27)
    pscudoscicncc (and/or scicncc as a means to
        an end). *See* "science"
    the seeking of eternal life through, 146
"science for sale," 152–53, 185

"science," 11–12, 15–17, 22, 27, 29, 31, 34–37,
    42, 43, 45, 47, 57, 63–64, 67–68,
    70–71, 133, 201n33. *See also ch. 5,
    "Quantum Confusion: A Postmodern
    Science?"* (105–27)
scientific inquiry, 57
Schmidt, Bernhard, 113
Schmidt, Gavin, 134, 136
Seethaler, Sherry, 4, 6–7
Seligman, Martin, 34, 36
separatism, 94
Serrano, Andreas, xix
sexual orientation, 14
Sex Week, 95
Shahzad, Faisal, 52
Siebert, Frederick, 167
Singularity University, 159–60
slavery, 80
smoking, 43, 45–46, 147, 150, 151–52
Snowden, Edward, 51
social Darwinism, 66, 69
social sciences, 9, 49–50, 89, 92, 105, 107
Socrates, 23, 80, 117
Sokal, Alan, 107, 108, 122
Soviet Union, 30, 96
Sowell, Thomas, 2–3
special interests, 185
Spencer, Herbert, 65n
Spengler, Oswald, 138
Spinoza, Baruch, 56
Springer Handbook of Special Pathology, 151
"stakeholders," 6
Stalin, Joseph, 30, 32, 63, 96
Steyn, Mark, 8, 176
stimulus package, 137
Stone, The (philophers forum), 22
Strategic Engineered Negligible Senescence
        (SENS) Research Foundation, 160
Students' Society of McGill University (SSMU),
        99–100
Study of History, A (Toynbee), 130, 178
Sucralose, 148
suicide, xv, 150, 178
Summer, Lawrence, 92–93
Supplemental Nutrition Access Plan, 41
"survival of the fittest," 59, 65n, 66, 68
systems, four different ways in which they can be
        ordered, 132

T

Temples of Reason, 56, 57, 59, 75
Tenured Radicals (Kimball), 107
Tetlock, Philip, 27, 50, 52, 53, 54
Thatcher, Margaret, 65
theory of natural selection, 64, 65, 67
Thomas Aquinas, Saint, 129, 141
Thornhill, Randy, 68
Thunder at Twilight (Morton), xiv–xv
Time magazine, 81, 130
Tipler, Frank J., 119, 174
tobacco, 147, 151–52
tolerance, 91, 93
Tonight Show, 102
totalitarianism, 23–24, 64
Tower of Babel, 122, 125
Toynbee, Arnold J., 130, 137, 138, 142, 143,
    178, 187
traditional morality, postmodernism's attack on,
    92
traditions, xiv, 18, 56, 57, 58, 91, 94, 98, 127
transcendental principles, 60, 75
Transcendent Man (documentary), 162
True Believer (Hoffer), 85
Tsarnaev, Tamerlan, 52
Tucker, Robert C., 62
Twitter, 158, 177
tyranny, 22, 24, 97

U

"Underwear Bomber," 52
unemployment rate, 41–42
United States Congress, 73, 108, 110, 137
United States Constitution, 90
University of California–Berkeley, 147
University of California–Los Angeles, 102
University of Connecticut, 81–82
university enrollment and tuitions, 81
University of Minnesota, 95
University of New Mexico, 33
University of Washington, 84, 193
USDA, 39
utopia, 24, 32, 117, 161

V

values, 10, 13, 15, 16, 17, 18, 31, 58, 59, 71, 80,
    81, 87, 90, 94, 98, 106, 114, 116,
    117, 136, 137, 185, 186, 188, 191
Van Gijseghem, Hubert, 14, 15
Velasco, Guillermo, 47

Victorian age, 71, 72
Vienna, Austria, xiii–xv, 126
Vietnam War, 72, 73
virtue, xvi, 11, 80
Voegelin, Eric, 59
Vozick-Levinson, Simon, 45

W–X

Wallace, Alfred Russel, 68
Washington Navy Yard shooting, 95
Washington Post, ix, 180
Weekly Standard, 160
Wells, H. G., 31
"Western canon" of literature, postmodern attack
    on the, 92
WHO (World Health Organization), 172, 175
Whose Justice, Which Rationality? (MacIntyre), 123
Wikipedia, 119
Witt, Josephine, 76
Wolfe, Tom, 38
Wolin, Richard, 93
women, percent of world population, 91
Wood, Graeme, 40
World Health Organization (WHO), 172, 175
World War I, xiv, 72, 126, 139
World War II, 72, 97, 127, 156, 168, 176, 188
Wrong: Why Experts Keep Failing Us (Freedman),
    26, 49

Y

Yahoo! News, 145
Yale University, 12, 95, 99, 120
Yeats, William Butler, 58
Y2K panic, 38–39

Z

zeitgeist, 100, 176
Zuckerberg, Mark, 84